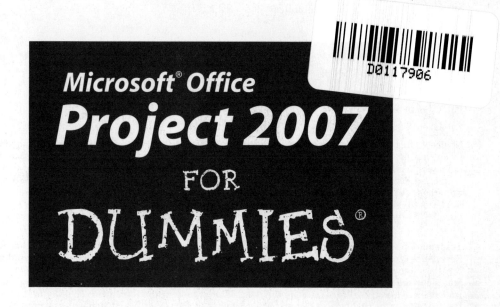

Microsoft® Office Project 2007 FOR DUMMIES®

by Nancy Muir

BICENTENNIAL
1807 WILEY 2007
BICENTENNIAL

Wiley Publishing, Inc.

Microsoft® Project 2007 For Dummies®

Published by
Wiley Publishing, Inc.
111 River Street
Hoboken, NJ 07030-5774
www.wiley.com

Copyright © 2007 by Wiley Publishing, Inc., Indianapolis, Indiana

Published by Wiley Publishing, Inc., Indianapolis, Indiana

Published simultaneously in Canada

For general information on our other products and services, please contact our Customer Care Department within the U.S. at 800-762-2974, outside the U.S. at 317-572-3993, or fax 317-572-4002.

For technical support, please visit www.wiley.com/techsupport.

Wiley also publishes its books in a variety of electronic formats. Some content that appears in print may not be available in electronic books.

Library of Congress Control Number: 2006934842

ISBN-10: 0-470-03651-6

ISBN-13: 978-0-470-03651-8

Manufactured in the United States of America

10 9 8 7 6 5 4 3 2 1

1B/RS/RS/QW/IN

WILEY

About the Author

Nancy Muir has written dozens of books on topics ranging from desktop applications, project management, and distance learning, to an award-winning book on character education for middle-schoolers. Prior to her freelance writing career, Nancy taught workshops in project management to Fortune 500 companies and was a manager in both the computer and publishing industries. She lives in the Pacific Northwest with her husband Earl, with whom she has collaborated on three books, including Electronics Projects For Dummies.

Dedication

To Earl for putting up with my hectic book schedule in our first year of marriage. You're the best! That long-promised cutting back on work time is almost here, my love.

Author's Acknowledgments

First, many thanks to my friend Elaine Marmel, author of the Microsoft Project Bible from Wiley. Her advice and insight into the workings of Project always help me see the forest for the trees. Did the chocolate arrive okay, Elaine?

Second I thank the folks at Wiley, including Kyle Looper, my able acquisitions editor, and Blair Pottenger, the book's project editor who was incredibly supportive and patient and helped me hold all the pieces together. Thanks also to development editor Linda Morris, copy editors Teresa Artman and Becky Whitney, and technical editor Jennifer Pendleton for keeping the prose accurate and intelligible.

Publisher's Acknowledgments

We're proud of this book; please send us your comments through our online registration form located at www.dummies.com/register/.

Some of the people who helped bring this book to market include the following:

Acquisitions, Editorial, and Media Development

Project Editor: Blair J. Pottenger

Development Editor: Linda Morris

Acquisitions Editor: Kyle Looper

Senior Copy Editor: Teresa Artman

Copy Editor: Becky Whitney

Technical Editor: Jennifer Pendleton

Editorial Manager: Kevin Kirschner

Media Development Specialist: Steven Kudirka

Media Project Supervisor: Laura Moss

Media Development Manager: Laura VanWinkle

Editorial Assistant: Amanda Foxworth

Senior Editorial Assistant: Cherie Case

Cartoons: Rich Tennant (www.the5thwave.com)

Composition Services

Project Coordinator: Ryan Steffen

Layout and Graphics: Carl Byers, Denny Hager, Stephanie D. Jumper, Barry Offringa, Lynsey Osborn, Alicia South

Proofreaders: Jessica Kramer, Techbooks

Indexer: Techbooks

Anniversary Logo Design: Richard Pacifico

Special Help

Jodi Jensen

Publishing and Editorial for Technology Dummies

Richard Swadley, Vice President and Executive Group Publisher

Andy Cummings, Vice President and Publisher

Mary Bednarek, Executive Acquisitions Director

Mary C. Corder, Editorial Director

Publishing for Consumer Dummies

Diane Graves Steele, Vice President and Publisher

Joyce Pepple, Acquisitions Director

Composition Services

Gerry Fahey, Vice President of Production Services

Debbie Stailey, Director of Composition Services

Contents at a Glance

Table of Contents

Introduction

. . . .

Project management probably started back when a few cave dwellers got together and figured out how to work as a team to bag a wooly mammoth for their Sunday dinner. Some fellow — I'll call him Ogg — probably took the lead as the very first project manager. He drew things in the dirt with a stick to help his team members understand the strategy of the hunt, and communicated with them in ughs and grunts. Unlike you, he had no boss to report to, no budget, and no deadlines (lucky Ogg), but the fundamental spirit of a project was there.

Over the years, project management has evolved as a discipline that involves sophisticated analyses and techniques, projections, tracking of time and money, and reporting. Project management software — which has been around only about 25 years or so — has brought a new face and functionality to project management that would have left our friend Ogg ughless.

About This Book

Microsoft Office Project 2007, the most recent incarnation of the world's most popular project management software, offers a tremendous wealth of functionality to users. However, it's probably not like any other software you've ever used, so mastering it can seem a daunting process. One trick is to understand how its features relate to what you do every day as a project manager. Another is to get someone like me to tell you all about its features and how to use them.

In *Microsoft Office Project 2007 For Dummies,* my goal is to help you explore all that Project offers, providing information on relevant project management concepts while also offering specific procedures to build and track your Project plans. But more importantly, I offer advice on how to make all these features and procedures mesh with what you already know as a project manager to make the transition easier.

Foolish Assumptions

I've made some assumptions about you, gentle reader. I figure that you are computer literate and know how to use a mouse, a keyboard, software menus, and toolbars. I assume you know how to use most common Windows functions (such as the Clipboard) as well as many basic software functions (such as selecting text and dragging and dropping things with your mouse).

I do not assume that you've used Project or any other project management software before. If you're new to Project, you'll find what you need to get up to speed, including information on how Project works, finding your way around, and building your first Project plan. If you've used an earlier version of Project, you'll find out about Project 2007 and all the new features it provides.

Conventions Used in This Book

I should explain a few odds and ends to make using this book easier:

- ✔ Web site addresses, known as URLs, are highlighted like this: www.microsoft.com.
- ✔ Menu commands are given in the order in which you select them, for example, "Choose Tools⇨Resource Sharing⇨Share Resources."
- ✔ Options in dialog boxes use initial caps even if they aren't capitalized on your screen to make it easier to identify them in sentences. For example, what appears as Show summary tasks in the Options dialog box will appear as Show Summary Tasks in this book.

How This Book Is Organized

This book is designed to help you begin to use Microsoft Office Project 2007 to plan, build, and track progress on projects, keeping in mind tried-and-true project management practices and principles. I divided the book into logical parts that follow the process of building and tracking a typical project plan.

Part I: Setting the Stage for Project

Part I explains what Project 2007 can do for you as well as what types of input you have to provide to use it successfully on your projects. You'll get your first glimpse of Project views and discover how to navigate around them. You'll begin to build Project plans by making calendar settings, building a task outline, and then entering timing and timing relationships for those tasks.

Part II: People Who Need People

Part II is the Project resources section: You discover all you need to know about creating and assigning work resources, material resources, and fixed costs to tasks in a project. You also discover how using resources on your project relates to the costs you accrue over time.

Part III: Well, It Looks Good on Paper

Up to now, you've been mapping out your project plan. Now it's time to see whether that plan meets your needs in terms of budget and timing. Project offers a whole toolbox to help you modify resource assignments and task timing to trim your costs and meet your deadlines so you can finalize your plan. You also get briefed on how to modify the format of items in your project to make your plan look as polished as possible, both on-screen and in print.

Part IV: Avoiding Disaster: Staying on Track

As any experienced project manager knows, projects just about never happen the way you thought they would. In this part, you save a picture of your plan — a *baseline* — and then begin to track actual activity against your plan. You also take a look at methods of reporting your progress, and how to get back on track when you find yourself derailed. In the final chapter, I provide advice on how to use what you glean from your projects to make better planning choices going forward.

Part V: Working with Enterprise Projects

With all that Project Professional has to offer the enterprise via its Project Server and Project Web Access functionalities and SharePoint online services, you can share documents online with your project team, have your human resources report their work time, and even integrate Project information with Outlook. This part shows you the basics of what Project Server can do, and how to use Project Web Access from both the manager and users' perspective.

Part VI: The Part of Tens

Ten seems to be a handy number of items for humans to put into lists, so this part gives you two such lists: Ten Golden Rules of Project Management and Ten Project Management Software Products to Explore. The first of these chapters tells you about some dos and don'ts that can save you a lot of grief when you're using Project for the first time (or the fifth time, for that matter). The second offers a look at some add-on products and complementary software products that bring even more functionality to Microsoft Office Project.

Part VII: Appendixes

This book is accompanied by a handy CD filled with project management goodies, including project management add-on software and Microsoft Project templates. Appendix A is where I explain how to work with the CD and exactly what you can find there.

Earned value? Budgeted cost of work performed? Work breakdown structure? I'm telling you, project management has more terminology than a medical textbook. That's why I provide a Glossary that contains a lot of terms, some from the discipline of project management and some project-specific. Definitions of key terms are included throughout this book, but when you need a refresher course, look here.

What You're Not to Read

First, you don't have to read this book from front to back unless you really want to. If you want to just get information about a certain topic, you can open this book to any chapter and get the information you need.

That said, I have structured the book to move from some basic concepts that equip you to understand how Project works through the steps involved in building a typical project. If you have an overpowering need to find out the whole shebang, you can start at the beginning and work your way through the book to build your first Project plan.

Icons Used in This Book

One picture is worth . . . well, you know. That's why *For Dummies* books use icons to give you a visual clue as to what's going on. Essentially, icons call your attention to bits of special information that might very well make your life easier. Following are the icons used in this book.

Remember icons signal either a pertinent fact that relates to what you're reading at the time (but is also mentioned elsewhere in the book), or a reiteration of a particularly important piece of information that's, well, worth repeating.

Tips are the advice columns of computer books: They offer sage advice, a bit more information about a topic under discussion that might be of interest, or ways to do things a bit more efficiently.

Warning icons spell trouble with a capital *T:* When you see a Warning, read it. If you're not careful, you might do something at this point that could cause disaster.

Where to Go from Here

Time to take what you've learned in the project management school of hard knocks and jump into the world of Microsoft Office Project 2007. When you do, you'll be rewarded with a wealth of tools and information that help you to manage your projects much more efficiently.

Here's where you step out of the world of cave-dweller project management and into the brave, new world of Microsoft Office Project 2007.

Part I
Setting the Stage for Project

"Look you've got Project Manager, Acct. Manager, and Opportunity Manager, but Sucking Up to the Manager just isn't a field the program comes with."

In this part . . .

Part I explains the types of input you have to give Project to make best use of its capabilities. You get a briefing on using Project views, using calendar settings to build Project plans, creating task outlines, and then specifying the timing and relationships that organize your project's tasks.

Chapter 1

Project Management: What Is It, and Why Should You Care?

*W*elcome to the world of computerized project management with Microsoft Project. If you've never used project management software, you're entering a brave, new world. It's like walking from the office of 25 years ago — with no fax, voicemail, or e-mail — into the office of today with its wealth of high-tech devices.

Everything you used to do with handwritten to-do lists, word processors, and spreadsheets all magically comes together in Project. However, this transition won't come in a moment, and you need a basic understanding of what project management software can do to get you up to speed. If you've used previous versions of Project, this little overview can help you refresh your memory as well as ease you into a few of the new features of Project 2007.

So, even if you're a seasoned project manager, take a minute to review this chapter. It provides the foundation for how you'll work with Project from here on.

The ABCs of Project Management

You probably handle projects day in and day out. Some are obvious, because your boss named them so that any fool would know that they're projects: the Acme Drilling Project or the Network Expansion IT Project, for example. Others are less obvious, such as that speech thing you have to do on Saturday for your professional association or washing the dog.

If you need to organize a company holiday party, it's a project. If you were handed a three-year Earth-exploration initiative to find oil in Iowa, coordinate subcontractors and government permits, and work with a team of 300 people, that's definitely a project. Yes, even that speech you have to present is a project because it has certain characteristics.

Understanding what your projects, large or small, have in common is the basis of understanding what Project can do for you. All projects have

- An overall goal
- A project manager
- Individual tasks to be performed
- Timing for those tasks to be completed (such as three hours, three days, or three months)
- Timing relationships between those tasks (For example, you can't put a new manufacturing process in place until you train people in how to use the process.)
- *Resources* (people, equipment, facilities, and supplies, for example) to accomplish the work
- A *budget* (the costs associated with those people, equipment, facilities, and supplies)

Project management is simply the process of managing all the elements of a project, whether that project is large or small.

The three Ts: Tasks, timing, and dependencies (well, two Ts and a D)

As Lewis Carroll said, "If you don't know where you're going, any road will get you there." So, first things first: You have to understand the goal of your project so you can begin to build the tasks that have to be performed to get you there.

A *task* is simply one of those items you used to scribble on your handwritten to-do lists, such as *Write final report* or *Apply for permits.* Tasks are typically organized into *phases* (appropriate stages) in Project, arranged in an outline-like structure, as you can see in the project shown in Figure 1-1. Because timing is essential in any project, Project helps you set up and view the timing relationships among tasks.

Becoming a task master

A task can be as broad or as detailed as you like. For example, you can create a single task to research your competition, or you can create a project phase that consists of a *summary task* and *subtasks* below it. For example, the summary task might be Competitive Research, with the subtasks Researching Online Business Databases, Assembling Company Annual Reports, and Reviewing Competitive Product Lines.

Adding tasks to a Project file doesn't cost you a thing (except a nanobit of memory), so a project can have as many tasks and as many phases as you like. You simply use the outlining structure in Project to indent various levels of tasks. The more deeply indented in an outline a task is, the more detailed the task.

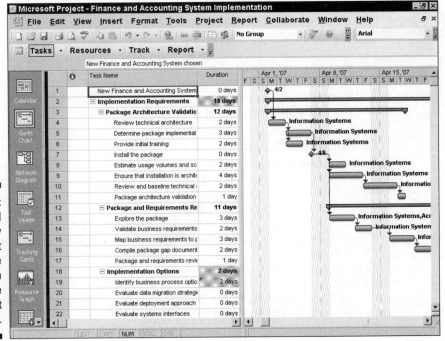

Figure 1-1: You'll probably spend most of your time in Project in outline-like Gantt Chart view.

One handy thing about this outlining structure is that you can roll up all the timing and cost data from the subtasks within your phases into summary-level tasks. Three sequential subtasks that take a day each to complete and cost you $200 apiece result in a summary task that spans three days and costs $600. You can view your project at various levels of detail or get automatic tallies of timing and costs if you prefer to simply view the summary level of tasks.

For more about defining and creating tasks, check out Chapter 4.

All in the timing

They say that timing is everything: Rome wasn't built in a day, a stitch in time saves nine, and don't even ask me about choosing exactly when to sell your high-tech stocks. The importance of timing applies to Project tasks, too. Almost all tasks have timing — referred to as *duration* — which is the amount of time needed to complete the task.

The only tasks without duration are milestones. A *milestone* is a task of zero duration; in essence, it simply marks a moment in time that must be reflected in your Project outline. Typical milestones are the approval of a brochure design and an assembly line startup.

Project doesn't provide magic formulas for duration: You assign duration based on your own experience and judgment. Does designing a product package take three days or three weeks? Will obtaining a building permit happen in a day or a month? (Remember that you're dealing with city hall, so think before you answer!) Project isn't an oracle: You have to provide facts, figures, and educated guesses to build your Project schedule. After that information is entered, though, Project can do some wonderful things to help you maintain your schedule and monitor your progress.

Task co-dependencies

The final piece in the puzzle of how long your project will take is the concept of *dependencies,* or the timing relationships among tasks. If you have a schedule that includes ten tasks that all begin at the same time, your entire project will take as long as the longest task (see Figure 1-2).

After you define and implement timing relationships among tasks, your schedule can stretch over time like a long rubber band. For example, one task might begin only after another is finished. Another task can start halfway through the preceding task. The second task cannot start until a week after the first task is finished. Only after you start to assign these relationships can you begin to see a project's timing as related to not just each task's duration but also the specific ways in which the tasks relate to each other.

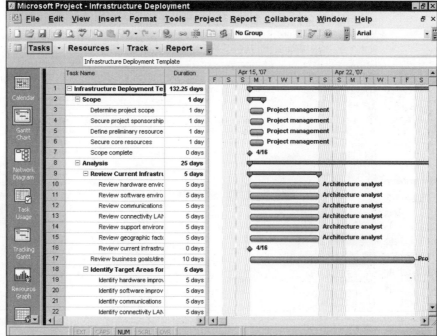

Figure 1-2:
This
schedule
includes
tasks with
timing but
no depend-
encies.

Here are some examples of dependencies:

- ✔ You can't begin to use a new piece of equipment until you install it.
- ✔ You must wait for a freshly poured concrete foundation to dry before you can begin to build on it.
- ✔ You can't start to ship a new drug product until the FDA approves it.

Figure 1-3 shows a project plan where each task's duration and the dependencies among tasks have been established, and the resulting overall timing of the project.

One other brief note about the timing of tasks: In addition to applying dependencies to tasks, you can apply *constraints.* For example, say that you don't want to start shipping your new cake flavor until you get the ad for it in your Christmas catalog, so you set a dependency between those two events. You can also set a constraint which says that you must start producing the cakes no later than November 3. In this case, if you don't make the catalog deadline, the product will still ship on November 3; that task will not be allowed to slip its constraint because of this dependency relationship.

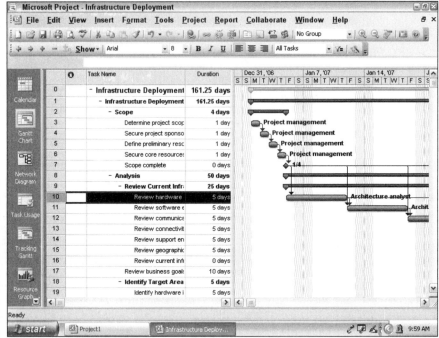

Figure 1-3:
This
schedule
includes
tasks with
both timing
and
depend-
encies.

You can find out more about constraints in Chapter 4 and about the fine art of managing dependencies in Chapter 6.

Lining up your resources

When people first use Project, some get a bit confused about resources. Resources aren't just people: A *resource* can be a piece of equipment you rent, a meeting room that you have to pay an hourly fee to use, or a box of nails or a software program you have to buy.

Project allows for three kinds of resources: work resources, material resources, and cost resources. A *work resource* is charged by how many hours or days the resource (often human) works on a task. A *material resource,* such as sewing supplies or steel, is charged by a per-use cost or by a unit of measurement (such as square yards or linear feet or tons). A *cost resource* has a set cost, such as a conference fee of $250; this cost doesn't vary by how much time you spend at the conference or how many people attend.

Some resources, such as people, perform their work according to a working calendar. If a person works an 8-hour day and you assign him to a task that takes 24 hours to complete, that person has to put in three workdays to complete the task. In comparison, someone with a 12-hour workday takes only two days to complete the same task. In addition, you can set working and nonworking days for your human resources, which accommodates variations such as 4-day weeks or shift work.

You can set different rates for resources, such as a standard hourly rate and an overtime rate. Project applies the appropriate rate based on each resource's calendar and work assigned. For more about resources and costs, see Chapter 7.

Several views in Project let you see information about resources and how their assignment to tasks has an effect on project costs. Figure 1-4 shows you the Resource sheet which has columns of information about resources and their costs.

Here's one other important thing you should know about resources: They tend to have conflicts. No, I'm not talking about conference room brawls (although that happens). These conflicts have to do with assigned resources that become overallocated for their available work time. For example, if you assign one poor soul to three 8-hour tasks that must all happen on the same day — and in the same eight hours — Project has features that do everything but jump up on your desk and turn on an alarm to warn you of the conflict. (Luckily, Project also provides tools that help you resolve those conflicts.)

Microsoft Project - Infrastructure Deployment
File Edit View Insert Format Tools Project Report Collaborate Window Help
No Group
Arial
Tasks Resources Track Report
Architecture analyst
Resource Name Type Material Label Initials Group Max. Units Std. Rate Ovt. Rate Cost
1 Architecture analys Work A Arct 100% $110.00/hr $0.00/hr
2 Project manageme Work P Mgmt 100% $65.00/hr $0.00/hr
3 Deployment resource Work D 100% $35.00/hr $50.00/hr
4 Procurement Work P 100% $45.00/hr $0.00/hr
5 Management Work M Mgmt 100% $0.00/hr $0.00/hr
6 Blueprints Cost B
7 Cables Material C $35.00
Calendar
Gantt Chart
Network Diagram
Task Usage
Tracking Gantt
Resource Graph
EXT CAPS NUM SCRL OVR

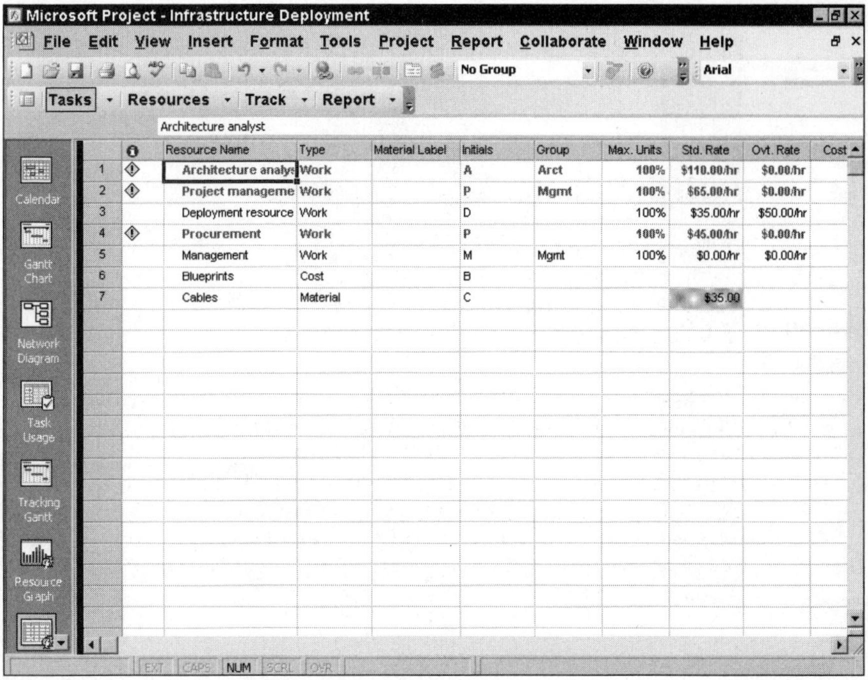

Figure 1-4: Resources charged at a rate per hour are the basis of how Project tallies costs.

Spreading the news

I'm one of those people who need instant gratification. One of the first things I ask about learning to use any new software product is, "What's in it for me?" Until now, I've told you about the type of information you have to put into Project: information about tasks, task dependencies, and resources. But isn't it about time you got something back from Project? Of course it is.

You finally reached one of the big payoffs for entering all that information: reporting. After you enter your information, Project offers a wealth of reporting options to help you view your project and communicate your progress to your project team, clients, and management.

You can generate predesigned reports based on information in your schedule or simply print any of the views you can display in Project. Project 2007 offers a set of Basic Reports and Visual Reports. (You must have the Microsoft .NET Framework installed in order to use Visual Reports, which is free and down-loadable from www.microsoft.com/downloads.) Figures 1-5 and 1-6 show you just two of the reporting options available in Project.

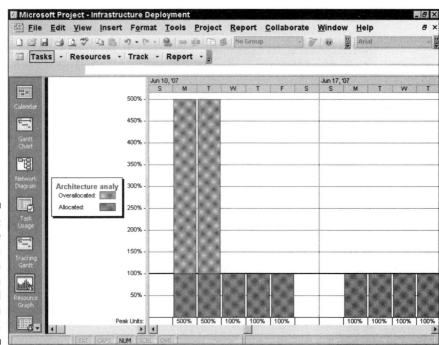

Figure 1-5:
Study resource usage with the graphical Resource Graph view.

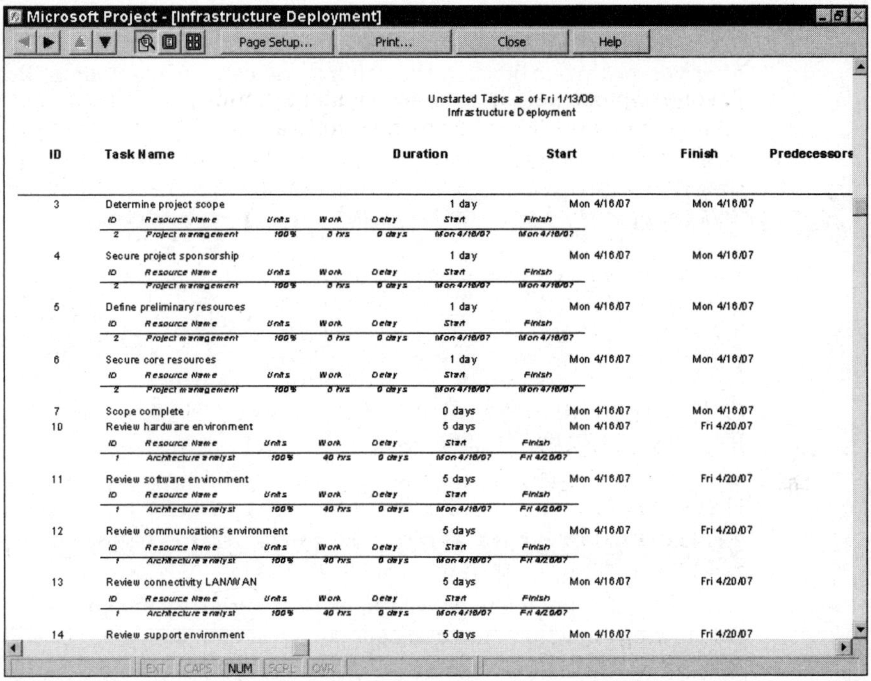

Figure 1-6:
An
Unstarted
Tasks
report.

Planning to keep things on track

Projects aren't frozen in amber like some organizational mosquito: They go through more changes than a politician's platform in a campaign year. That's where Project's capability to make changes to your project data comes in handy.

After you build all your tasks, give them durations and dependencies, and assign all your resources and costs, you set a baseline. A *baseline* is a snap-shot of your project at the moment you feel your plan is final and you're ready to proceed with the project. After you set a baseline, you record some activity on your tasks. Then you can compare that actual activity with your baseline because Project saves both sets of data in your schedule.

Tracking activity in your project involves recording the actual timing of tasks and recording the time that your resources have spent on those tasks, as well as entering any actual costs that accrue. You can then display Project views that show you how far off you are at any time (compared with your baseline) in terms of the actual timing of tasks and cost of your project.

Whether you have good news or bad, you can use reports to show your boss how things are going compared with how you thought they would go. Then, after you peel your boss off the ceiling, you can use many more Project tools to make adjustments to get everything back on track.

The Role of the Project Manager

Although understanding the role (let alone the usefulness) of some managers isn't always easy, it's always easy to spot the value of a *project manager*. This person creates the master plan for a project and tries to ensure that it gets implemented successfully. Along the way, this key person uses skills and methods that have evolved over time, always seeking to manage how things get done and generally keeping schedules on track.

What exactly does a project manager do?

A project manager isn't always the highest authority in a project; often that role belongs to whomever manages the project manager, up to and including members of senior management. Rather, the project manager is the person on the front lines who makes sure that the parts of the project come together and assumes hands-on responsibility for successes as well as failures.

In project management parlance, the person who champions (and has the ultimate responsibility for) a project is the *project sponsor*.

A project manager manages these essential pieces of a project:

- ✔ **The project plan or schedule:** This is what you create with Microsoft Project. It includes the estimated steps and associated timing and costs involved in reaching the project goal.
- ✔ **Resources:** Managing resources involves resolving resource conflicts and building consensus as well as assigning resources and tracking their activities on the project. This part of the job also involves managing nonhuman resources, such as materials and equipment.
- ✔ **Communication with the project team, management, and customers:** Communicating the project's status to everyone who has a legitimate stake in its success *(stakeholders)* is a key responsibility.

Although a project manager might work for a project sponsor, the project often also has a *customer* for whom the end product is produced. That customer can be outside the project manager's own company, or within.

Understanding the dreaded triple constraint

You've seen the signs at the copy store or the auto repair place: You can have it fast, cheap, or right; pick two. That, my friend, is the triple constraint of project management in a nutshell.

In a project, you have timing, resources (which are essentially costs), and quality of the product or service produced at the end of the project. Microsoft Project helps you manage the resources and timing of your project. The quality of your project is often affected directly by how well you manage them. If you add time, costs increase because resources are working longer hours at a certain wage. If you take away resources, you save money, but this can affect quality — and so on.

Coming to a logical balance of time, money, and quality is at the core of what a good project manager does throughout the life of a project.

Applying tried-and-true methodologies

Microsoft Project incorporates some scheduling and tracking tools that are the result of many years of developing project management methods. A few of these are worth noting:

- The **Gantt Chart** (shown in Gantt Chart view of Figure 1-7), which is the main view of Project, shows you a spreadsheet with columns of data along with a graphical representation of the tasks in the project arranged along a horizontal timeline. By using the data in the columns (such as task name, start date, finish date, and resources assigned to tasks), you can understand the parameters of each task and see its timing in the graphical area. Being able to view all this information on one page helps you understand what's happening in your project in terms of time and costs.

- The **Network Diagram (also called a logic diagram)**, shown in Figure 1-8, is essentially the Microsoft version of a PERT chart. PERT (Program Evaluation and Review Technique) was developed during the construction of the Polaris submarine in the 1950s. This mostly graphical representation of the tasks in your project reflects the flow of work in your project rather than the literal timing of tasks. This view helps you to see how one task flows into another and to get a sense of where you are — not so much in time, but rather in terms of the work you have to accomplish.

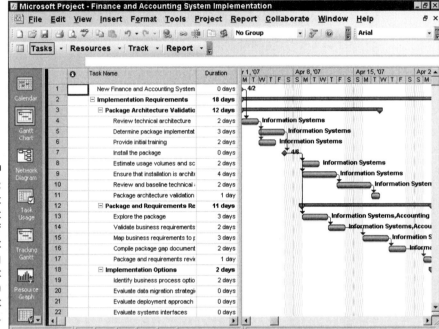

Figure 1-7:
The Gantt Chart method of project scheduling as it appears in Microsoft Project.

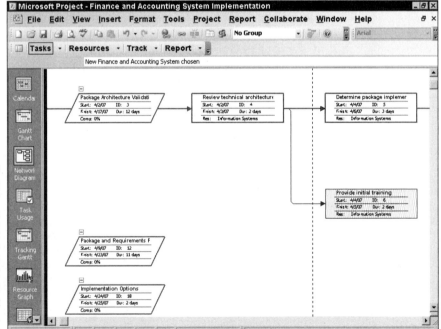

Figure 1-8:
A kissin' cousin to the original PERT chart, the Network Diagram focuses on work, not on time.

✔ **Risk management** is a central part of project management because, frankly, projects are chock-full of risk. You run the risk that your resources won't perform, that materials will arrive late, that your customer will change all the parameters of the project halfway through — well, you get the picture.

Risk management is the art of anticipating risks, ranking them from most to least likely, and determining strategies to prevent the most likely ones from occurring. Project helps you with risk management by allowing you to try out *what-if scenarios:* You can change the start date or length of a task or phase of tasks (for example) and see just what that change does to your schedule, such as the delays, cost overruns, and resource conflicts that might occur in such a scenario, down to the last hour and penny. Having this kind of information at your fingertips makes risk management easier and (almost) painless.

✔ **Resource management** consists of using resources wisely. A good project manager finds the right resource for the job, assigns that person a reasonable workload, stays alert for shifts in the schedule that cause that resource to be overbooked, and during the life of the project makes adjustments that keep all resources most productive. In Project, tools are available, such as a *resource graph* (traditionally called a *histogram*) and the resource usage chart (shown in Figure 1-9), which reflects resource workload.

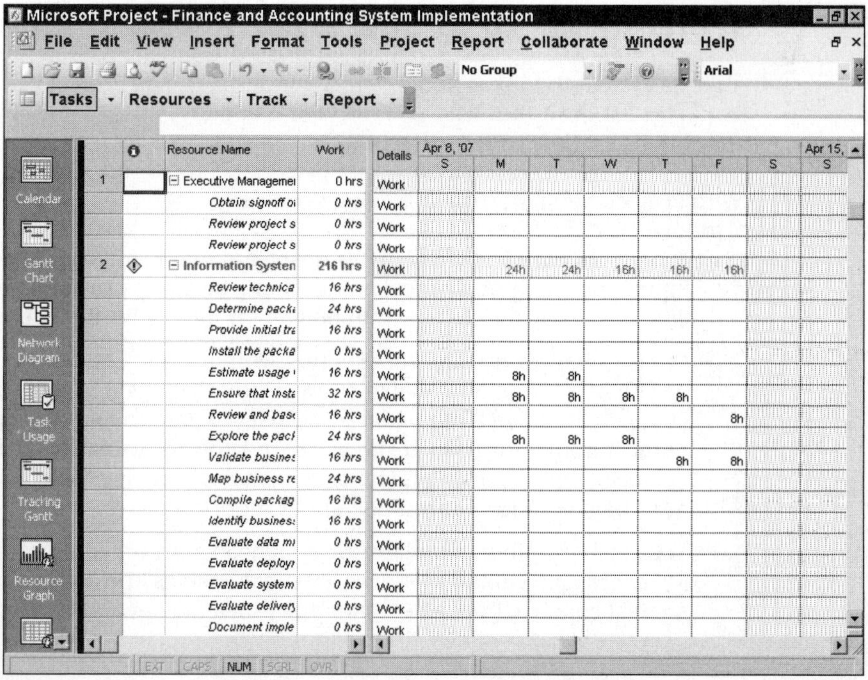

Figure 1-9: A resource usage chart helps you spot resource-scheduling problems.

Figure 1-9 also shows *resource leveling* (a calculation that automatically reschedules resources to resolve overbooking), which can enable you to manage resources much more effectively. You can see how overbooked the Information Systems Analyst is on this date.

You can use codes for resources that designate skill levels or abilities so that finding the right resource for each job is as simple as performing a search.

From To-Do List to Hard Drive

If you're reading from start to finish in this chapter, you're probably shaking your head and saying, "Boy, handwritten to-do lists look pretty good right now. Beats creating hundreds of tasks, assigning them durations, establishing dependencies among them, creating resources, entering resource calendar and rate information, assigning resources and costs to tasks, entering activity performed on tasks . . ." and so on.

Well, you're right *and* wrong about that. You do have to enter a lot of information into Project to get the benefit of its features. But you can also get a lot out of Project.

Getting up to speed with Project

Take a moment to look at some of the wonderful things Project can do for you. This list describes why you (or your company) bought it and why you're investing your time to read this book.

With Project, you enjoy the following benefits:

- ✔ Project automatically calculates costs and timing for you based on your input. You can quickly recalculate what-if scenarios to solve resource conflicts, get your costs within budget, or meet your final deadline.

- ✔ Project offers views and reports that, with the click of a button, make a wealth of information available to you and those you report to. No more manually building a report on total-costs-to-date to meet a last-minute request from your boss. If she wants to know total-costs-to-date, you can just print your Tracking Gantt view with the Tracking table displayed. See Chapter 16 for information about reporting.

- ✔ You can use built-in templates to get a head start on your project. Project *templates* are prebuilt plans for a typical business project, such as commercial construction, an engineering project, a new product rollout, software development, or an office move. See "Starting with templates" later in this chapter for more about this time-saving feature.

You likely do similar types of projects all the time. After you create one project, you use it as a template for future projects.

✔ You can create resources for your project according to information you already created in your Outlook Address Book. You can even create one set of company resources and give access to every project manager in the company (see Chapters 18 and 19 for how to set up centralized enterprise resources).

✔ A number of tools in Project employ complex algorithms (that you couldn't even begin to figure out) to do such tasks as level resource assignments to solve resource conflicts, filter tasks by various criteria, model what-if scenarios, and calculate in dollars the value of work performed to date.

Collaborating with your project team online

You can take advantage of all the Internet has to offer by using Project features to collaborate with others. In fact, Project 2007 begins to step into the world of Enterprise Project Management (EPM), where easily sharing ideas, information, and documents across your enterprise becomes possible.

For example, Project allows you to request updates on a task's progress from team members via e-mail. You can post documents and ask for team input. You can even publish your project on the Web.

The Professional version of Project includes Project Server and Project Web Access, which enhance workgroup collaboration. You can take advantage of an online project center and resource center with areas for discussions, progress tracking, document exchange, and more.

Part V of this book, "Working with Enterprise Projects," looks at how to take advantage of the enterprise-wide features of Project Server and Project Web Access.

Getting Started

As Shakespeare said, "In delay there lies no plenty." I don't know about you, but I need all the plenty I can get, so it's time to jump in and start using Project.

You have three choices when starting a new project. You can use Project Guide to get Project's assistance creating a project, you can build a project on your own from scratch by entering individual task and resource details, or you can use a project template that already contains data related to your industry or the type of project you're doing.

Getting going with help from Project Guide

Project Guide is like some of those wizards you see in Microsoft products: It walks you through a series of steps that ask you to enter some information and then automates a process for you. However, in many ways, Project Guide is like no wizard you've ever seen.

Taking a first look at the Guide

Project Guide has four different sections: Tasks, Resources, Track, and Report. Within each of those categories might be ten or so links for you to click to initiate an action. When you do so, you might have to choose a variety of subactions, depending on your particular project. Also, the sections of Project Guide span the entire life of your project, from the time you first enter task information to the time you generate your final report.

If you've never used project management software (or Project itself), you might find it helpful to run through Project Guide to set up your first schedule, enter resources, track activities on tasks, or generate reports. However, to know how to make intelligent choices in Project Guide, you have to have some basic understanding of how a project is built, which I provide in the next few chapters. My advice is to walk with me through many of the steps in this book and then use Project Guide to practice building your first project. Then you can see whether its structure works the way your mind does — or not.

Using Project Guide

A Project Guide toolbar displays by default in the toolbar area at the top of your Project screen. The toolbar has an icon you click to show or hide the Project Guide, so if the Project Guide doesn't appear on the left side of your screen, just click the Show/Hide Project Guide button.

To use the Project Guide, you click a category (such as Tasks) and then click a link (such as List the Tasks in the Project) in that category. This action displays additional information in the Project Guide pane (see Figure 1-10) asking you to enter data or choose or accept a setting and move through a series of screens. When you finish working through one set of screens, you return to the Project Guide pane and can click another task or category to proceed.

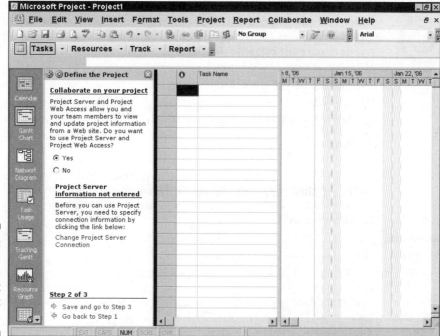

Figure 1-10:
A typical
information
request
from Project
Guide.

Microsoft laid out these categories and tasks in the logical order in which you should tackle them to build most projects. Thus, when you start to use Project Guide, just click the categories and the tasks within them in sequence. They should remind you of all the things you should consider, even if you choose to skip a few steps here and there for your particular project.

Starting from scratch

Although you can use Project Guide to start a project, you don't have to. You can enter information on your own at any time.

When you open Project 2007, you see a blank project file on-screen along with the Project Guide task pane. You can start building your new project directly in this blank schedule. Starting to create a new project usually involves entering some general project information and then adding some task information.

You can open a new, blank project schedule at any time by choosing File⇨ New and clicking the Blank Project link in the New Project task pane.

You need to enter much more information in addition to general project information and tasks in order to build a complete project, as you discover in the next few chapters. Entering general project information and task information is your usual starting point, however.

Tell Project about your project

With a blank project open, a logical first step is to enter some general project information, such as the project start date. To do so, you choose Project⇨ Project Information. The Project Information dialog box appears, as shown in Figure 1-11.

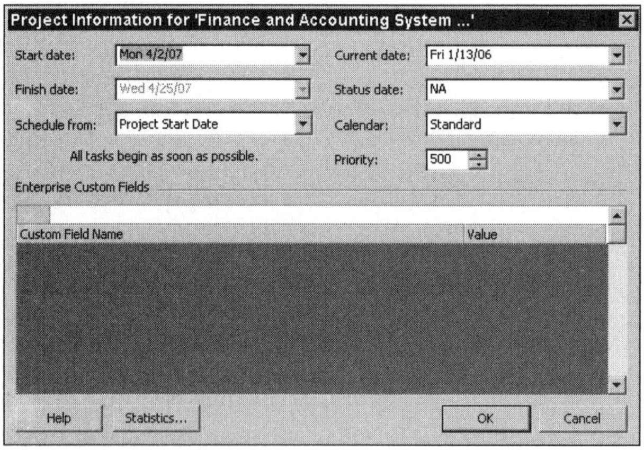

Figure 1-11: Use the Project Information dialog box for some basic project settings.

Here's what you can do in this dialog box:

- ✔ **Set the start date for the project.** If you're not sure when the project will start, set the start date about a month from today. Then, after you build some tasks and have a better handle on the entire length of your project, you can come back and set a real start date. Project automatically recalculates all dates when you do.

- ✔ **Set the finish date for the project.** Especially if you have a *drop-dead date* (an attention-getting term!) beyond which the project cannot wander and still reach completion, you can set the finish date. In such a case, be sure to look at the next setting in this list — and change it accordingly.

- ✔ **Schedule from the start or finish of the project.** Most projects work forward from the start date. However, if you have an absolute drop-dead date for the end of your project (for example, if you're organizing a sports event that must occur on New Year's Day next year), you might want to set the finish date and then work backward to fit all your tasks into the allotted length of time. If you change this setting to Project Finish Date, the Finish Date field becomes available.

✔ **Set the current date.** You can fill in the current date according to your computer calendar. Or, you can choose another date if you like, but that usually doesn't make much sense unless you're in a different time zone from where the project will occur.

✔ **Set a status date.** By default there is no status date set for the project. You use a *status date* when you're tracking the progress of your project at regular intervals. If you set a status date, your computer assumes that any activity you record in your project is being tracked as of this date. You can find out more about this feature in Chapters 12, 13, and 14.

✔ **Set the working calendar for your project.** You have three choices: Standard, Night Shift, and 24 Hours. Base your choice on the working habits of your organization. For example, if your company uses resources in three shifts per day — a total of 24 hours of straight working time — and all those shifts would contribute work to your project, choose 24 Hours. If you use a day shift and a night shift, choose Night Shift. If you work a standard 8-hour day, choose Standard. (Most projects use a standard calendar with a typical 8-hour workday.)

Calendars can get a little confusing. A project calendar that you set in this dialog box indicates what the usual workday is like in your company, but you can set up individual calendars for each resource you create. You can then more easily accommodate both shift workers and nine-to-fivers in the same schedule. See Chapter 3 for more about resource calendars.

✔ **Assign a priority to your project.** Assigning a priority (such as 500 for high priority or 100 for a lower priority) can be especially useful if you use the same resources across several projects. With your priorities set on all projects, Project tools can then automatically reallocate resources.

You can also create custom project information fields for your organization in the Enterprise Custom Fields section of this dialog box. For example, you might want a field that explains which department in the company is running the project.

Clicking the Statistics button in this dialog box presents an overview of your project, as shown in Figure 1-12.

Project Statistics for 'PROJOFF'

	Start		Finish
Current	Thu 1/1/04		Wed 8/4/04
Baseline	Thu 1/1/04		Wed 8/4/04
Actual	NA		NA
Variance	0d		0d

	Duration	Work	Cost
Current	155d	2,308h	$78,820.00
Baseline	155d	2,308h	$78,820.00
Actual	0d	0h	$0.00
Remaining	155d	2,308h	$78,820.00

Percent complete:

Duration: 0%   Work: 0%

Close

Figure 1-12:
You can
review
a summary
of the
information
you entered.

Perusing the project schedule

After you choose settings in the Project Information dialog box and then click
OK, you're faced with a blank Project schedule, as shown in Figure 1-13. As a
writer, I can tell you that nothing is as daunting — or as inspiring — as facing
a blank page. It's the canvas on which you create your Project plan. Note the
Project Guide pane to the left of the spreadsheet section.

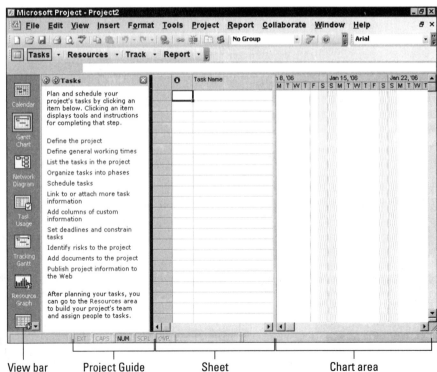

Figure 1-13:
Begin with a
new Project
schedule.

View bar   Project Guide   Sheet   Chart area

In Figure 1-13 you see Gantt Chart view. You can discover more about various views in Chapter 2. For now, note the following:

- ✔ **View bar:** To go to different views, click the bar of icons on the far left: the *View bar.* If this bar isn't displayed, choose View⇨View Bar to do so.
- ✔ **Project Guide:** To the right of the View bar is the *Project Guide task pane,* which is an informational area with step-by-step guidance on how to build your project. If Project Guide isn't displayed, click the Show/ Hide Project Guide button on the Project Guide toolbar to display it.
- ✔ **Sheet:** In the middle of the view is the sheet section. You can use this spreadsheet interface to enter, edit, and view information about your project.
- ✔ **Chart area:** Finally, the *chart area* on the far right reflects your task information graphically as soon as you begin to add tasks.
  - *Taskbars* in this area indicate the duration and timing of tasks in addition to the progress you record on them.
  - The *timescale* — the indications of time increments across the top of the chart area — helps you interpret the timing of each taskbar. You can adjust the increments to show your project in larger or smaller increments of time. Figure 1-12, for example, shows increments in days.

You start building a project by entering tasks. Simply click a cell in the Task Name column of the sheet section and then type the name. You can enter and edit details of a task by entering information directly into various columns (which you can display in many views) or by double-clicking the task name in the sheet to access the Task Information dialog box (see Figure 1-14). I get into more detail about entering task information in Chapter 2.

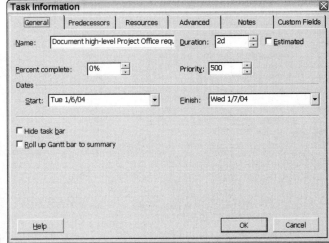

Figure 1-14:
The various tabs in this dialog box hold a wealth of information about a single task in your project.

Starting with templates

Reinventing the wheel has never been one of my favorite sports, so I'm grateful that Microsoft provides some convenient project templates. These include projects by type: for example, an engineering project or office move. Templates already have many tasks appropriate to the task type created for you.

Figure 1-15 shows the Project Office template. Templates typically contain sample tasks broken into logical phases, with task durations and dependencies in place. The templates from Microsoft often include resources, but you can create your own resources as well as use, edit, or delete the ones provided.

You can open a template from the New Project task pane. To do so, follow these steps:

1. **Choose File⇨New.**

   The New Project task pane appears, as shown in Figure 1-16.

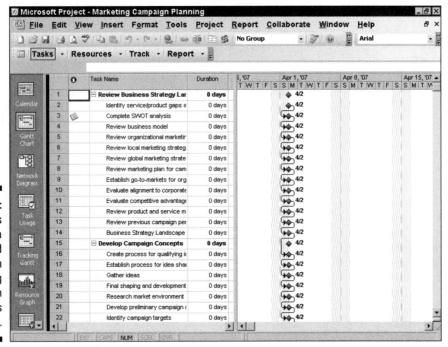

Figure 1-15: Templates provide a great head start in building common business projects.

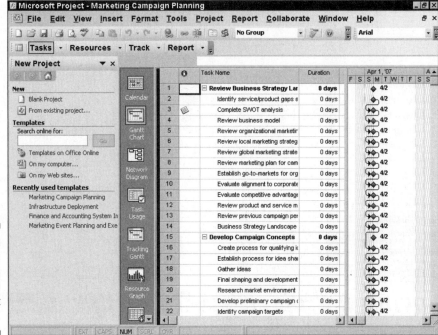

Figure 1-16:
Open a
template
from the
New Project
task pane.

2. Click the On My Computer link.

The Templates dialog box opens. You can also use the On My Web Sites and Templates on Office Online links to access online templates.

3. Click the Project Templates tab, which is shown in Figure 1-17.

4. Click a template to display a preview.

5. When you find the template you want to use, click OK.

The template opens in Project document format (MPP). You can then save the file with a new name. You can also delete tasks, move them around, or add tasks as necessary for your project.

After opening a template, be sure to check its Project Information (choose Project➪Project Information) to make sure that the Start Date and Calendar options are set as you want.

If you modify a template and think that you might use that set of tasks again for future projects, consider saving the file as a custom template. Just choose File➪Save As, and then select Template in the Save As Type list.

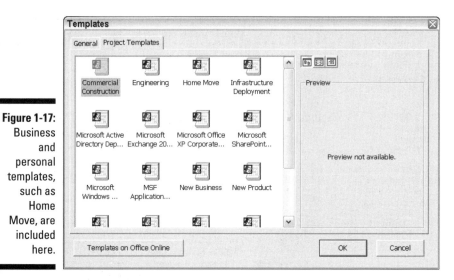

Figure 1-17:
Business
and
personal
templates,
such as
Home
Move, are
included
here.

Saving a Project for Posterity

Saving Project files works just as saving does in most other software you've used. Here's a reminder.

To save a Project file that you haven't saved before, follow these steps:

1. **Choose File⇨Save As.**
2. **Use the Save In list to locate the folder where you want to save the file; then click to select it.**
3. **In the File Name text box, type a name for the project.**
4. **Click Save.**

It's good organizational practice to create a folder for your project where you save in one place not only your Project files but also supporting documents, e-mails, and other items. You can create a new folder from within the Save As dialog box by clicking the Create New Folder button.

Getting Help from Project

If you can get to work without mishap and turn on your computer, you probably know how to use a help system in software, too. Table 1-1 offers a rundown of the type of help you can find in Project 2007 when you click the Help button on the Standard toolbar.

Table 1-1	Project Help Features
Help Option	*How to Use It*
Microsoft Project Help	This option displays the full Help feature with a table of contents and a search field.
Show the Office Assistant	Displays the annoying little icon that asks you to enter your question in a natural-language style (that is, a sentence) and offers topics to try to address your questions.
Contents and Index	Displays the same thing as Microsoft Project Help. Go figure.
Reference	Provides reference information such as a comprehensive list of all fields in Project, a glossary, and a table of mouse and keyboard shortcuts.
Getting Started	A side menu for this Help menu option offers a tutorial and project map. The tutorial provides a set of topics explaining Project from the basics of what is project management through creating a plan. The project map is another take on the phases involved in building your project.
Microsoft Office Online	Because Project is part of the Office family of products, this link is provided to the Office online Assistance Center.
Microsoft Office Diagnostics	This option automatically identifies errors and tries to correct them. Use it if you have serious problems using the software (for example, if the software continually shuts down and gives you error messages).
Project Guide	The one option not accessed from the Help menu, Project Guide is new in Version 12. Project Guide, which appears when you open a new project, offers links to step-by-step information on how to build your project.

As you can see, you could spend a year just working your way through all the help topics in Project. Don't worry: They're there when you need them, and some, such as Project Guide, even pop up automatically to offer help.

Chapter 2

The Best-Laid Plans

*H*omer (not Simpson — the other one) once said, "The evil plan is most harmful to the planner." In the interest of helping you avoid the evils of bad planning, take a moment to get comfortable with various aspects of your Project plan.

The file that you create in Project is called a Project *plan,* or *schedule.* This plan is like a multidimensional chess game from *Star Trek,* with a plethora of data about various aspects of your project as well as graphical representations of that information.

To see that information, Project provides more views than the Grand Canyon. These views help you observe the structure of your plan and see the progress in your project. Project also offers many ways to move around and display different information in your views. Navigating Project and displaying (and modifying) its views are the topics covered in this chapter.

Navigating Project

Having a lot of views from which to observe your project information is great, but all those views don't do you any good if you don't know how to get from one to the other or how to move around in a view after you find it.

Changing views

You can move from one view to another in Project by using the View bar or the View menu. The View bar runs along the far left side of every view, as shown in Figure 2-1. Simply click any view icon there to display that view.

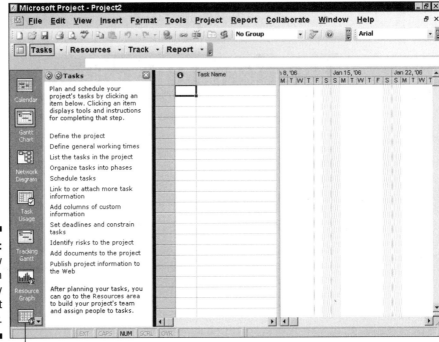

Figure 2-1:
The View bar location in every Project view.

View bar

TIP

If the View bar doesn't appear on your screen, choose View⇨View Bar to display it.

There are eight commonly used views already displayed on the View bar; Calendar, Gantt Chart, Network Diagram, Task Usage, Tracking Gantt, Resource Graph, Resource Sheet, and Resource Usage. In addition to these views, you might need to use a few dozen other views as you work through your project. To display views not shown on the View bar, follow these steps:

1. **Click the arrow at the bottom of the View bar to scroll down to the bottom.**

2. **Click the More Views icon.**

   The More Views dialog box appears, as shown in Figure 2-2.

   You can also access the More Views dialog box by choosing View⇨More Views.

3. **Use the scroll bar to locate the view you want.**

4. **Select the view you want and click Apply.**

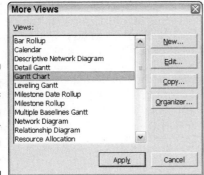

Figure 2-2:
Dozens of
views are
available for
display in
Project.

Scrolling around

The simplest views, such as Calendar view, have a single pane, with horizontal and vertical scroll bars. Other views, such as Resource Usage view (see Figure 2-3), have two panes. In that case, each pane has its own horizontal scroll bar; they share the vertical scroll bar, so the panes move up and down together.

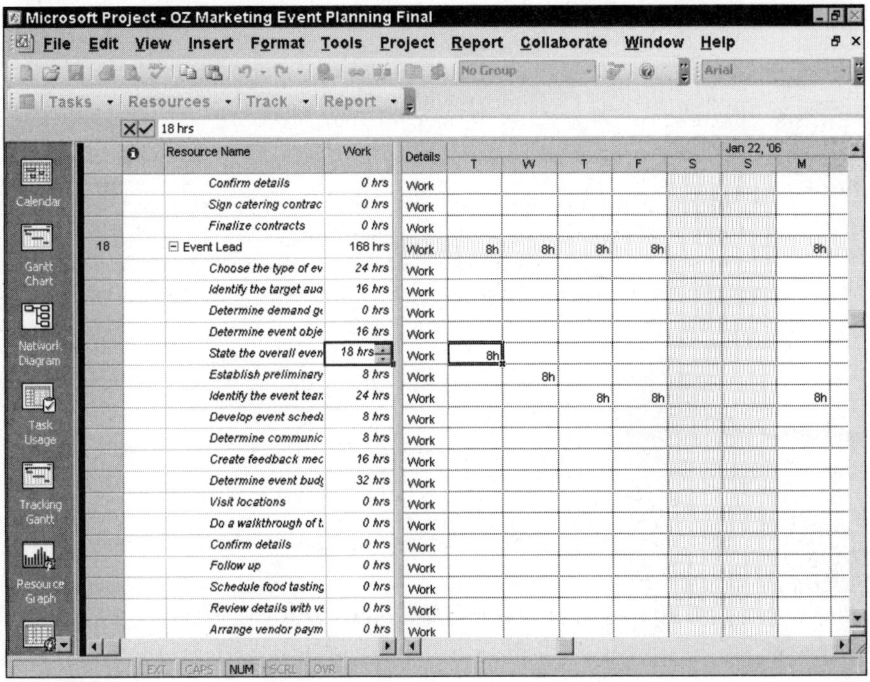

Figure 2-3:
Multiple
panes of
information
maximize
space in
many views.

In most views with two panes, the pane to the left is called the *sheet,* which is a spreadsheet-like interface with columns of information. To the right of this view is the chart. The *chart* uses bars, symbols, and lines to represent each task in your project and the dependency relationships among them.

At the top of the chart area is the *timescale.* This tool is used as a scale against which you can interpret the timing of the taskbars. To see your plan in greater or lesser timing detail, you can modify the time units used in the timescale. For example, you can look at your tasks in detail over days or in a broader overview in months. Figure 2-4 shows a two-pane view with a sheet, chart, and timescale.

See the "Changing the timescale" section, later in this chapter, to find out how to change the time increments displayed in the timescale.

By using the horizontal scroll bars in each pane, you can view additional columns or additional time periods in any pane with a timescale. Timescale panes cover the life of the project; in longer projects, you can scroll through years of time.

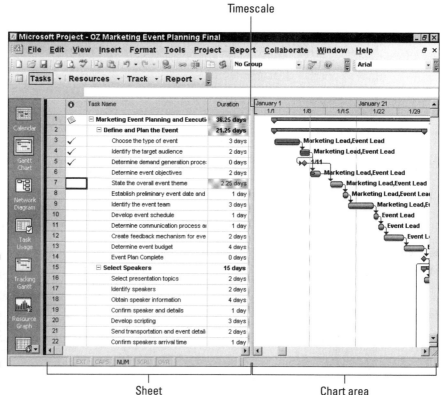

Figure 2-4:
The sheet, chart, and timescale of Gantt Chart view.

Use these different methods to work with scroll bars:

- ✔ **Click the scroll box and drag it until you reach the location in the pane that you want to look at.** When you click and drag the scroll box to move through a timescale display, the date display indicates where you are at any time in your scrolling calendar. Release the mouse button when the date display matches the date you want to view.

- ✔ **Click to the left or right of the horizontal scroll box to move one page at a time.** Note that a page in this instance is controlled to some extent by how you resize a given pane. For example, with a timescale pane and a timescale set to weeks, you move one week at a time. In a sheet pane displaying three columns, you move to the next (or preceding) column.

- ✔ **Click the right or left arrow at either end of a scroll bar to move in smaller increments.** With a sheet pane, you move about one-half column per click. In a timescale view with weeks displayed, you move about one day at a time.

Getting to a specific spot in your plan

To reach a particular area of your Project plan, you can also use the Go To command on the Edit menu. With the Go To command, you can enter either of two items in the Go To dialog box when you want to find a task:

- ✔ A date from a drop-down calendar
- ✔ A task ID

You can also click the Go To Selected Task tool (or press Ctrl+Shift+F5) to scroll the timescale to show the taskbar for a selected task in the sheet pane.

The task ID is assigned automatically when you create tasks; this number provides a unique identifier for tasks in the plan.

A Project with a View

Views are one way software designers organize information so that you can get to it in logical ways. Because of the complexity of information in a typical Project plan, many views are available to examine it. If an average word-processed document is as complex as a cookie, your average Project plan is more like a five-tier wedding cake adorned with intricate flowers and garlands in delicate swirls of sugary icing.

In a typical Project plan, you have information about the following:

- ✔ **Resources:** The resource name, resource type, rate per hour, overtime rate, assignments, department, cost per use, and more
- ✔ **Tasks:** The task name, duration, start and finish date, assigned resources, costs, constraints, and dependencies, for example
- ✔ **Project timing and progress:** Several types of calendars, project start and finish dates, percentage of tasks completed, resource hours spent, baseline information, critical path information, and more
- ✔ **Financial information:** Earned value, time and cost variance, and projected costs for uncompleted work, for example

Want to get closer? In every view, you can use the Zoom command on the View menu to see more or less detail in your schedule. Read more about using the Zoom command in the sidebar "Zooming in and out," later in this chapter.

Finding out how to use the many Project views to enter, edit, look at, and analyze Project data is important. Don't worry that you'll be overwhelmed: After a while, using all those views is . . . well, a piece of cake.

For more about modifying the format of elements displayed in a view, see Chapter 11.

Home base: Gantt Chart view

Gantt Chart view is like a favorite room in your house, the place where most people end up. It's the view that appears first when you open a new project. This view, shown in Figure 2-5, is a combination of spreadsheet data and a graphical representation of tasks; it offers a wealth of information in one place.

Gantt Chart view has two major sections: the sheet pane and the chart pane. This view is an electronic version of the original Gantt Chart, developed by engineer Henry L. Gantt in 1917 to deal with production-control projects in manufacturing. (See? Invent a project management tool, and you too can become immortal.)

In Gantt Chart view (and any view with a sheet pane), you can change what information is shown in the sheet by using tables. *Tables* are preset combinations of columns of data that you can easily display by choosing View⇨Table and then choosing a table (such as Entry or Cost) from the submenu that appears.

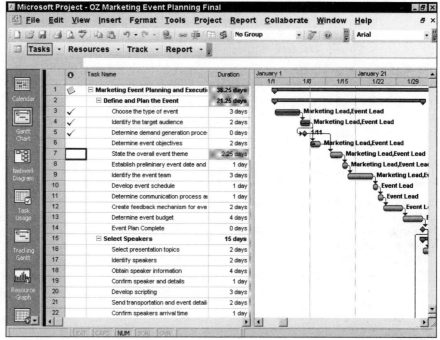

Figure 2-5:
Gantt Chart
view can
display any
combination
of columns
of data that
you want.

You can also customize the column display for any table by displaying or hiding individual columns of data one by one. (See the section "Displaying different columns," later in this chapter, for information about this procedure.)

Going with the flow: Network Diagram view

Another view that you're likely to use often is Network Diagram view, which is shown in Figure 2-6. The organization of information represents the work-flow in your project, with a series of task boxes. The boxes include dependency lines running between them to reflect the sequence of tasks (see Chapter 6 for more about dependency relationships). You read this view from left to right, with the earlier tasks on the left flowing into later tasks and sub-tasks to the right. Tasks that happen in the same timeframe are aligned vertically above each other. Tasks with an X through them have been marked as complete.

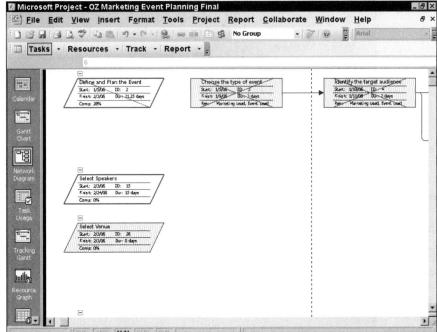

Figure 2-6:
Network
Diagram
view puts
important
task
information
in task
boxes.

Traditionally called a *PERT chart,* this method of diagramming workflow was developed by the United States Navy in the 1950s for use in building the Polaris submarine.

Network Diagram view has no timescale because the view isn't used to see specific timing but rather to see the general order of tasks in a plan. However, each task box holds specific timing information about each task, such as the start date, finish date, and duration. (You can customize the information in the task boxes, as described later in this chapter, in the "Customizing Views" section.)

Calling up Calendar view

Who can conceive of creating a schedule without opening up a calendar? This familiar view of time is one of the many views offered in Project. Calendar view, as shown in Figure 2-7, looks like a monthly wall calendar, with boxes that represent days on a calendar in rows that represent the days in a week.

You can modify Calendar view to display from one to six weeks (or more, by using a Custom setting in the Zoom dialog box) on the screen at a time. Calendar view also includes a timescale that you can modify to show a 7-day or 5-day week and shading to indicate working and nonworking days based on a selected base or resource calendar.

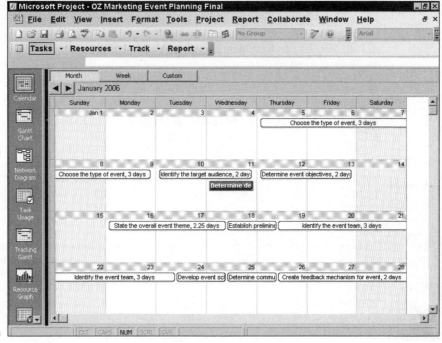

Figure 2-7:
The familiar
calendar
interface
shows you
how one
task can
straddle
several days
(or even
weeks).

Dozens of views are built into Project. You encounter many more as you work through specific elements of Project in this book.

Customizing Views

Just when you thought you were starting to get a handle on the two dozen or so views available in Project, I dazzle you with even more possibilities: Every one of those views can be customized to show different information. Now the possible view variations become astronomical.

You can customize every view in Project to show different information; for example, you can choose to show different columns of information in spread-sheets, different labels in Network Diagram boxes or taskbars, or different sets of data in graph views. You can modify the size of panes of information and adjust the timescale.

Why all this flexibility with what you see on-screen? At various times in a project, you need to focus on different aspects of your tasks. Having a problem with costs? Take a look at Resource Usage view and insert several columns of cost information, such as resource rates and total actual costs. Is your plan taking longer than the Hundred Years' War? You might want to display Tracking

Gantt view and look at a bunch of columns with timing and dependency data or examine the project's critical path in the chart pane. Need to display more of the sheet area so that you can read those columns without having to scroll? You can do that, too. In this section, you find out how to do all the things you need to do to show a variety of information in each view.

Working with view panes

In addition to Gantt Chart view, several other views have two panes, such as Task Usage, Tracking Gantt, and Resource Usage. You can modify the information that you see in the sheet pane as well as the scale for timing in the chart pane. You can also display information near taskbars in the chart pane.

Resizing a pane

In views that show more than one pane, you can reduce or enlarge each pane. This capability helps you see more information in one area, depending on what your focus is at the time.

The overall area taken up by the two panes is constant, so when you enlarge one pane, you reduce the size of the other.

Follow these steps to change the size of a pane in a view:

1. **Place your mouse cursor over the edge of a pane.**

2. **When you see a cursor that's a line with two arrows (one pointing left and one pointing right), click and drag.**

    • Dragging to the left enlarges the pane on the right.

    • Dragging to the right enlarges the pane on the left.

3. **Release the mouse button.**

    The panes are resized.

Note that if you display the Project Guide or another task pane, such as New Project or Search Results, Project automatically resizes the sheet and chart panes to accommodate the additional pane.

Because the Project Guide takes up space on-screen, a quick way to see more of any of the project information in any view is to hide the Project Guide; this advice also applies for the View bar. The Project Guide toolbar offers a Hide/Show Guide button that you can click to hide or display it, and you can choose View⇨View Bar to turn the View bar on and off.

Changing the timescale

I wish I could tell you that Project actually lets you change time and give your project lots more of it, but it doesn't. What it does allow you to do is modify the timescale to display your plan in larger or smaller time increments.

A timescale consists of a possible total of three tiers, as you can see in Figure 2-8. You can use them to display different time increments. For example, the top tier could mark off months, while the middle tier marks off weeks, and the bottom tier marks off days. This variety of detail lets you easily observe overall task length as well as points in time during the life of the task. You can use all three tiers, only the middle tier, or the middle and bottom tiers.

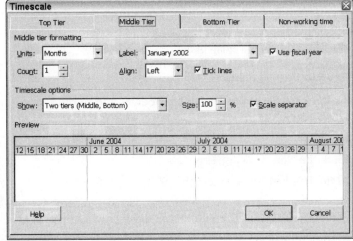

Figure 2-8: The timescale is comprised of three tiers, so you can view time from several directions.

You can modify the units of time and the alignment of each tier and also include tick lines to mark the beginning of each increment on the timescale. You also have the option to include or not include nonworking time on the timescale. For example, if you include an indication of nonworking time on a project for which weekends are nonworking, Saturdays and Sundays are indicated by a shaded area in the display, which can make a useful visual divider between weeks.

You can also display text labels near taskbars and change what data is included. Labels can be placed above, below, inside, or to the left or right of the taskbars. Especially in projects where you display many columns of data and a lengthy schedule, a taskbar can be placed far to the right of the sheet pane data. You can then include information, such as task name or start date, alongside the taskbar to help you read your plan more easily.

To modify the timescale, follow these steps:

1. **Right-click the timescale in any view that contains one and then click Timescale.**

   The Timescale dialog box appears. (Refer to Figure 2-8.)

2. **Click a tier tab and select a style for Units, Label, and Align.**

3. **Set the count.**

   For example, if your Units choice is weeks and you change the Count option to 2, the timescale appears in two-week increments.

4. **If you don't want to display a certain tier, select One Tiers or Two Tiers from the Show drop-down list (under the Timescale Options section).**

5. **If you want Project to use fiscal year notation in the timescale, select the Use Fiscal Year check box.**

   For example, if your 2006 fiscal year begins July 1, 2006, 2007 is used on all months in the fiscal year. The fiscal year is set in the Options dialog box on the Calendar tab.

6. **To show marks at the beginning of each unit of time, select the Tick Lines check box.**

7. **Repeat Steps 2–6 for each tier you want to modify.**

8. **Click the Non-working Time tab.**

9. **In the Draw options, select the one you prefer.**

   Your choices are to have the shaded area for nonworking time appear behind taskbars or in front of them or just not appear.

10. **In the Color or Pattern list, select different options for the shading format.**

Zooming in and out

One way to modify your display for any Project view is to use the Zoom In and Zoom Out buttons on the Standard toolbar. This feature shows you a longer or shorter period of time in your project without having to change the timescale settings. When you need to see several years at a time in your project, for example, click Zoom Out several times until you fit as many months or years as you like in the view. You can also choose View➪Zoom and specify periods of time to display in the Zoom dialog box, or even choose to have the entire project appear on-screen.

11. **Click the Calendar setting and select a different calendar to base the timescale on.**

    You can find out more about calendar choices in Chapter 3.

12. **Click OK to save your new settings which apply only to the timescale for the currently displayed view.**

You can use the Size setting on the three tier tabs to shrink the display proportionately to get more information on your screen or the printed page.

Displaying different columns

Each spreadsheet view has certain default columns of data that are stored in tables. Gantt Chart view with the Tracking table displayed, for example, has data related to the progress of tasks. The Resource sheet contains many columns of data about resources that can be useful for entering new resource information. In addition to displaying predefined tables of columns, you can modify any spreadsheet table to display any columns you like.

Follow this procedure to show selected columns of data:

1. **Right-click the column heading area and then choose Insert Column.**

    The Column Definition dialog box appears, as shown in Figure 2-9.

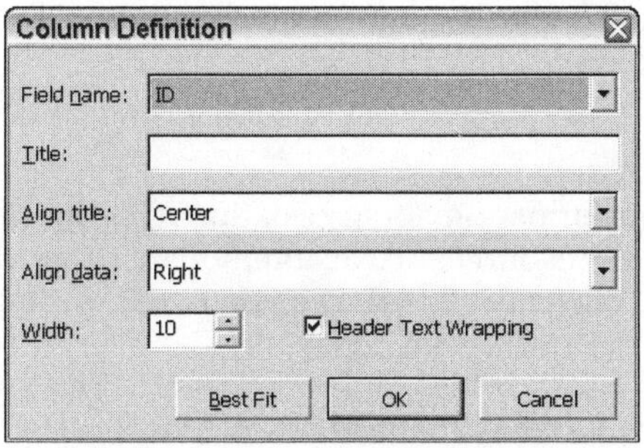

Figure 2-9:
Here you can select new columns to insert.

Column Definition

Field name: ID
Title:
Align title: Center
Align data: Right
Width: 10   ☑ Header Text Wrapping

Best Fit   OK   Cancel

2. **In the Field Name list, select the field that contains the information you want to include.**

3. **If you want to enter a different title for the field, type it in the Title box.**

    The title in the current view appears in the column heading for this field.

4. **Use the Align Title, Align Data, and Width options to modify the column format.**

5. **Click OK to insert the column.**

To hide a column, right-click its heading in the sheet pane and then choose Hide Column.

You can also display preset tables of sheet data, such as Tracking for recording activity on tasks or Entry for entering new task information. You do this by simply choosing View➪Table and then clicking the name of the table you want to display.

Modifying the contents of the Network Diagram boxes

When you first display Network Diagram view, you see rectangular boxes, one for each task in your project. You can change the information contained in those boxes and change the box formatting.

By default, a typical subtask contains the task name, task ID, start date, finish date, duration, and resource names. For a milestone, you get only the milestone date, milestone name, and task ID number.

See Chapter 4 for more about adding information about tasks and milestones.

Different categories of tasks (such as *critical* or *noncritical*) can contain different information, and you can change the information contained in any individual box or category of boxes.

Changing what's in the box

Sometimes you want to see information about task timing; other times, you focus on other issues, such as resources. To accommodate these various information needs, Network Diagram view allows you to use various templates for what's contained in the diagram boxes.

To modify the information included in these boxes, follow these steps:

1. **Right-click anywhere in Network Diagram view outside any box and then choose Box Styles.**

   The Box Styles dialog box appears, as shown in Figure 2-10.

2. **In the Style Settings For list, select a task category.**

3. **To modify the data included in the task boxes, select a different template from the Data Template list.**

   You can choose additional templates (and edit any template to include whatever data you like) by clicking the More Templates button.

   A preview of the data included in the template appears in the Preview area.

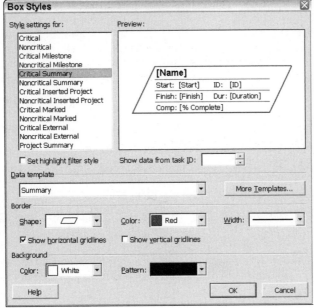

Figure 2-10:
You can use
templates of
data for
Network
Diagram
view task
boxes.

4. **Click OK to save the new template.**

You can also apply different templates to each box separately by right-clicking a box (rather than clicking outside a box), choosing Format Box, selecting a different template from the Data Template drop-down list, and then clicking OK.

Making boxes pretty

Are you the creative type? Don't like the shape or color of the boxes in the Network Diagram boxes? Want to add shading to the background of the boxes? Project lets you do all that and more.

Follow these steps to modify the format of Network Diagram boxes:

1. **Right-click anywhere in Network Diagram view outside any box and then choose Box Styles.**

   The Box Styles dialog box appears, as shown in Figure 2-11.

2. **Click the Shape drop-down list and select a different shape from the list that appears.**

3. **Click the Color drop-down list and select a different color from the list of colors.**

   Note: This choice specifies the color of the line that forms the box, not a background color. For that, see Step 5 of this list.

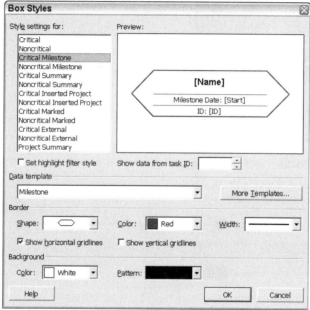

Figure 2-11:
Modify the
format of all
boxes by
using the
settings in
this dialog
box.

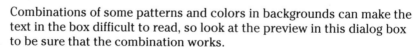

4. **Click the Width drop-down list and select a line width from those displayed.**

5. **Click the Color drop-down list in the Background section and select a color for the background that fills the inside of each box.**

6. **Click the Pattern drop-down list and select a pattern of lines to fill the interior of each box.**

Combinations of some patterns and colors in backgrounds can make the text in the box difficult to read, so look at the preview in this dialog box to be sure that the combination works.

7. **Click OK to save the new settings.**

You can also format individual boxes by right-clicking a box, choosing Format Box, and then making the settings outlined in this set of steps.

Chapter 3

Mark It on Your Calendar

*M*ost people live their lives based on clocks and calendars. Think about it: You wake up, and your first thoughts are about what day it is, what time it is, and whether it's a working day.

You have a familiar definition for what your typical workday is, whether you're a 9-to-5 kind of person or your particular job calls for you to work from midnight to 8 a.m. You also vary from that routine now and then by putting in a 12-hour marathon in a crunch or slipping away after half a day to go fishing on a nice summer day.

Project 2007 calendars are sort of like your life in that they set some standards for a typical working time and then allow for variation. Unlike you, Project 2007 has several types of calendars to account for.

Mastering Base, Project, Resource, and Task Calendars

Bear with me because I won't kid you: Mastering the four calendars in Project 2007 can be tricky. Understanding how calendars work in Project 2007, however, is essential to mastering the software. Tasks are scheduled and resources are assigned based on the calendar settings that you make. Thus, the costs accumulated by resource work hours won't be accurate if you don't understand your calendar settings from the get-go.

Because the use of the term "project" can get confusing as it refers to the software, your project plan, and one of the calendar types (the Project calendar), I need to explain the terminology I use in this chapter. I use Project 2007 when referring to the software itself, Project calendar when referring to the calendar, and just plain project when talking about your project plan.

How calendars work

Here's the lowdown on the role of each of the four calendars in Project 2007 (with more in the next section about how they interact with each other):

- ✔ **Base calendar:** This is the calendar template that all other calendars are built on top of. Three Base calendars are available: Standard, 24 Hours, and Night Shift. (You read more about them shortly.)

- ✔ **Project calendar:** This is the default calendar for scheduling. This is where you choose which Base calendar template this particular project should use.

- ✔ **Resource calendar:** This combines the Base calendar settings with any exceptions (nonworking times) that you set for a particular resource.

- ✔ **Task calendar:** This is where you can set exceptions for a particular task.

When you create tasks and assign resources to work on them, Project 2007 has to base that work on a timing standard. For example, if you say that a task should be completed in one workday, Project 2007 knows that a *workday* means 8 hours (or 12 hours or whatever) because that's how you set up a standard workday in your Project calendar. Likewise, suppose that you assign a resource to put in two weeks of work on a task in a company that uses a standard five-day workweek. If that resource's own calendar is set for a standard four-day workweek, the two weeks of work put in by that resource defer to the timing of the Resource calendar for a total of only eight workdays.

The nature of a task can have an effect on resource time. A two-week, effort-driven task isn't complete until its resources have put in two weeks (according to the Project or Task calendar) of effort. Find out more about effort-driven tasks in Chapter 4.

Not everyone in a company works the same schedule, and not every task can be performed in the same eight-hour workday. To deal with the variations in schedules that occur in most workforces, Project 2007 offers various calendar settings. As I mentioned earlier in this chapter, Project, Resource, and Task calendars can be set to use one of three Base calendar templates built into Project 2007. The three Base calendar templates are as follows:

- ✔ **Standard:** The default setting. Sets a working day as 8 a.m.–5 p.m. with an hour for lunch and a five-day, Monday–Friday workweek.

- ✔ **24 Hours:** Allows work to go on around the clock every day of the week.

- ✔ **Night Shift:** Sets the working time as 11 p.m.–8 a.m. with an hour for dinner and a six-night, Monday–Saturday workweek. Working times for a Night Shift calendar are shown in Figure 3-1.

Check out the legend in Figure 3-1; it explains how different hours are shaded in the calendar display.

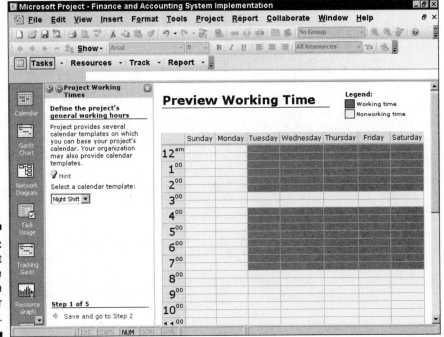

Figure 3-1: Different hours are shaded in the calendar display.

You can modify the three Base calendar templates and create new templates from them. See the section "Creating a Custom Calendar Template," later in this chapter.

How one calendar relates to another

All calendars in your project are controlled, by default, by the Project calendar setting. Here's the tricky part, though: When you change a Task or Resource calendar (this type of change is referred to as an *exception*), you have to understand which setting takes precedence.

Here's how this precedence thing works:

- ✔ With no other settings made, the Base calendar template you select for the Project calendar when you first create the project controls the working times and days of all tasks and resources.

- ✔ If you make changes in the working hours for a resource, those settings take precedence over the Project calendar for that resource when you assign it to a task. Likewise, if you assign a different Base calendar for a task, that calendar takes precedence over the Project calendar for that task.

- ✔ If you apply one calendar to a resource and a different calendar to a task that the resource is assigned to, Project 2007 uses only common hours to schedule the resource. For example, if the Task calendar allows work from 8 a.m.–5 p.m. and the Resource calendar allows work from 6 a.m.–2 p.m., the resource works from 8 a.m.–2 p.m., which is the only period the calendars have in common.

- ✔ You can set a task to ignore Resource calendar settings by opening the Task Information dialog box (double-click the task name in Gantt Chart view) and selecting the Scheduling Ignores Resource Calendars check box on the Advanced tab. (This setting isn't available if the Task calendar is set to None.) You might make this setting if you know that all resources are required to be involved in a task (such as a quarterly company meeting), regardless of their usual work hours.

Calendar Options and Working Times

Just when you thought that you were out of the woods, I'll throw two more timing elements at you — calendar options and working times.

Calendar options are used to change the standards for a working day, week, and year. If you set a Project calendar to Standard (by default, 8 a.m. to 5 p.m., five days a week), for example, the Calendar tab of the Options dialog box is where you can designate which five days are working days or modify the working hours to 9 a.m.–6 p.m.

Working time is used to adjust the time available for work on a particular date or days. Suppose you make a change to the calendar options so that you have 8-hour days and 32-hour workweeks. You should also check your working time and be sure that you specify three days of the seven-day week should be nonworking to jibe with the 32-hour week. If you want to set a certain date as *nonworking* for your project, such as your company offsite meeting day, you can do that with the working time settings.

If you use Project Server for enterprise-wide project management, you can make settings in the Enterprise Global Template, which sets the working time for all projects across your company. See Chapter 18 for more about enterprise settings.

Setting calendar options

When you make changes to a Resource or Task calendar, you simply adjust the times that a resource is available to work or the time during which a task occurs. You don't change the length of a typical workday for the project. A day is still eight hours long if that's the Project calendar setting, even if you say that a task that takes place on that day uses the 24-hour Base calendar template.

If you want to change the length of a typical workday to ten hours rather than eight, for example, you must do so on the Calendar tab of the Options dialog box.

Follow these steps to modify the calendar options:

1. **Choose Tools⇨Options.**

   The Options dialog box appears.

2. **Click the Calendar tab, as shown in Figure 3-2.**

   You can also display these settings by clicking the Options button in the Change Working Time dialog box. Read about the settings there in the following section.

3. **From the Week Starts On drop-down list, choose a day.**

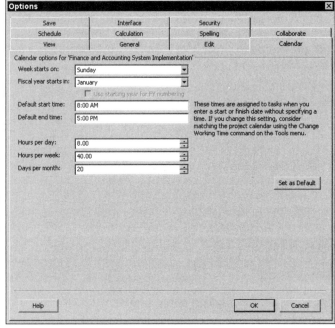

Figure 3-2:
Define your typical working day, week, month, and year.

4. **To modify the start of your fiscal year, select the month you want from the Fiscal Year Starts In drop-down list.**

5. **To change the working hours for a typical day, type new times in the Default Start Time and Default End Time fields.**

   If you change the Default Start or End Time setting, you should also change the corresponding working times. See the following section to discover how to do this.

6. **Modify the Hours Per Day, Hours Per Week, and Days Per Month fields as needed.**

7. **Click OK to save the settings.**

If your company uses these settings for most projects, you can click the Set As Default button on the Calendar tab of the Options dialog box to make your settings the default settings for any new project you create.

Setting exceptions to working times

If you want to change the available working hours for a particular day (such as December 24), you use the working time settings. For example, if you want the day before Christmas to be a half day, you can modify the working time settings for that day; then any resources assigned to a task on this date put in only one-half day of work. You also use these settings to specify global working and nonworking days to match the calendar options settings.

Here's how to change working times:

1. **Choose Tools⇨Change Working Time.**

   The Change Working Time dialog box appears, as shown in Figure 3-3.

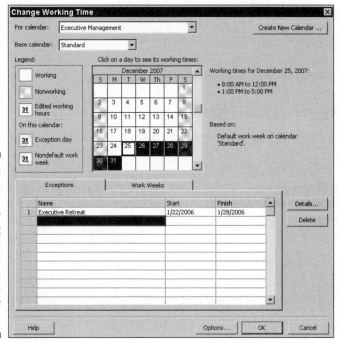

Figure 3-3:
The working times you set here for your project should correspond to settings in the calendar options.

2. **In the Click On a Day to See Its Working Times calendar section, click the day you want to change.**

3. **Click the Exceptions tab to display it; then click a blank row and type a name for the exception.**

4. **Click the Details button.**

   The Details box for this calendar dialog box appears (see Figure 3-4).

5. **Select either the Nonworking or Working Times radio button.**

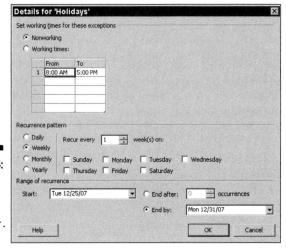

Figure 3-4:

calendar.

6. **Enter a time range in the From and To fields.**

   If you want to set nonconsecutive hours (for example, to build in a lunch break), you have to put two or more sets of numbers here (such as 8 to 12 and 1 to 5).

7. **Select a recurrence pattern and then set an interval in the Recur Every *x* Week(s) On field.**

   For example, if you select Weekly and click the arrows to set the interval field to 3, this pattern recurs every three weeks.

8. **Set the range of recurrence.**

   You can do this step by entering Start and End By dates or by selecting the End After radio button and setting the number of occurrences there.

9. **Click OK twice to close the dialog boxes and save your changes.**

The Nondefault Work Week legend item that you find in the Change Working Time dialog box (refer to Figure 3-3) designates working time that isn't part of the working time established by the Base calendar template for this calendar.

Setting the Project calendar

The first calendar that you should set up for your project is the Project calendar. You set the Project calendar in the Project Information dialog box (shown in Figure 3-5), which you can display at any time by choosing Project⇨Project Information.

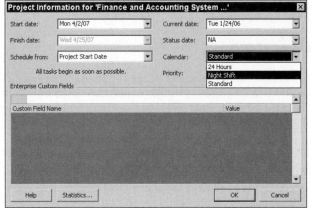

Here are the settings that you can make in the Project Information dialog box:

- ✓ **Calendar:** Select the Base calendar template to use for the Project calendar from this drop-down list. I list this setting first because it's the only one you *have* to deal with when you start a new project.

- ✓ **Start Date and Finish Date:** You might want to wait to set these dates until you build in most of your tasks and resources. Then, when you really know when you can start work, set the start date and let Project 2007 calculate the finish date based on your tasks' timing and dependencies. See more about these settings in Chapter 4.

- ✓ **Schedule From:** You can choose to have tasks scheduled backward from the finish date or forward from the start date. Most folks go forward from the start date.

- ✓ **Current Date:** By default, this setting matches your computer clock setting. However, you can change this so that it does not match your computer clock setting. Changing this date is useful for looking at what-if scenarios or for tracking progress as of a certain date in the past.

- ✓ **Status Date:** You typically set this to the current date to track progress on your project. When tracking you usually want to see the status of your project as of now, so you don't really need to deal with this setting. However if you want to track as of the end of a fiscal period or another timeframe, you can change this to track the status of your tasks as of any other date.

- ✓ **Priority:** This field is useful if your organization has many projects and you create links among them. If you use a tool such as resource leveling (see Chapter 10 for more about this topic) to resolve conflicts, it can consider this project priority setting when making its calculations about what to delay and what to keep on track.

Using Project Guide to Make Calendar Settings

Project Guide offers a useful Calendar Wizard that can help you set both calendar options and working time settings, which can be useful when you're new to Project 2007. Follow these steps to make calendar options and Project calendar settings using this wizard:

1. **If Project Guide isn't already visible, you can display it at any time by choosing View➪Toolbars➪Project Guide.**

   If the Project Guide toolbar is displayed and you want to hide it, you can click the Show/Hide Project Guide button on the Project Guide toolbar to hide it.

2. **Click the Task button if the task pane isn't already displayed.**

3. **Click the Define General Working Times item listed in the Project Guide task pane.**

   The Preview Working Time calendar appears, as shown in Figure 3-6.

4. **From the Select a Calendar Template drop-down list, choose the Base calendar that you want your project to use.**

   The Calendar setting offers the three Base calendar templates: Standard, Night Shift, and 24 Hours, as described in the "How calendars work" section, earlier in this chapter.

5. **Click the Save and Go to Step 2 option at the bottom of the Project Guide pane.**

   The task pane contents change to show check boxes for each day of the week (see Figure 3-7). If you want to change the working days in your calendar for this project, click to select or deselect any day.

6. **Click the Save and Go to Step 3 option, and then click Change Working Time in the task pane.**

   The Change Working Time dialog box, described in the preceding section, appears. Refer to that section to find out about changes you can make here.

7. **Click OK to close the Change Working Time dialog box and then click the Continue to Step 4 option.**

8. **Use the three text boxes that appear in the task pane to change the Hours Per Day, Hours Per Week, and Days Per Month settings, if you want.**

9. **Click the Continue to Step 5 option.**

   A message appears in the task pane to say that the Project calendar is now set. If you want to work with other calendars at this point, you can click the Define Additional Calendars option.

10. **Click Save and Finish.**

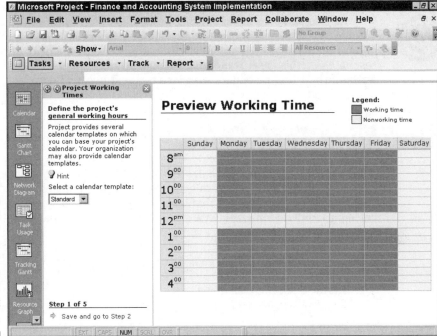

Figure 3-6:
You can choose your Base calendar and see a graphical view of it here.

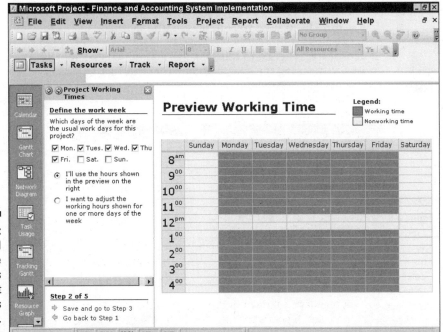

Figure 3-7:
Click and choose which days you want resources to work.

When you choose a Base calendar template, it sets the typical working time for your company. If a few resources on your project work the night shift but the majority of your resources work a standard workday, you may want to choose the Base calendar template that applies to the majority of your resources (in this case, Standard). You can make changes to specific Resource and Task calendars later (see the next two sections).

Modifying Task Calendars

You can set a Task calendar to use a different Base calendar template than the one you selected for the Project calendar. Doing so takes precedence over the Project calendar for that task. Suppose that you select the Standard calendar template for a project and a 24 Hours Task calendar template. If you then specify that the task has a duration of one day, its one 24-hour day.

To modify settings for a Task calendar, follow these steps:

1. **Double-click the task name.**

   The Task Information dialog box appears.

2. **Click the Advanced tab.**

3. **From the Calendar drop-down list, choose a different Base calendar, as shown in Figure 3-8.**

4. **Click OK to save your new calendar setting.**

If a resource assigned to this task has a modified calendar, that resource works only during the specific hours that the Task calendar and Resource calendar have in common.

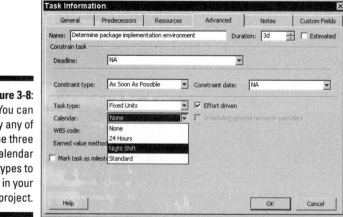

Figure 3-8: You can apply any of the three calendar types to tasks in your project.

Making Resource Calendar Settings

Even the most resourceful resources have only so many hours in a day to work. When you have to deal with variations in resource schedules, consider modifying the Resource calendars.

Which resources get calendars?

Projects can have three types of resource: work, material, and cost, which you can read more about in Chapter 7. For now, you should know that only one resource type — the work resource — has its own calendar. That's because material resources are charged not by time worked but rather by units used, and a cost resource gets assigned a set cost that also doesn't relate to any time worked on a task.

You can change the Base calendar template for each work resource and set specific dates as working or nonworking. These exceptions take precedence over your Project and Task calendars, and control when a specific resource can work.

I have one word of caution about modifying Resource calendars: Unless a resource truly has a unique working schedule, don't change its Base calendar template. For example, if a resource usually works a day shift but works a night shift for only a few days during the life of the project, don't change that resource's Base calendar template to Night Shift. If one person works from 10 a.m.–7 p.m. because the company allows him to, you probably don't have to vary his schedule from the typical 8-to-5 work schedule that's set in the Project calendar because he puts in eight hours a day like everyone else. Unless your project deals with the most detailed level of time, where hours and not days are the typical units of measure for tasks, making these types of changes is more work than it's worth.

Making the change to a resource's calendar

To modify a resource's calendar settings, follow these steps:

1. **Display a view that includes a resource column, such as the Resource sheet.**

   Just click the view in the View bar. Chapter 1 covers how to display different views.

2. **Double-click a resource name.**

   The Resource Information dialog box appears.

3. **Click the Change Working Time button to display the Change Working Time dialog box, shown in Figure 3-9.**

   The Exceptions and Work Weeks tabs have settings identical to the ones in the Change Working Time dialog box I discussed for tasks, but changes made here affect this resource rather than the task.

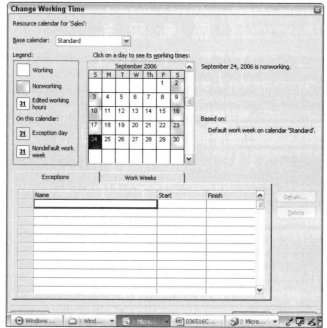

Figure 3-9:
Making
changes
here affects
this
resource.

4. **In the Click On a Day to See Its Working Times calendar section, click the day that you want to change.**

5. **Click the Work Weeks tab to display it; then click a blank row and enter a name for the exception.**

6. **Click the Details button.**

   The Details dialog box for this calendar appears (see Figure 3-10).

7. **Select either the Nonworking or the Working Times radio button.**

8. **Enter a time range in the From and To fields.**

   If you want to set nonconsecutive hours (for example, to build in a lunch break), you have to put two or more sets of numbers here (such as 8 to 12 and 1 to 5).

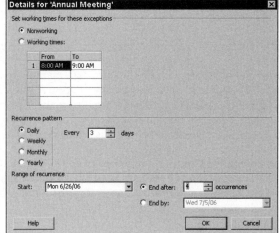

Figure 3-10:
Modify the
default
calendar
settings
here.

9. **Click to select a recurrence pattern and then set an interval in the Every *x* Days box.**

   For example, if you choose Daily and click the arrows to set the interval field to 3, this pattern recurs every three days.

10. **Set the range of recurrence.**

    You can do this by entering Start and End By dates or select the End After radio button and set the number of occurrences.

11. **Click OK twice to close the dialog boxes and save your changes.**

Can resources work overtime even if their calendars say that they're 9-to-5'ers? Yes, but you have to tell Project 2007 to schedule overtime work. You can also set a different rate to be charged for overtime work for that resource. To find out more about overtime, see Chapter 8.

Do It Yourself: Creating a Custom Calendar Template

If you ever wanted to make your own time, here's your chance. Although Project 2007's three Base calendar templates probably cover most working situations, you might want to create your own calendar template. For example, if your project involves a telemarketing initiative and most project resources work six hours, from 4 p.m.–10 p.m. (that's when they all call me!), it might be useful to create a new calendar template named Telemarketing.

If you want to save some time when creating a template (and time is what this chapter is all about), start with an existing Base calendar template that most closely fits your needs. Then, modify it as you like by making changes to the working times and calendar options (see the section "Calendar Options and Working Times," earlier in this chapter) to make sure that they're in agreement. After you create a new calendar template, it's available for you to apply in all three calendars: Project, Task, and Resource.

Because the Project calendar is the basis of your entire project, it should represent the most common working schedule in your project. If only some resources in your project work odd hours, change the Resource calendars and not the Project calendar.

Follow these steps to create a new calendar template:

1. **Choose Tools⇨Change Working Time.**

   The Change Working Time dialog box appears.

2. **Click the Create New Calendar button.**

   The Create New Base Calendar dialog box appears, as shown in Figure 3-11.

Figure 3-11:
Start your
new
calendar
here.

3. **In the Name box, type a unique name for the new calendar.**

4. **Select either the Create New Base Calendar or the Make a Copy Of *x* Calendar radio button. Then select an existing Base calendar from the list to base your calendar template on.**

In Step 4, if you choose Create New Base Calendar, Project creates a copy of the Standard calendar with a new name. If you choose Make a Copy Of and select 24 Hours or Night Shift, your new calendar is based on that choice. Whichever you choose, it's your starting point, and you can make changes to make the calendar unique after making this choice.

5. **Click OK to return to the Change Working Time dialog box.**

   Now you make changes to the working time for the new calendar template.

6. **Click Options.**

   The Options dialog box appears with the Calendar tab displayed.

7. **Make changes to the start of the week or year, the start and end times for a workday, and the hour or day settings.**

8. **Click OK twice to save the new calendar settings.**

Sharing Copies of Calendars

You can make a calendar available for all projects in two ways:

 ✔ **Set a calendar as the default for all new projects by making that choice in the Change Working Time dialog box.**

 ✔ **Make calendars from one project available for use in another project.**

   This second method is especially useful when you want to share calendars with other project managers in your company and don't want to change your own default calendar.

To copy a calendar from one project to another, follow this procedure:

1. **Open the project to which you want to copy a calendar.**

2. **Choose Tools⇨Organizer.**

   The Organizer dialog box appears.

3. **Click the Calendars tab, as shown in Figure 3-12.**

Figure 3-12:
You can copy your calendar to other projects.

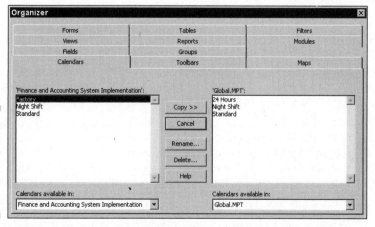

4. **From the Calendars Available In drop-down list (lower left), select the Project 2007 file that contains the calendar you want to copy. In the Calendars Available In drop-down list (lower right), choose whether you want to make the calendar available in another currently open project or the Global template.**

5. **In the list on the left, click the calendar you want to copy and then click the Copy button.**

   The calendar is copied to the current project.

6. **If you want to give the calendar a different name, click the Rename button, type a new name in the Rename dialog box that appears, and then click OK.**

7. **Close the Organizer by clicking the close button (the X) in the upper-right corner.**

Here are a few pointers about copying calendars from project to project:

✓ **Make sure that the name you give the calendar is descriptive.** Providing an appropriate name helps you remember the calendar's general parameters.

✓ **If your company has standard calendars, try having one resource create and disseminate them.** If ten versions of a management calendar float around and you grab the wrong one, it can cause problems.

✓ **Put the project manager's initials in each calendar template name you create.** That way, you know which ones you created.

Chapter 4

A Tisket, a Task Kit

A project manager is, by necessity, a taskmaster because tasks form the to-do list of your project. Tasks incorporate the What, When, Who, and Where information of your plan. Resources work on a project by getting assigned to tasks. The timing of tasks and the relationships between them form the schedule for your project. By tracking the activity on tasks, you can see the progress of your project over time.

You can create tasks in a few different ways: by typing information in the sheet area of Gantt Chart view (or any other view that displays information in columns) or by using the Task Information dialog box. You can also import tasks from Outlook or Excel.

You have to make some choices when you create tasks. For example, you have to determine and specify settings for a task that control its timing and its priority, as well as certain constraints regarding how its timing might or might not shift during the life of your project.

In this chapter, you find out all about tasks and the various settings that give each task its own, unique personality.

Tackling Your First Task

The first step in creating tasks is to identify the individual action items in your project. Then you can create each of those steps as individual tasks in Project.

After you create some tasks, you begin to build some structure to your to-do list by creating phases consisting of summary tasks with subtasks below them in an outline structure. For example, you might have a summary task named Permits with two subtasks: Submit Application and Pay Fees.

You can find out how to organize tasks into outlines in Chapter 5. All you have to focus on in this section is making the settings that are required to simply create tasks.

Identifying what makes up a task

Determining all the settings that characterize a task is a bit more complicated than writing an item on a to-do list. Think of each task in your project as a record — like a database record that lists a person's name, address, birthday, and shoe size. In a similar way, a task in Project contains data about that task: not only a task name but also other vital data about how that task fits into your project.

To create a task, you enter information such as

> Task name
>
> Task duration
>
> Task type
>
> Task priority
>
> Constraints for scheduling the task

Some settings, such as task type (fixed duration) and priority (none), can often be left at default settings. Others, such as task duration, almost always require some input from you.

Pretty much everything that you enter about a task (except the task name and resources assigned to the task) involves how the task timing is controlled. Several of these settings work in combination, with Project performing complex algorithms to set the timing of the task according to the value of each setting. Other elements, such as the task finish date, don't determine timing but rather cause Project to display a symbol in the Indicator column (the column to the right of the task number column with a small blue circle containing an "i" at the top) to alert you when a task has moved beyond its estimated deadline.

You can also specify a unique Task calendar in the Task Information dialog box; calendars are covered in Chapter 3.

Creating a task

You can create a task, on the simplest level, by entering a name for it. You can fill in the details of task duration and task type, for example, at the same time or later.

You can enter task names in three ways:

- ✔ Enter names in a Gantt Chart view sheet pane.
- ✔ Enter names in a Task Information dialog box.
- ✔ Import tasks from Excel or Outlook.

Generating tasks in Gantt Chart view

Many people who work on lengthy projects find that entering all task names in the sheet pane of Gantt Chart view is the quickest and easiest way to go. You can simply enter one task name in the Task Name column, press the down arrow on your keyboard to move to the next blank row, enter another task, and so on.

Follow these simple steps to enter a task in Gantt Chart view:

1. **In the Task Name column, click a blank cell.**

2. **Type a task name.**

   You can edit what you type by clicking in the entry box above the sheet and pressing the Delete or Backspace key to clear characters (see Figure 4-1). You can also click the X and check mark buttons to the left of the entry box to clear or accept your entry.

3. **Press the down arrow on your keyboard to move to the next cell in the column and then type the next task name.**

   When you move to the next task cell, Project automatically assigns a sequential task number in the far-left column. This number is a handy way to identify tasks in larger schedules.

4. **Repeat Step 3 until you enter all task names.**

   You can display whatever columns you like in Gantt Chart view to enter additional task information, such as duration, type, start date, and finish date. To display additional columns, simply right-click any column heading, choose Insert Column, and select the column to display from the Field Name list.

   You can also use the Entry table (choose View➪Table➪Entry to display it) to access the most common task information columns.

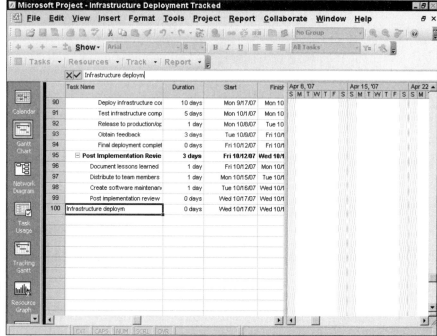

Figure 4-1:
You can
clear or
accept text
in the entry
field.

Producing tasks via the Task Information dialog box

If dialog boxes provide the kind of centralized information form that fits the way you like to work, consider using the Task Information dialog box to enter task information. The series of tabs in this dialog box contain all the information about a task.

Follow these steps to create a task via the Task Information dialog box:

1. **In the Task Name column, double-click a blank cell.**

   The Task Information dialog box appears, as shown in Figure 4-2. The General and Advanced tabs in this dialog box contain various timing settings for the task.

2. **In the Name field, type a task name.**

3. **Click OK to save the new task.**

   The task name appears in Gantt Chart view in the cell you clicked in Step 1.

4. **Press the down arrow key to move to the next cell.**

5. **Repeat Steps 1–4 to add as many tasks as you like.**

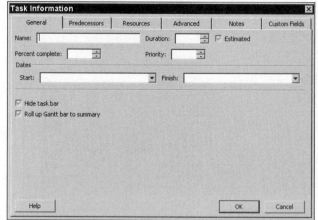

Figure 4-2:
Determine
various task
timing
settings
here.

As you name tasks, try to the keep task names in your project both descriptive and unique. However, if you can't make all the names unique (for example, you have three tasks named Hire Staff), you can use the automatically assigned task number or the work breakdown structure (WBS) code (see Chapter 5) to identify tasks; these numbers are always unique for each task.

Importing tasks from Outlook

After you get started thinking about what has to be accomplished in your project, tasks are like rabbits breeding. What might start as a series of simple to-do tasks in Outlook often becomes a full-fledged project with hundreds of tasks. When that happens, you'll be glad to know that Microsoft provides an easy-to-use import feature that puts the tasks you create in Outlook into Project.

Although the Project import-mapping feature allows you to map fields in a file created in another application to fields in Project to import data, the process can be tedious. The *Import Outlook Tasks* feature is essentially an import map that's preset to work with Outlook task fields.

Follow these steps to import Outlook tasks into Project:

1. **Open the plan that you want to insert tasks into, or open a new project (choose File⇨New).**

2. **Choose Tools⇨Import Outlook Tasks.**

   The Import Outlook Tasks dialog box appears, as shown in Figure 4-3.

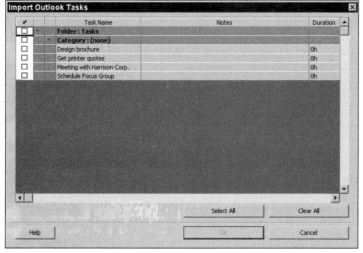

Figure 4-3:
Task names,
notes, and
durations
entered in
Outlook all
come along
for the ride.

   3. **Select the options for the tasks you want to import, or click Select All
      to import all Outlook tasks.**

      By default, Outlook keeps tasks in a Tasks folder. Selecting the check box
      for the Folder: Tasks item is another way to select all tasks in Outlook.

   4. **Click OK.**

      The tasks are imported and appear at the end of your list of tasks with
      change highlighting applied

When you import tasks from Outlook, the task name, the task duration, and
any task notes are brought over. If a task in Outlook has no duration, Project
creates the task with an estimated one-day time frame.

Project 2007 enhances Outlook integration that goes way beyond importing
tasks. See Chapter 19 for more information.

Importing an Excel task list

I am a firm believer that you should make things easy on yourself. If you like
to noodle around with your task list for a project in Excel, you shouldn't have
to retype everything into Project to build a Project plan. For that reason,
Microsoft has provided an Excel Task List template. This template, located in
the Microsoft Office template folder, can be opened from Excel.

The template provides four Excel worksheets, as shown in Figure 4-4, in
which you can enter tasks, resources, and resource assignments, and then
export that data from Excel to Project.

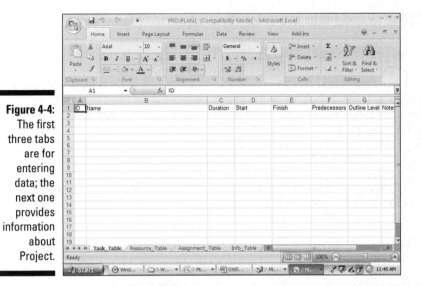

Figure 4-4:
The first
three tabs
are for
entering
data; the
next one
provides
information
about
Project.

Follow these steps to use this template:

1. **In Excel, open the template called Microsoft Project Task List Import Template.**

2. **Fill in information about Tasks, Resources, and Dates in the appropriate columns, and then save the file.**

3. **Open Project and choose File➪Open.**

   The Open dialog box appears.

4. **Locate the Excel Project Template file you just saved and then click Open.**

   The Import Wizard appears.

5. **Click Next to begin the wizard.**

6. **Choose the second option, Project Excel Template, for the format of the data you're importing. Then click Next.**

7. **On the next wizard screen, choose the method for importing the file.**

   You can import the file As a New Project, to Append the Data to the Active Project, or to Merge the Data into the Active Project. If you choose the third option, you have to create a *merge key* that delineates how the data should merge with existing tasks.

8. **Click Finish.**

   The project appears with whatever tasks, resources, and assignment information you entered in a project plan format.

Linking to tasks that live somewhere else

You can insert hyperlinks in a project outline, which provides a handy way to quickly open another project.

Inserting a hyperlink creates a task that you can use to represent the timing or costs of another project or subproject in your plan. However, you have to enter timing and cost information yourself — it isn't brought over from the hyperlinked project.

To insert a hyperlink to another Project file in your project, follow these steps:

1. **Click to select the blank task name cell where you want the hyper-linked task to appear.**

2. **Choose Insert⇨Hyperlink.**

   The Insert Hyperlink dialog box appears, as shown in Figure 4-5.

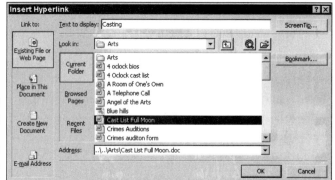

Figure 4-5:
Choose a
linking
destination.

3. **In the Text to Display box, type a name for the hyperlinked file.**

   Make sure that this text makes clear what information is being summarized.

4. **In the Link To area, click the Existing File or Web Page icon.**

   You can link to a document, an e-mail address, or a Web page.

5. **In the Look In list, locate and select the file to which you want to insert a hyperlink.**

6. **Click OK.**

   The link text is inserted, and a hyperlink symbol appears in the Indicator field. You can simply click that link symbol to open the other file.

Inserting one project into another

You can also insert tasks from one project into another. You accomplish this by inserting an entire, existing project into another project; The project that is inserted is known as a *subproject*. This method is useful when various project team members manage different phases of a larger project. The capability to assemble subprojects in one place allows you to create a master schedule from which you can view, all in one place, all the pieces of a larger, more complex project.

Follow these steps to insert another Project file into your plan:

1. **In Gantt Chart view, select the task in your task list above which you want the other project to be inserted.**

2. **Choose Insert⇨Project.**

    The Insert Project dialog box appears, as shown in Figure 4-6.

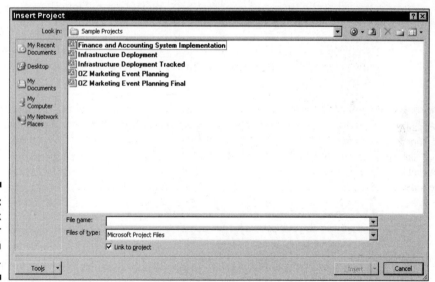

Figure 4-6:
Insert a link to another project from here.

3. **From the Look In list, locate the file that you want to insert and click it to select it.**

4. **If you want to link to the other file so that any updates to it are reflected in the copy of the project you're inserting, select the Link to Project check box.**

5. **Click Insert to insert the file.**

    The inserted project appears above the task you selected when you began the insert process.

Note that the inserted project's highest-level task appears at the level of the task you selected when you inserted the project, with all other tasks below it in outline order. If you need to, use the Indent and Outdent tools on the Formatting toolbar (arrows pointing to the left and right, respectively) to place the inserted tasks at the appropriate level in your project. You can find out more about how to organize tasks into outlines in Chapter 5.

You're in It for the Duration

In projects, as in life, timing is everything. Timing in your projects starts with the durations that you assign to tasks. Although Project helps you see the effect that the timing of your tasks has on the overall length of your plan, it can't tell you how much time each task will take: That's up to you.

Estimating the duration of tasks isn't always easy; it has to be based on your experience with similar tasks and your knowledge of the specifics of your project.

If you often do projects with similar tasks, consider saving a copy of your schedule as a template that you can use in the future, thereby saving yourself the effort of re-estimating durations every time you start a similar project. Find out about saving templates in Chapter 17.

Tasks come in all flavors: Identifying task type

Before you begin to enter task durations, you need to be aware of the three task types. These types have an effect on how Project schedules the work of a task.

Essentially, your choice of task type determines which element of the task doesn't vary when you make changes to the task:

 ✔ **Fixed Duration:** This task type takes a set amount of time to complete, no matter how many resources you add to the mix. For example, a test on a substance that requires that you leave the test running for 24 hours has a fixed duration, even if you add 20 scientists to oversee the test.

✔ **Fixed Units:** This is the default task type. With this task type, when you assign resources to a task with a certain number of *units* (hours of work expressed as a percentage of their working day), the resources' assignments don't change even if you change the duration of the task and the work amount.

✔ **Fixed Work:** The number of resource hours assigned to the task determines its length. If you set the duration of a Fixed Work task at 40 hours, for example, and assign two resources to work 20 hours each (simultaneously) at units of 100 percent, the task will be completed in 20 hours. If you take away one of those resources, the single resource must put in 40 hours at units of 100 percent to complete the task. Understanding how the choice of task type causes your task timing or resource assignments to fluctuate is an important part of creating an efficient project.

Follow these steps to set the task type:

1. **Double-click a task.**

   The Task Information dialog box appears.

2. **Click the Advanced tab, if necessary, to display it (see Figure 4-7).**

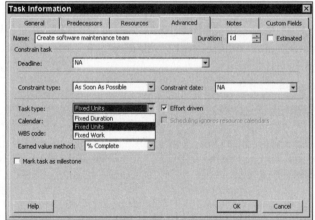

Figure 4-7:
Set the task
type here.

3. **Choose one of the three choices from the Task Type list (see the preceding list of choices).**

4. **Click OK.**

You can also display the Type column in a Gantt Chart sheet and make this setting there.

Setting task duration

Most tasks in a project have a duration, whether it's ten minutes or a year or something in between. (For milestone tasks, which have no duration, see the next section.) Deciding how finely to break down your tasks can affect how efficiently you track progress on those tasks: Tasks that wander on for a year are usually too broad, and tasks that take ten minutes are too narrow. Whatever your best guess at task duration is, Project can accommodate you.

If your project is to run a one-day event, getting to the level of ten-minute tasks might make sense. In most projects, however, such finely detailed timing doesn't make sense because it defeats the point of all the tracking and reporting features of Project. (That's true unless you have people tracking their progress minute by minute, but in that case, what else would they have time to do?) On the flip side, creating a 12-month-long task suggests that you might be defining your project too broadly to accurately keep track of all that can happen in a year.

As with all task information, you can enter a duration in a Gantt Chart sheet (see the section "Generating tasks in Gantt Chart view," earlier in this chapter) or in the Task Information dialog box. Follow these steps to enter a duration by using the dialog box:

1. **Double-click a task to display the Task Information dialog box.**

2. **If necessary, click the General tab to display it (refer to Figure 4-2).**

3. **In the Duration box, use the spinner arrows to increase or decrease the duration.**

4. **If the current duration units aren't appropriate (for example, days when you want hours), type a new duration in the Duration box.**

   New tasks are created with an estimated duration of one day unless you change the duration. You can use the following abbreviations for various time units:

   - **m:** Minutes

   - **h:** Hours

   - **d:** Days

   - **w:** Weeks

   - **mo:** Months

Don't assume that changing the start and finish dates of a task changes its duration — it doesn't. You have to manually change the duration; if you don't, your project plan will not be what you intend it to be.

5. **Click OK to accept the duration setting.**

If you aren't sure about the timing of a particular task and want to alert people to your lack of certainty or if you need a way to find such tasks and enter more solid timing when you have better information, select the Estimated check box (on the General tab) when you enter the duration. Then apply a filter for tasks with estimated durations (see Chapter 15 for more about using filters).

Setting tasks with no duration: Milestones

I mention in the preceding section that almost all tasks have durations; the exception is a *milestone* — a task with no duration. (Now, that's the type I *like* to be assigned to.) In fact, milestones are less like tasks than they are like signposts that mark moments in time. Examples of milestones are the approval of a prototype (although the deliberations to make that decision might have taken months) or the completion of a phase of tests.

Some people include tasks such as Design Complete or Testing Complete at the end of each phase of their project. They can then create timing relationships to the moment of completion — for example, allowing production of a drug to proceed after the testing and approval is complete. Such milestones also alert you and your team members to a moment of progress in your project that can help to keep the team motivated.

Note that new tasks are created with an estimated duration of one day unless you enter a duration. To create a milestone, you indicate that the task has zero duration. The quickest way to do that is to simply type 0 in the Duration column in Gantt Chart view. Or, you can click the Advanced tab of the Task Information dialog box (refer to Figure 4-6) and select the Mark Task as Milestone check box. When you do, the milestone is designated in Gantt Chart view with a black diamond shape rather than a task bar.

Showing up again and again: Recurring tasks

Some tasks occur again and again in projects. For example, attending a monthly project debriefing or generating a quarterly project report is considered a recurring task.

No one wants to create all the tasks for the monthly debriefing in a project that will take a year to complete. Instead, you can designate the recurrence, and Project automatically creates the 12 tasks for you.

Here's how you create a recurring task:

1. **Choose Insert⭢Recurring Task.**

   The Recurring Task Information dialog box appears, as shown in Figure 4-8.

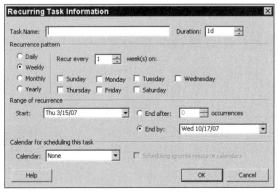

Figure 4-8: When you enter this information, Project creates multiple occurrences of a task automatically.

2. **In the Task Name box, type a name for the task.**

3. **In the Duration box, click the spinner arrows to set a duration, or type a duration, such as** `10d` **for 10 days.**

   You can read about the abbreviations you can use for units of duration — such as *d* for days — in the earlier section, "Setting task duration."

4. **Select a recurrence pattern by selecting the Daily, Weekly, Monthly, or Yearly option.**

   What you select here provides different options for the rest of the recurrence pattern.

5. **Depending on the selections offered to you, make choices for the rest of the pattern.**

   For example, if you select the Weekly option, you must choose a Recur Every *x* Week(s) On setting, and then choose a day such as Friday. Or, if you select Monthly, you must specify which day of every month the task will recur.

6. **In the Range of Recurrence area, type a date in the Start box. Then select and fill in either the End After or End By option.**

   For example, you might start on January 1 and end after 12 occurrences to create a task that occurs every month for a year.

7. **Click OK to save the recurring task.**

If your settings cause a task to fall on a nonworking day (for example, if you choose to meet on the eighth day of every month and the eighth day is a

Sunday in one of those months), a dialog box appears, asking you how to handle this situation. You can choose not to create the task, or you can let Project adjust the day to the next working day in that period.

To assign resources to a recurring task, you can use the resource column in Gantt Chart view. (The Recurring Task Information dialog box doesn't have a Resources tab.)

Starting and Pausing Tasks

When most people start using Project, one of the first things they try to do is enter a start date for every task in their project. After all, you always include dates when you write up a to-do list, right? Well, for one thing, you're jumping the gun — and missing out on one of the great strengths of project management software: the capability to schedule tasks for you according to sometimes-complex combinations of factors, such as dependencies between tasks and task constraints. By allowing Project to determine the start date of a task, you allow it to make adjustments automatically when changes occur.

If you enter a task duration and don't enter a start date for the task, that task starts by default as soon as possible after the project start date you set in the Project Information dialog box, based on any dependencies you set up between tasks.

Typically, to establish a task's start date, you look for something in the project that would dictate its timing; for example, if you don't want construction to begin until you obtain permits, set a dependency between the permits task and the construction task in such a way that construction can't start before the permit task ends.

Certain tasks, however, must start on a specific date. Examples are a holiday, an annual meeting, or the start of the fishing season.

Project sets the finish date of a task based on when that task starts as well as the task duration. If a task must finish on a certain date, however, you can set a finish date and let Project determine the start date.

Entering the task start date

Setting a start date or a finish date for a task applies a kind of constraint on it that can override dependency relationships or other timing factors. Task constraints, discussed in the upcoming "Constraints You Can Live With" section, are the preferred way to force a task to start or end on a certain day. If you determine, however, that a particular task must begin or end on a set date no matter what, you can enter a specific start or finish date. Setting the start or finish date is simple.

To enter a start or finish date for a task, simply follow these steps:

1. **Double-click a task.**

   The Task Information dialog box appears.

2. **Click the General tab if it's not already displayed; refer to Figure 4-2.**

3. **Click the arrow on the Start or Finish box.**

   A calendar appears.

4. **Click a date to select it, or click the forward or backward arrow to move to a different month and select a date.**

   If the current date is the date you want, use the shortcut of clicking the Today button on the drop-down calendar.

5. **Click OK.**

Note that setting a start date isn't quite as strong a factor in how Project determines timing as applying the Must Start On constraint. You can find out more about how constraints work in the "Constraints You Can Live With" section, later in this chapter.

Taking a break: Splitting tasks

Did you ever start something — your taxes, for example — and find that you just had to drop everything before you were done and go do something else? (In the case of taxes, I usually need a break for a good cry.)

It's the same in projects. Sometimes tasks start and then you have to put them on hold before they can start again later — for example, if you experience a work shutdown due to labor negotiations. Or, perhaps you can anticipate a delay in the course of a task and want to structure it that way when you create it. In that case, you can use a Project feature to split a task so that a second or third portion starts at a later date, with no activity between. You can place as many splits in a task as you like.

Follow these steps to split a task:

1. **Click the Split Task button on the Standard toolbar.**

   A box appears, as shown in Figure 4-9. The box provides a readout to guide you as you set the start date for the continuation of the task.

2. **Click the task at the date where you want to split the task, and then drag until the box contains the date on which you want the task to begin again.**

Split Task button

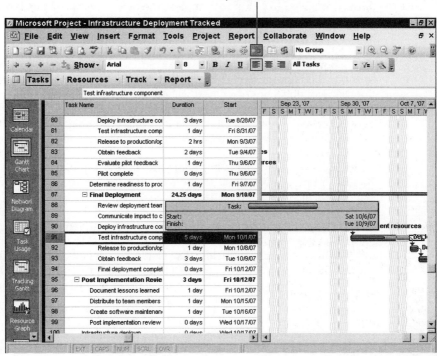

Figure 4-9:
Check out
this guide to
setting the
start date
for the
continuation
of the task.

3. Release the mouse button.

The task is split.

You can rejoin a split task by placing your mouse over the taskbar until the
move cursor appears and then clicking the split taskbar and dragging it back
to join with the other portion of the taskbar.

Don't use the split-task approach to put an artificial hold on a task until some
other task is complete. Suppose that you start testing a product but then
have to wait for final approval before finalizing the test results. In that case,
you should create a Testing task, a Final Approval milestone, and a Finalize
Test Results task — and then create dependency relationships among them.
That way, if one task runs late, your final task shifts along with it instead of
being set in stone (as a split task can be).

It's Such an Effort: Effort-Driven Tasks

When you hear the word *effort* in Project, you can think *work.* When you create
a task, by default it is *effort driven,* which means that if you adjust resource

_____

assignments, the duration might change but the number of hours of effort (work) you need to put in to complete the task stays the same. When you add or delete a resource assignment on an effort-driven task, work is spread around equally among resources.

Here's how an effort-driven task works. Suppose that you have a two-day task to set up a computer network in a new office. With one resource assigned to the task, working 8 hours a day, it will take 16 hours to complete the work (two 8-hour days). If you assign a second resource, the task no longer takes two days because the hours of effort required will be completed more quickly by the two people working simultaneously — in this case, in one 8-hour period.

An example of a task that is not effort driven is attending a daylong seminar. No matter how many people attend or how many people are present, the seminar takes one day to complete.

Effort Driven is a simple check box choice on the Advanced tab in the Task Information dialog box (refer to Figure 4-6). Select this check box to enable or disable the Effort Driven setting; it's selected by default. When you clear this setting, the same task that you set to run two days takes two days, no matter how much effort your resources put in. In other words, adding resources doesn't cause the task to be completed sooner.

Constraints You Can Live With

A constraint is more than something you're forced to live with, such as dandruff or noisy neighbors. In Project, *constraints* are timing conditions that control a task. You tell Project what, if anything, to constrain for each task.

Understanding how constraints work

When you create a task, the As Soon As Possible constraint is selected by default. In other words, the task starts as soon as the project starts, assuming that no dependencies with other tasks exist that would delay its start.

Task start and finish dates — working with dependencies, the task type, the Effort Driven setting, and constraints — set the timing of each task. However, when Project performs calculations to try to save you time in a project that's running late, it considers constraints to be the most sacred timing settings. For example, if you set a constraint that a task must finish on a certain date, Project shifts around almost any other task in a schedule in recalculating timing before it suggests that that task might finish on another date.

Here's a word to the wise: Use constraints only when you absolutely need to force a task's timing.

Table 4-1 lists all the constraints and an explanation of their effects on your task's timing.

Table 4-1	Task Constraints
Constraint	*Effect*
As Soon As Possible	The default setting; the task starts as early in the schedule as possible based on dependencies and the project start date.
As Late As Possible	The task occurs as late as possible in your schedule, based on dependencies and the project finish date.
Finish No Earlier Than	The end of the task cannot occur any earlier than the date you specify.
Finish No Later Than	The end of the task cannot occur any later than the date you specify.
Must Finish On	The task must finish on an absolute date.
Must Start On	The task must start on an absolute date.
Start No Earlier Than	The task cannot start any earlier than the date you specify.
Start No Later Than	The task cannot start any later than the date you specify.

Establishing constraints

You can set only one constraint for a task. Setting a constraint involves selecting the type of constraint you want in the Task Information dialog box. Some constraints work together with a date you choose. For example, if you want a task to start no later than a certain date, you need to select a date by which the task must start. Other settings, such as As Soon As Possible, work off a different date — in this case, the start date you set for the whole project or any dependency relationships you set up with other tasks. (See Chapter 6 for more about dependency relationships.)

To set a task constraint, follow these steps:

1. **Double-click a task.**

   The Task Information dialog box appears.

2. **Click the Advanced tab; refer to Figure 4-6.**

3. **Select a constraint from the Constraint Type list.**

4. **If the constraint requires a date, select one from the Constraint Date list.**

5. **Click OK to save the settings.**

Setting a deadline

I don't know about you, but sometimes I think deadlines were made to be overlooked. Project agrees because strictly speaking, deadlines aren't constraints (although the setting for the deadline is in the Constraint Task area of the Task Information dialog box, on the Advanced tab). Deadlines aren't the same as constraints because they don't force the timing of your tasks in any sense. If you set a deadline, it simply causes Project to display a symbol in the Indicator column if the task has run past the deadline to alert you so that you can panic (I mean, take action) appropriately.

To set a deadline, follow these steps:

1. **Double-click a task.**

   The Task Information dialog box appears.

2. **Click the Advanced tab; refer to Figure 4-6.**

3. **Click the arrow in the Deadline field to display a calendar, and then select a date.**

   If necessary, use the forward or backward arrow to move to a different month.

4. **Click OK to save the deadline setting.**

You can also display a deadline column in your Gantt Chart sheet pane to enter the deadline or to show yourself and others what your targeted deadline date is.

Making a Task Note

Despite the wealth of information that you can enter about a task and its timing, not everything can be said with settings. That's why every task includes an area to enter notes. You might use this feature, for example, to enter some background information about changes in timing or other changes that occur during the schedule, or to list vendor contact information relevant to the task.

To enter task notes, do the following:

1. **Double-click a task.**

   The Task Information dialog box appears.

2. **Click to select the Notes tab (shown in Figure 4-10).**

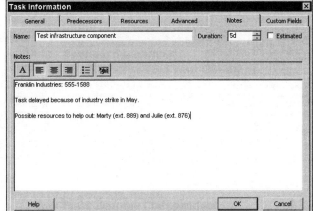

Figure 4-10:
Enter useful
information
about the
task here.

3. **In the Notes area, type any information you like.**

   You can enter contact information, notes about resources, or other useful information about the task.

4. **Format the note.**

   Click the buttons at the top of the Notes area to change the font. You can also

   - Left-align, center, or right-align text
   - Format text as a bulleted list
   - Insert an object

5. **Click OK to save the note(s).**

Saving Your Project — and Your Tasks

After you have some tasks in your project, don't lose 'em! It's a good idea to save your project regularly.

You save a Project file by using the same process you've used hundreds of times to save files in other software applications.

To save a Project file, do this:

1. Choose File⇨Save.

The Save As dialog box appears, as shown in Figure 4-11. If you use other software, you've probably seen this dialog box about 2 million times.

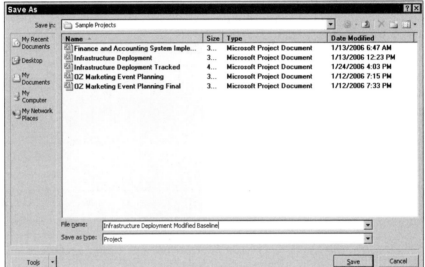

Figure 4-11:
Save your
tasks here.

2. From the Save In list, locate the folder in which you want to save the file.

3. In the File Name box, type a name.

4. Click Save.

If you want to save changes to a previously saved Project file by using a different filename or file format (for example saving as an Excel spreadsheet or a Project template), choose File⇨Save As and provide a new filename or file type at the bottom of the Save As dialog box.

If you want to share your file with others and you have Project Server set up in your organization, you can do so by using Project Web Access to publish it online. See Chapter 19 for the lowdown on this useful collaborative tool.

Task Information in Action: Planning Your Next Space Launch

If you want to tie together all the task-setting information covered in this chapter, you can look at it in the context of a specific project. Suppose that you're managing a space shuttle launch and you have these main tasks:

- ✔ Train personnel
- ✔ Launch public relations
- ✔ Check equipment
- ✔ Launch operation

Under the public relations task, suppose that you have three subtasks:

- ✔ Write press releases
- ✔ Hold press conference
- ✔ Set up interviews with astronauts

Your first step is to set durations for each task. They're determined to a great extent by your experience with similar projects, but suppose that you determine that writing press releases will take two days, a press conference will take two hours, and setting up interviews will take three days. You enter these durations in one of two locations: in the Durations column or in each individual Task Information dialog box.

Next, you have to determine the task types. Write Press Releases is an effort-driven, fixed-work task. (If you get somebody to help you, it takes less time to complete the work.) Hold Press Conference, on the other hand, has a fixed timing (after two hours, you cut off the press); in this case, it's a fixed-duration task. Finally, Set Up Interviews with Astronauts could be a fixed-units task: It takes a certain number of hours to make all the phone calls and arrangements, but when the arrangements are done, you might still want the resources available for confirmations or to deal with changes. With a fixed-units task (which is the Project default), completing the number of units of work doesn't change the resource hours you assigned.

Finally, what task constraints might you apply to these tasks? Although I'm not a fan of applying too many constraints to any project, here are a couple of possibilities:

✔ The press conference might take place **no later than** the task to launch the shuttle. After the shuttle has left orbit, the press conference to brief the press on the mission must already have been completed.

✔ You could set the interviews with astronauts so that they **must start on** the day before the launch — when the members of the media hold the most interest in the event and the astronauts are still available.

If, in the end, the entire launch is scrubbed because of unexpected weather or a faulty hatch door, won't you be glad that you used the Project dependency structure to cause all tasks to move out when you change the start date for the project for the sixth time?

Chapter 5

Getting Your Outline in Line

· ·

· ·

Certain things bring order to the universe: Clocks, stop signs, and outlines, to name just a few. Whereas clocks bring order to time and stop signs bring order to rush hour, outlines bring order to information by imposing a hierarchy. An outline breaks down one idea or topic or category of information into smaller units with some logical sequence.

Project uses an outline structure to organize tasks in your project, as well as tools and functionality to help you build, reorganize, and view the outline structure. Learning how to create an outline is something you did back in Mrs. Plotkin's fourth-grade English class, and now, showing you how to use an outline to organize the many tasks in your project is my job. Welcome to Outlining 101.

Summary Tasks and Subtasks

When you take a look at a project outline, such as the one shown in Figure 5-1, you see that it organizes tasks into levels; each level represents a phase of your project. A task that has other tasks indented below it in this outline structure is a *parent task,* or *summary task.* The tasks indented below it are *child tasks,* or *subtasks.* Summary tasks are indicated in bold in your Project outline. You can tell when a summary task has a family of subtasks clinging to its skirts: When a subtask is hidden, a little plus-sign symbol is displayed next to its summary task. When you click the plus sign, the task expands to show its whole clan of subtasks.

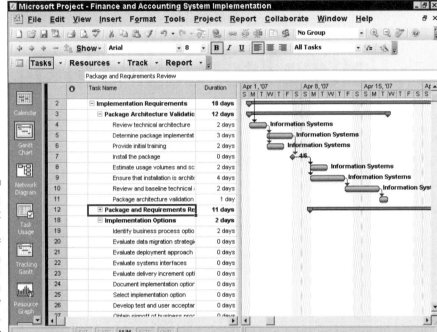

Figure 5-1:
A project
outline is a
collection of
subtasks
nested
within
summary
tasks.

You can build several of these little families of tasks to represent project phases in your outline. Think of a project outline as a set of little wooden nesting dolls, with each successively smaller doll representing a deeper level of detail. The highest-level task is the outer doll, which is the biggest of the bunch. The next doll in the group is a little smaller, just as the next level of tasks in an outline reflects a little narrower level of detail, and so on, right down to the littlest baby doll. The largest task in a project might be Build New Plant, and the smallest detailed task might be Empty Dumpster, with a whole lot of tasks in between.

Project phases

All information about a family of tasks (that is, a *phase* of your project) is rolled up into its highest-level summary task. Therefore, any task with sub-tasks has no timing or cost information of its own: It gets its total duration and cost from the sum of its parts.

You can, though, assign resources and costs to a summary task; for example, you might assign a project manager for an entire phase of tasks. However, a summary task also includes the total of the costs of any tasks below it.

This roll-up functionality is cumulative: The lowest-level task rolls up to its parent, which might roll up into another summary task, which rolls up (for example) into a project summary task. Any task with tasks below it gets its duration and cost information from its subtasks, no matter how deeply nested it might be in the hierarchy.

The structure of phases in an outline is also useful when you need to reorganize an outline: When you move a summary task, all its subtasks come right along for the ride!

How many levels can you go?

You have no real limit on how many levels of tasks you can create in an outline (except perhaps how much memory you have in your computer to accommodate a monster schedule!). Remember, though: At some point, you have to deal with assigning timing and resources to each of these tasks — and then track their progress. Too much detail can make your project plan difficult to manage.

Also, if you find that you build in three, four, or five levels of detail throughout your plan, consider that you might really be building several projects at a time. Having too many levels suggests that a few of these project phases might be more manageable if you break them off and make them projects on their own — with their own project managers. Unless you want the maintenance of your Project plan to become a project in and of itself, don't overdo the level of detail in your outline; two or three levels are usually sufficient.

The One-and-Only Project Summary Task

Just as a ship has only one captain, only one task summarizes all other tasks in each project. I strongly suggest that you create a *project summary task,* which represents the highest (least detailed) level of information and is often simply the title of the project, such as New Product Rollout or Space Shuttle Launch. A project summary task is created when every task in the project falls under it in the outline and is indented to become subordinate, as shown in Figure 5-2. You can see in the figure that Implementation Requirements is the project summary task.

When you think about it, an upper-level headline in an outline is the sum of its parts; the headline reflects the overall topic for all the items below it. The project summary task takes this concept a step further: This task rolls up all the actual data from other tasks into one line item. Thus, the project summary task's duration reflects the duration of the entire project. From a monetary angle, the project summary task's total cost reflects the total costs for the entire project. Figures like these can be handy to have at your fingertips — and that's one value of a summary task.

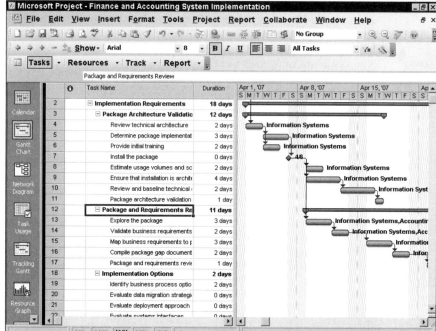

If you're confused about the length of your summary task, remember that the *summary task duration* is the difference between the earliest task start date and latest task end date. However, nonworking days aren't counted in the summary task duration. The length of the summary task, therefore, equals the number of days of work over the course of the subtasks, not the number of calendar days between the start of the first task and end of the last.

Not everyone uses project summary tasks. You can simply create, at the highest level of your outline, tasks that represent major project phases — with subphases and subtasks below them — and not create one task that's higher in the order than all others. However, my advice is to always have a project summary task, for two reasons:

✔ **You can quickly view totals for the project at a glance in the columns of data in Gantt Chart view and other views.**

✔ **You can place a link to your project summary task in another project so that all data for one project is reflected in another.** For example, if you create five schedules for new product launches in your company, you can easily create a master schedule for all company product launches by linking to the project summary tasks in each of the projects. (Neat, huh?)

As you build your project, you can easily create a project summary task yourself (indent other tasks beneath it) or use a Project feature to generate one automatically at any time — even after you build all the phases of your project. To have Project automatically create a project summary task, follow these steps:

1. **Choose Tools⇨Options.**

    The Options dialog box appears.

2. **Click the View tab to display it.**

3. **Select the Show Project Summary Task option.**

4. **Click OK to insert the upper-level task.**

Structuring the Project's Outline

If you already read the first few pages of this chapter, your tantalizing glimpse of how outlines work in Project has doubtlessly left you eager to start building your own, but project outlines take a little upfront thought. You have to settle two important matters about your project before you start building a logical project outline:

- ✔ **The goal:** What do you want to achieve at the completion of your project? Is your goal to manage an entire space shuttle mission? Then you need as many tasks as it takes to get from here to splashdown. If your goal is only to launch the space shuttle, however, your focus is narrower, and the level of detail of certain tasks will probably be different.

- ✔ **The scope:** Scope is a little more specific than the goal. Do you want to build a new warehouse from scratch, outfit it with equipment and furniture, and deal with moving people into their offices by December 1 within a budget of $20 million? Or, is the scope of your project to hook up the computer network by November 1 within a budget of $50,000? Understanding what your overall deliverables are helps you further define where to start and stop your project.

To help you to sketch the early draft of your project, Project lets you create a proposal schedule with major deliverables and no specific tasks. See Chapter 6 for more about deliverables and proposals.

Look around your own office: You'll be surprised to find that many projects that go off track never had a clear goal. In fact, entering project data into project management software is a waste of time if you don't know what your mission is. Go ahead: Ask three people working on the same project in your company to state the goal of the project. I would bet the farm that you get three different answers. For an IT project, for example, the IT director might tell you the goal is to reduce tech support calls, the project manager might say the goal is to upgrade all server software to the latest version, and the technician might specify that the goal is to get all the software installed by next Thursday. (Sound familiar?)

To define a goal and scope for your project, answer these questions:

✔ **For a goal:**

- What will be different when the project is complete?
- What will the project achieve? Will a building be built, a workforce trained, or a space shuttle launched?

✔ **For the scope:**

- What will the project cost?
- How many people will be involved?
- Whom does the project affect: A workgroup, division, company, or clients?
- What deadlines does the project have?

Everything but the kitchen sink: What to include

After you have a clear picture of your project goal and the scope of the work to be done, you can begin to think about what your outline should contain. For example, here's the first of three approaches to an outline of tasks for planning a company party:

   I. Send invitations

  II. Reserve Conference Room B

 III. Order food

Perhaps a little more detail would be helpful:

  I. Company Christmas party

    A. Invitations

      1. Design invitations

      2. Mail invitations

B. Location

    1. Reserve Conference Room B

    2. Order extra chairs

    3. Decorate space

C. Food

    1. Hire caterer

    2. Clean up

Or, you can take a really detailed approach:

I. Company events

  A. Company Christmas party

    1. Planning

      a. Set party date

      b. Invitations

        1) Design

        2) Send out

      c. Budget

        1) Research costs

        2) Create budget

        3) Obtain budget approval

    2. Location and furniture

      a. Location

        1) Reserve Conference Room B

        2) Arrange for carpet cleaning

        3) Pick decoration theme

        4) Decorate space

      b. Furniture

        1) Order extra chairs

        2) Arrange for serving table

    3. Food

      a. Research caterers

      b. Set food budget

    c. Hire caterer

    d. Provide kitchen access to caterers

    e. Assign clean-up committee

    f. Clean up

  B. Halloween party

    1. And so on . . .

Which one of these outlines is best for this project? That depends on how complex these arrangements are — and on how narrowly you define the project. Are you planning the entire year of company events or only one party? How many people will perform the tasks and over what period of time? Will one person research, budget, and hire the caterers in a single hour? If so, a single task — Hire Caterer — might be enough. Will one person do the research, another set the budget, and another hire the caterer — and might these tasks be separated by days (or even weeks)? If so, having several tasks might be the way to go.

If one task must happen before another can start, you might have to break down the tasks to reflect the causality between certain events. For example, if you can't begin a new manufacturing process before people are trained, it's probably not prudent to lump training and the implementation of the new process into a single task.

Too little detail might let some tasks slip through the cracks, while too much detail might cause your project team to be inefficient, spending more time reporting progress and breaking down activities than doing the work. Here's the bottom line: When you understand the scope of your project and the relationship of each task as you create your project outline, you're likely to build in the right level of detail.

Building the outline

People approach building a project outline in different ways. Some create all the tasks they can think of in random order and then promote and demote tasks to different levels and move them around to appear in the correct order. Other people create upper-level tasks first and then go back and fill in details below each task. Still other people work one phase at a time, by creating one upper-level task and filling in every possible task underneath it. Then they go on to the next phase and create every task under that, and so on.

The approach that you use depends to some extent on how you think. Some people think chronologically, and others group like information. You eventually have to deal with all levels of structure in your final outline, but which level you tackle first is up to you.

Moving Tasks All around Your Outline

You discover how to create tasks in Chapter 4. In this section, you move those tasks around to create the outline structure. If you use any word processing outlining feature, this stuff is pretty easy. If this is new turf for you, it's still easy!

The outdent-and-indent shuffle

Outdenting and indenting are the functions that you use to move tasks to higher or lower levels of detail in your outline. In some software programs, these terms are *promoting* and *demoting,* respectively.

- ✔ **Outdenting** a task moves it up a level in the outline (literally shifting it to the left in the outline). When outdented, a task is moved to a higher level of detail; in other words, it's less detailed.

- ✔ **Indenting** a task moves it down a level in the outline (literally indenting the task to the right in the outline) and puts it at a deeper level of detail.

You use tools on the Formatting toolbar (shown in Figure 5-3) to outdent and indent tasks in a project outline. The Outdent tool is a left-facing arrow; the Indent tool is a right-facing arrow.

You can outdent and indent tasks from any view, even Network Diagram view. However, seeing the effect in Network Diagram view is tricky, and I recommend using Gantt Chart view when manipulating tasks in an outline structure.

If you use an outlining feature in other software, you might be tempted to press Tab to indent a task in an outline and Shift+Tab to outdent a task. In Project, though, don't. It doesn't cause disaster, but it doesn't do you much good either. It only moves your cursor from one column to the other in a columnar view (like Gantt Chart view). And in Network Diagram view, it moves the cursor from field to field in a single task box.

To outdent or indent a task, follow these steps:

1. **Click a task in a columnar view to select it.**

2. **Click the Outdent or Indent button according to what action you want to take.**

Outdent and Indent tools

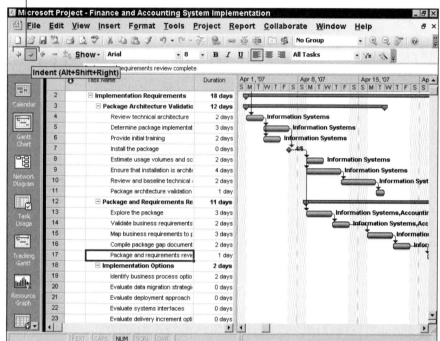

Figure 5-3:
Click these
tools to
move a task
in or out in
the outline.

Moving tasks up and down

A maxim of project management says that things change: Tasks that you thought you could do early on can't happen yet because the people, materials, or money are in short supply. Or, a task that you thought you couldn't start until next July gets bumped up in priority when your customer changes his mind (again) about deliverables. Because of this changeability, when you enter tasks in a project outline, odds are that you'll need to move those tasks around at some point. You can move subtasks to other phases of the outline by simply clicking and dragging them.

You should understand that moving a task can change its outline level. A task retains its level in the outline only when you move the task to follow a task at the same level. (Okay, there's an exception, which I get to in a minute.) Comparatively, if you move a lower-level task to a section of tasks at a higher level — for example, move a third-level task to a section of second-level tasks — the moved task takes on the level of the task preceding it. And the converse is true when you move a higher-level task to follow a lower-level task.

The exception I hinted at happens when you move a lower-level task to follow a summary task. For example, a second-level task that you move to immediately follow a summary task stays at the second level rather than take on the summary task level of the task that now precedes it because there's only one summary task.

Using the click-and-drag method

If you ask me, click-and-drag is to computing what the remote control is to television. It's a quick, no-brainer method of moving stuff around in software that just makes life simpler. Here's an example: The quickest way to move a task in an outline is to use the click-and-drag method.

To move a task up and down with the click-and-drag method, follow these steps:

1. **Display a columnar view, such as Gantt Chart view.**

2. **Select a task by clicking its task ID number.**

3. **Drag the task to where you want it to appear in the outline.**

   A gray line appears, indicating the new task position, as shown in Figure 5-4.

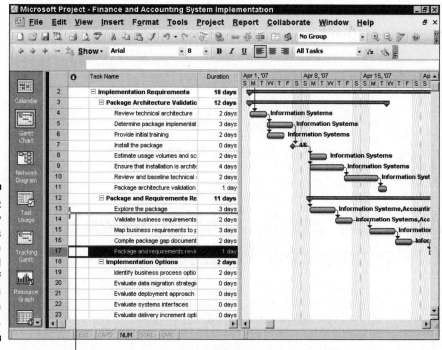

Figure 5-4: This gray line shows you where the task will appear if you release the mouse button.

Gray line

4. **When the gray line is located where you want to insert the task, release the mouse button.**

   The task appears in its new location. If you want the task to be at a different level of the outline, you can now indent or outdent it as needed.

To move more than one task at a time, click and drag to select multiple task IDs, and then drag them *en masse* to a new location. You can also use the standard Shift+click and Ctrl+click selection methods to select multiple tasks in a Project outline. Use Shift+click to select contiguous tasks, and use Ctrl+click to select discrete tasks.

Using the cut-and-paste (or copy-and-paste) method

Clicking and dragging works fine in most cases, but in very large projects — with a few hundred or more tasks, for example — this method can be like dragging a peanut to Tibet: It's not the process; it's the distance you have to travel.

In a larger outline, simply use the cut-and-paste method to move tasks:

1. **Select a task by clicking its task ID number.**
2. **Click the Cut Task tool on the Standard toolbar.**

   The task is removed from its current location and placed on the Windows Clipboard.

3. **Scroll to display the location where you want the task to appear.**
4. **Click the task after which you want to insert the task.**
5. **Click the Paste tool.**

If you want to insert a copy of a task in a project outline, you can follow the preceding steps and click Copy Task rather than Cut Task.

If you're cutting and copying only a single cell and not a whole task, click in the cell — the toolbar buttons will be named Cut Cell and Copy Cell instead.

Now You See It, Now You Don't: Collapsing and Expanding Tasks

Since caveman days (or whenever the first fourth-grade teacher taught the first set of kids how to outline their book reports), outlines have allowed you to focus on different levels of detail. Outlines do this on paper by essentially ordering information so that you can more easily focus on the level of information you need and ignore the rest.

With the invention of computer outlining, the capability to focus on only certain portions of an outline comes into its own because you can easily open and close an outline to show or hide different levels of information — or entire sections of your outline. The minus symbol next to the "Analysis" summary task shown in Figure 5-5 indicates that all subtasks below it are displayed.

This capability means that you can hide all but the upper level of tasks in a project to give your manager an overview of progress. Or, you can close every phase of your project except the one in progress, so your team can focus on just those tasks in a status meeting. Or, you can close most of your outline so that jumping to a late phase of a very large schedule doesn't involve more scroll work than a Baroque fireplace.

A summary task with all tasks displayed has a minus sign to its left. A summary task with hidden subtasks sports a plus sign to its left. All summary tasks are indicated in bold in the project outline. When a summary task has a minus sign next to it, you can select the summary task and do one of three things:

✔ Click the minus sign to hide all subtasks.

✔ Click the Hide Subtasks button on the Formatting toolbar to hide all subtasks below the selected summary.

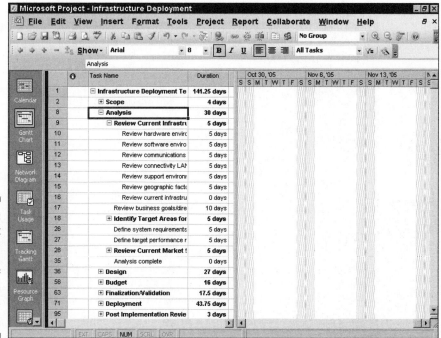

Figure 5-5: This project outline shows you details of just one phase of the project.

✔ Click the Show button on the Formatting toolbar and then click the level of detail you want to leave open in the entire outline, as shown in Figure 5-6. (For example, you can click Outline Level 1 for only the highest level in the outline to show the fewest details.) Figure 5-6 also shows the location of the Hide Subtasks and Show Subtasks buttons on the Formatting toolbar.

TIP

If you don't want to see plus and minus outlining symbols, you can remove them from all views by deselecting the Show Outline Symbol option on the View tab in the Options dialog box.

When a summary task has a plus sign next to it, you can select the summary task and do one of three things:

✔ Click the plus sign to display one level of subtasks.

✔ Click the Show Subtasks button on the Formatting toolbar to display one level of subtasks for the selected summary.

✔ Click the Show button on the Formatting toolbar and click the level of the outline you want to reveal for the entire outline.

Show Subtasks

Hide Subtasks

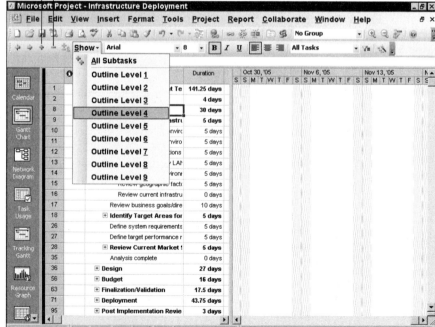

Figure 5-6:
Choose
whatever
level of
detail you
want to see
from this
drop-down
list.

To quickly reveal all subtasks in a project, click the Show button and then click All Subtasks.

Cracking the WBS Code

Some codes are used for disguising things (think of *The DaVinci Code*). In Project 2007, however, codes are used to make the elements of a project easier to identify. These codes — *work breakdown structure (WBS) codes* — can be generated automatically to give a unique identity to each task in your project by its order in the project outline.

For example, the second task in the second phase of a project has a code of 1.2.2. This code helps you identify all tasks that belong to Phase 1, no matter at what level of the outline they might lie, as shown in Figure 5-7. Quite simply, assigning a WBS code to an outline helps you to identify the location of individual tasks in the outline so that people can find and reference them easily. This concept is similar to how page numbers in a book's table of contents help you go right to a specific page.

The United States government often requires that subcontractors use this type of code, so companies doing business with the government should find this automatic application of a WBS code useful.

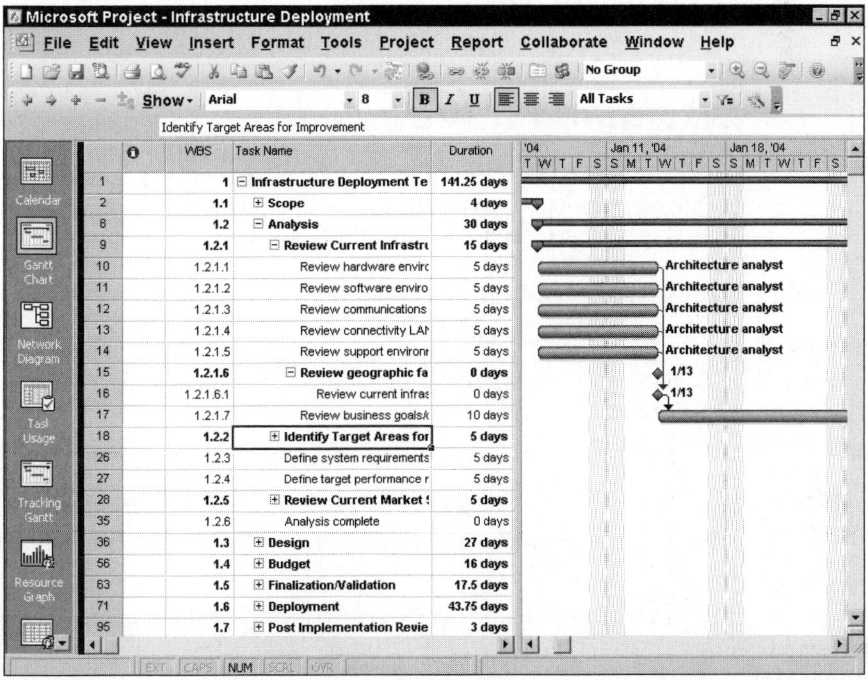

Figure 5-7: In larger projects, the WBS code can get quite lengthy!

RBS: Kind of like WBS, but for people

If you use the Enterprise Global Template, you can make use of the *RBS (resource breakdown structure)* field, which is a way of ranking resources in your organization. RBS represents the organizational structure for resources. RBS codes assigned by the project manager or enterprise administrator can help you to streamline the process of granting permissions to access online data or to filter for resources at a certain level in your organization.

The Resource Substitution Wizard and Portfolio Modeler also make use of RBS levels in their calculations. You can also use the Group feature to group tasks by the resource hierarchy of assignments. After an administrator with the ability to modify the Enterprise Global Template sets the RBS field, everybody and their brother (in your enterprise) can view it. All these tasks require Project Server, so see Chapter 18 for more about RBS.

Standard WBS code uses numbers for each level of the code. You can also create custom codes that provide a few options for how the code is defined. Read how in the upcoming section, "Customizing the code."

If you want to visualize your WBS code, consider using Visio WBS Chart Wizard. If Microsoft Visio is installed on your computer, you can use this wizard to generate a Visio WBS chart for selected tasks — or all the tasks in your project. You can use the settings in the wizard to generate a chart for a specified level in the project outline, such as only level-1 tasks, or level-1 and level-2 tasks, and so on.

Displaying a WBS code

Here's the good news: You don't really have to create a WBS code per se because the very structure of your outline creates the code. All you have to do is display it. To do that, follow these steps:

1. **Click the Gantt Chart icon on the View bar.**

   Gantt Chart view appears.

2. **Right-click anywhere in the column headings and then choose Insert Column.**

   The Column Definition dialog box appears, as shown in Figure 5-8.

   You use this dialog box to set options such as column width and alignment.

3. **Click the arrow for the Field Name drop-down list and then select WBS.**

   Use the scroll bar, if necessary, to locate the field name.

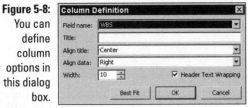

4. **Click OK.**

   The WBS column is displayed. If you add a task, or move, promote, or demote a task in your project outline, the WBS code is updated automatically.

Customizing the code

For the fourth task under the second phase of the first phase in the project, the WBS code would look like this, by default:

> 1.2.4

Such off-the-rack WBS code often works just fine for projects. For those times when you want to make changes, however, Project 2007 allows you to modify the code to use a prefix — the name of your project, a client ID, or your department number, for example — and to vary the use of numerals or letters to indicate the various levels of your code structure. An example of a customized code is shown in Figure 5-9.

The elements used to make up the code are *code masks.* You can specify the following choices for WBS code masks:

- ✔ **Numbers (Ordered)** uses a numerical code.

- ✔ **Uppercase Letters (Ordered)** uses letter codes (such as A, B, and C to correspond to the first, second, and third phases of a project) with uppercase formatting.

- ✔ **Lowercase Letters (Ordered)** also uses letters but with lowercase formatting.

- ✔ **Characters (Unordered)** is used for combinations of letters and numbers. This choice generates an asterisk; you can replace the asterisk with whatever characters you like in a columnar view.

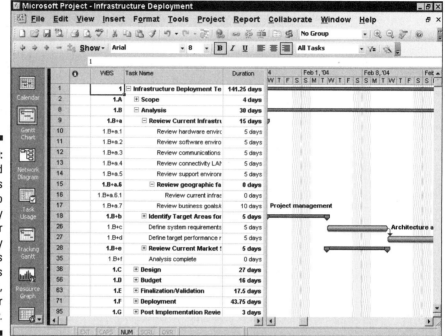

Figure 5-9:
Customized
WBS codes
can help
you identify
your
tasks by
categories
such as
division,
client, or
company.

To customize a WBS code, follow these steps:

1. Choose Project➪WBS➪Define Code.

The WBS Code Definition dialog box appears, as shown in Figure 5-10.

Project offers a Code Preview field so that you can see what your changes will do as you make them.

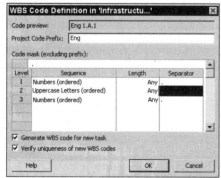

Figure 5-10:
The Code
Preview
field lets you
preview
your
changes.

2. **In the Project Code Prefix box, type a prefix.**

3. **Click at the top of the Sequence column and then select a mask for the first level.**

4. **Click the Length column and then select a length for the mask sequence that corresponds to the number of tasks you expect to have at that level.**

   Each number represents a single character. If you choose 4, for example, your first task at this level is numbered 0001. If you aren't sure, leave the default choice of Any, which allows for any length.

5. **Click under the Separator column and then select a separator.**

   The choices are a period, hyphen, plus sign, or forward slash.

6. **To define WBS code elements for additional levels of your outline, repeat Steps 3–5.**

7. **When you're finished, click OK to save the new code.**

The essential point of a WBS code is to provide a unique identifier for each task in your project. The WBS Code Definition dialog box offers the Verify Uniqueness of New WBS Codes option, which is active by default. If you turn off this option, you aren't alerted if you insert, for example, a subproject that contains duplicate WBS numbers.

If you don't want Project 2007 to automatically add a custom WBS code when you insert new tasks, clear the Generate WBS Code for New Task option in the WBS Code Definition dialog box. (Alternatively, choose Project⇨WBS⇨ Define Code.) If you later want to renumber all tasks to accommodate new tasks, changes, and subprojects you've inserted, choose Project⇨WBS⇨ Renumber. This technique can be useful if you want to try what-if scenarios and don't want all your tasks to change.

Chapter 6

Timing Is Everything

. . . .

. . . .

*I*magine this: If you create a hundred tasks and leave their default constraints so that they start as soon as possible and have no dependencies, all those tasks start on the project start date and occur simultaneously. The project consisting of a hundred tasks takes exactly as long to complete as the longest task.

Wander back over here to reality for a moment. When was the last time that every task in your project could be performed at the same time? When did you last have enough resources to even begin to make that feasible? When did you ever have a set of tasks in which not a single task had to be completed before another could start? Imagine what would happen if you poured a building's foundation before you got the building permit. Or, consider the chaos if you tried to train your employees to use a new piece of equipment before the equipment even arrived.

The reality is that tasks in a project don't all start at the same time. To reflect that reality in a Project plan, you have to build in a timing logic. That logic consists of setting dependency links between tasks. *Dependencies* are timing relationships between tasks — for example, when one task depends on the completion of another. Dependencies are caused by either

> ✔ **The nature of the tasks:** You can't frame a house, for example, until its concrete foundation is dry; otherwise, the building will sink.
>
> ✔ **A lack of available resources:** Your operations manager can't attend two plant inspections simultaneously.

How Tasks Become Codependent

In Chapter 4, I mention that you shouldn't set task start dates very often because projects are *fluid* — they change and grow faster than bad guys come at you in the average computer game. If you build in timing logic rather than assign specific dates to tasks, Project can reflect changes by adjusting your project based on that logic.

If the task of getting materials in-house is delayed by a week, for example, the dependent task of starting the manufacturing process moves out a week automatically. You can note the change when you're tracking activity in your plan, and Project makes adjustments accordingly. The alternative is to go in and change the start date of just about every task in your schedule *every time a task is running late* — you don't even want to think about doing that!

Dependent tasks: Which comes first?

As with human relationships, every dependency relationship involves roles: Every task is either a predecessor or a successor. Any two tasks with a timing relationship can be a predecessor-successor pair, even if the timing of the two tasks overlaps or they're set to happen concurrently.

Figure 6-1 shows you how the taskbars in Gantt Chart view graphically depict the predecessors and successors in dependency relationships between tasks. Notice how taskbars represent the relationship when a task starts after (or during the life of) another task. Also notice the lines drawn between tasks: These lines indicate *dependency links*.

Here's some important advice about dependencies, so listen up: You can have more than one dependency link to a task, but don't overdo it. Many people who are new to Project make the mistake of building every logical timing relationship that could exist. If things change and the dependencies have to be deleted or changed (for example, to shorten a schedule), the web of dependencies starts to get convoluted — and can easily create a nightmare.

For example, you must complete the tasks of obtaining a permit and pouring a foundation for a building before you can start framing it. However, if you set up a dependency between obtaining the permit and pouring the foundation, setting a dependency from foundation to framing is sufficient to establish the correct timing. Because you can't start pouring the foundation until you have a permit and you can't frame until you pour the foundation, framing cannot start before you have a permit.

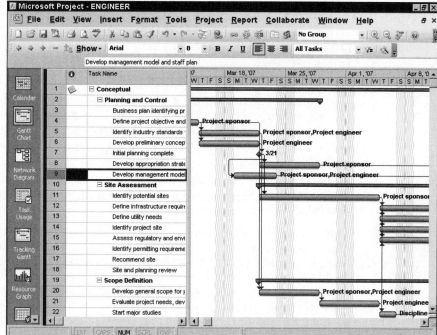

Figure 6-1:
In this view,
dependency
relationships
are shown
by the lines
between
taskbars.

You don't have to use dependencies to prevent resources from working on two tasks simultaneously. When you set the availability for resources and assign them to two tasks happening at the same time, you can use tools such as resource leveling (discussed in Chapter 10) rather than establish a dependency that forces one task to happen after another. This feature delays tasks whose scheduling causes a resource overallocation. See Chapter 10 for more about how resource assignments affect task timing.

Dependency types

You can establish four types of dependency links: finish-to-start, start-to-finish, start-to-start, and finish-to-finish. Using these types efficiently can mean the difference between a project that finishes on time and one that is still limping along long after you retire.

In Chapter 4, I cover task constraints and priorities. These settings work in concert with dependencies to determine the ultimate timing of tasks in your project.

Here's how the four dependency types work:

✓ **Finish-to-start:** A finish-to-start dependency is the most common type of dependency link. In this relationship, the predecessor task must be completed before the successor task can start. When you create a dependency, the default setting is finish-to-start.

An example of a finish-to-start dependency is when you must complete the Print Invitations task before you can begin the Send Out Invitations task. Figure 6-2 shows two tasks with the finish-to-start relationship indicated by a successor taskbar that starts where the predecessor taskbar leaves off.

✓ **Start-to-finish:** In a start-to-finish dependency, the successor task can finish only after the predecessor task has started. If the predecessor is delayed, the successor task can't finish.

Suppose that you're planning the building of a new cruise ship. You might start selling tickets for the ship's maiden voyage while the ship is being built, and you don't want to stop selling tickets until the ship is ready to leave. So, the predecessor task is Ship Ready for First Voyage (a milestone), and the successor is Sell Tickets for Maiden Voyage. If the ship isn't ready, you can keep selling tickets. When the ship is ready to go, the ticket windows close, and that task can finish. *Bon voyage!*

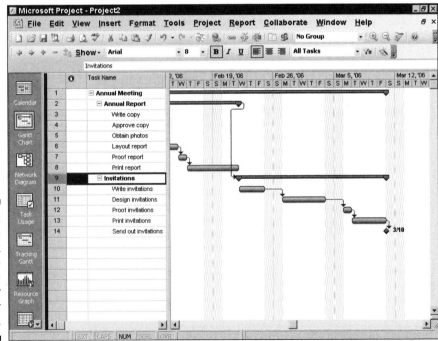

Figure 6-2:
Where one task ends, the milestone symbol for the other begins.

✔ **Start-to-start:** Start-to-start means what it says: Two tasks must start simultaneously. For example, even though they are being created by different designers, you might want to ensure that you send posters and invitations for your blockbuster event to the printer at the same time for cost efficiency.

Figure 6-3 shows the start-to-start relationship between the two tasks.

✔ **Finish-to-finish:** Finish-to-finish has nothing to do with warm relations between citizens of Finland. Finish-to-finish means that (you guessed it) two tasks must finish at the same time.

Suppose that you're preparing an annual report for your adventure-travel company. You have to obtain photographs of travel destinations and have the brochure copy laid out. You need both items in hand before you can forward the report to the printer. If you set a finish-to-finish dependency between these two tasks, you allow both tasks the greatest length of time to be completed. (Why have the photos sitting around for four weeks, for example, when the copy isn't ready?)

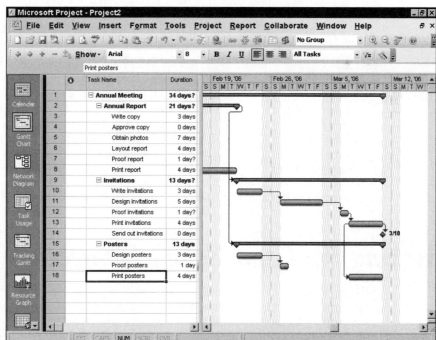

Figure 6-3:
The start-to-start relationship between two tasks.

Allowing for Murphy's Law: Lag and lead time

Dependencies can get a little more complex than simply applying the four types of dependency links I describe in the preceding section. You can use lag time or lead time to fine-tune your timing relationships:

- ✔ **Lag time** occurs when you add time to the start or finish of a predecessor task; lag time causes a gap in timing.

- ✔ **Lead time** is created when you subtract time from the start or finish of the predecessor; lead time causes an overlap between two tasks.

Here are a couple of examples:

- ✔ You want to launch a new toy product into the market and set up a start-to-start dependency relationship between the Begin Print Media Advertising predecessor task and the Begin TV and Radio Advertising successor task in your project. In a simple start-to-start relationship, both tasks start at the same time. If you want the TV and radio ads to come out a week after the print ads begin, though, you build in a week of lag time to the start-to-start relationship where Begin Print Media Advertising is the predecessor and Begin TV and Radio Advertising is the successor. TV and Radio ads will now start one week after print ads begin to appear.

- ✔ In a project to train a new set of volunteer docents to give tours of a historic mansion, suppose that you create a finish-to-start relationship between the two tasks Locate Recruits and Train Recruits. However, to save time in your project, you decide to incorporate two days of lead time — that is, allow the training of the earliest hires to start before all the recruits are hired. In that case, you essentially deduct time from the finish-to-start relationship that allows you to start training two days before the finish of the Locate Recruits predecessor.

Making the Dependency Connection

Making dependency relationships is simple. You simply create a dependency, make settings to select the dependency type, and build in any lag or lead time. The tricky part comes in understanding how each type of dependency affects your plan when your project goes live and you start to record actual activity that resources perform on tasks.

Adding the missing (dependency) link

When you create a dependency, by default, it's a finish-to-start relationship: One task must finish before another can start. If that's just the kind of dependency you want, that's all there is to it. If not, after you create this link, you can edit it to change the dependency type or to build in lag or lead time.

To establish a simple finish-to-start link, follow these steps:

1. **Display Gantt Chart view and make sure that the two tasks you want to link are visible.**

   You might have to collapse some tasks in your project or use the Zoom command on the View menu to fit more tasks on your screen.

2. **Click the predecessor taskbar and drag your mouse pointer to the successor taskbar.**

   As you drag, a box appears, as shown in Figure 6-4, and your cursor changes to the shape of a little chain link.

3. **When the readout indicates the task number you want to link to, release your mouse button.**

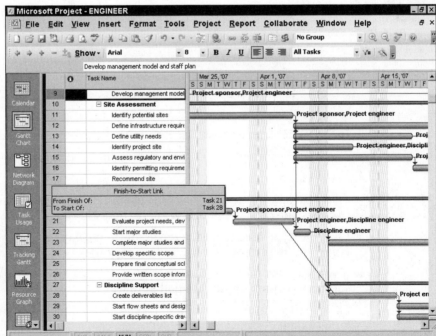

Figure 6-4:
This box lets you know when your cursor is resting over the task to which you want to link.

You can also establish a finish-to-start relationship by clicking the predecessor, pressing Ctrl, and then clicking the successor task; then just click the Link Tasks button on the Standard toolbar.

To establish a link in the Task Information dialog box or modify an existing relationship, make note of the task ID number of the predecessor task and then follow these steps:

1. **Double-click the successor task.**

   The Task Information dialog box appears.

2. **Click the Predecessors tab, as shown in Figure 6-5.**

   On this tab, you can build as many dependency relationships as you like.

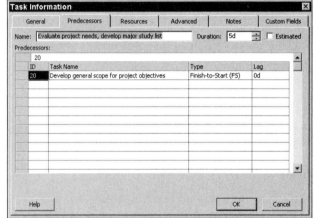

Figure 6-5:
Build
dependency
relationships
here.

3. **In the ID field, type a task ID number for the predecessor task.**

   Alternately, you could select the task from the Task Name drop-down list.

4. **Press Tab.**

   The task name and the default finish-to-start dependency type with 0d (no days, the default unit of time) of lag time are entered automatically.

5. **Click the Type field and click the arrow to display the dependency types, and then click the appropriate dependency for your situation.**

6. **If you want to add lag or lead time, click the Lag field and use the spinner arrows to set the amount of time.**

   Click up to a positive number for lag time or down to a negative number for lead time.

7. **Repeat Steps 3–6 to establish additional dependency relationships.**

8. **When you're finished, click OK to save the dependencies.**

   The Gantt chart displays your dependencies with lines and arrows, as shown in the project displayed in Figure 6-6.

Most dependency links are between tasks that are reasonably close to each other in the Project outline. However, if you have to link tasks that don't fit on a single screen of information, the click-and-drag method can be tricky. In that case, use the successor Task Information dialog box to create the relationship by entering the predecessor task ID number or name.

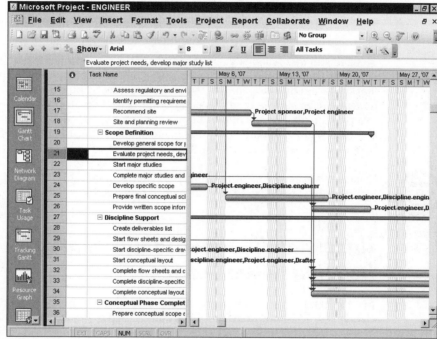

Figure 6-6: The more complex the project and its timing relationships, the more lines you see.

Extending your reach with external dependencies

No person is an island — and no project exists in isolation. Many times, another project you're managing or another project going on somewhere else in your organization affects your project. Perhaps resources or facilities are shared, or perhaps the timing of tasks in other projects affects the timing of tasks in yours. For example, if your project is to plan the opening of a new store, you might have to create a dependency from your Begin Move-In task to the Final Building Inspection Complete task in someone else's construction project.

When linked dependencies don't do a thing

If you want to set up important project dates and set up dependencies among them but you don't want those dates to cause any delay in your project (as a linked task might do), try deliverables. New to Project 12, *deliverables* are important dates in your project that you can use to build a proposal for your project before you even begin to add tasks. You can publish deliverables and report on them. They offer an alternative way to audit changes among several projects. Deliverables, which are essentially a Windows SharePoint Server list accessed through Project Web Access, provide a tool that you can use to control the effect of dependencies on your schedule. See Chapters 18 and 19 for more about Project Web Access.

To deal with this balancing act, you can create a hyperlinked task that represents the timing of the other project (or of a particular task in it). Enter a start date and duration for the task in your project. You can then create dependencies between that task and other tasks in your project to reflect the external timing. Use the hyperlink to jump quickly to the other project whenever you want to update your timing information. (See Chapter 4 for information about hyperlinking tasks and entering the start date and duration.)

You can also insert an entire project and add a link to it so that updates to the other file are reflected in your plan automatically.

Understanding that things change: Deleting dependencies

Just like the latest trend in fashion, dependencies in a project can suddenly change. For example, sometimes they're no longer needed because of a shift in resources or overall project timing. When you need to get rid of a dependency, you can undo what you did in either the Gantt Chart or the Task Information dialog box.

With Gantt Chart view displayed, follow these steps:

1. **Select the two tasks whose dependency you want to delete.**

   - **For two adjacent tasks:** Click and drag to select their ID numbers.

   - **For nonadjacent tasks:** Click one task, press and hold the Ctrl key, and then click a nonadjacent task.

2. **Click the Unlink Tasks button on the Standard toolbar.**

Be careful when you use this method: If you click only one task and then click the Unlink Tasks button, you get a somewhat drastic result: *All* dependency relationships for that task are removed.

To remove dependency relationships in the Task Information dialog box, here's the drill:

1. **Double-click a successor task name.**

   The Task Information dialog box appears.

2. **Click the Predecessors tab to display it.**

3. **Click the Type box for the dependency that you want to delete.**

   A list of dependency types appears, as shown in Figure 6-7.

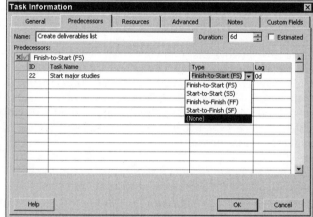

Figure 6-7:
You can use this tab to create and delete dependency links.

4. **Choose None.**

5. **Click OK to save the change.**

   The dependency line on the Gantt chart is gone; the next time you open that Task Information dialog box, the dependency is gone, too.

With the Change Highlighting feature turned on, you can clearly see the effect on your schedule of making this type of change. To turn on this feature, choose View➪Show Change Highlighting. Any tasks affected by adding or deleting a dependency now have either their start or finish date columns highlighted in the spreadsheet pane, depending on which date the change affected.

Just Look at All These Task Dependencies!

Project provides several ways to view dependencies in your project. The method you choose probably relates to how you visualize data, so there's no absolute right or wrong way here!

You might have already seen the dependency link lines that appear in the Gantt chart (refer to Figure 6-6). Another great way to see the flow of dependencies is in Network Diagram view. This workflow view uses similar lines and arrows to reveal dependency relationships, but it allows you to get a different perspective on them.

You can display the Task Drivers pane (choose Project⇨Task Drivers) to see a list of everything in the schedule that's driving the timing of a selected task. For more about the Task Drivers feature, see Chapter 10.

Figure 6-8 shows the Network Diagram view of an engineering project. Notice that each task has a node containing its vital statistics. Between the nodes are lines revealing dependency relationships among tasks. Although you can't see the effect in this black-and-white image, any task dependency links on the critical path are displayed in red by default, and noncritical tasks are displayed in blue. (*Critical-path* tasks have no slack: They can't be delayed without delaying the entire project.)

A neat trick in Network Diagram view is to edit the layout to show link labels. (Right-click outside any task nodes, choose Layout, and then select the Show Link Labels check box.) A code, such as FS for finish-to-start, is displayed to explain the type of dependency that each dependency line represents, as shown in Figure 6-8.

You can also display columns that itemize, by task ID number, successors or predecessors for each task in any view with a sheet area, such as Gantt Chart view. Figure 6-9 shows Gantt Chart view for the same engineering project with successor and predecessor columns displayed. These columns also display a notation of any type of dependency other than the default finish-to-start type and any lead or lag time using percentages or lengths of time. For example, 71SS+50% is a start-to-start link to task 71, with lag time set so that the successor begins halfway through the predecessor task. Similarly, 71SS+2 days is a start-to-start link to task 71, with lag time set so that the successor begins two days after the predecessor task starts.

Note that you can also edit the contents of Network Diagram nodes to include predecessor and successor data.

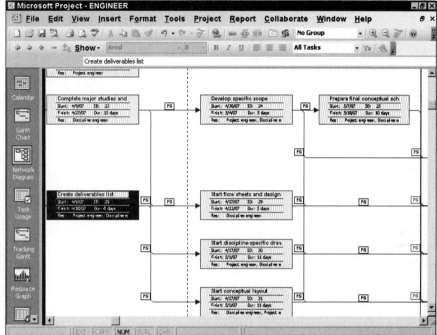

Figure 6-8:
Following the flow of dependency lines is a bit easier in Network Diagram view.

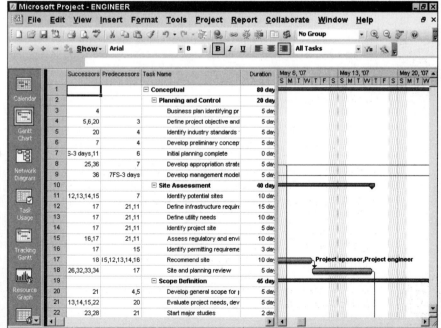

Figure 6-9:
Of course, you have to know which task number is which before you can use the information in these columns!

Part II
People Who Need People

The 5th Wave   By Rich Tennant

"And tell David to come in out of the hall. I found a way to adjust our project budget estimate."

In this part . . .

Here's where you get to know Project resources — human and otherwise — and how to orchestrate people, material and other costs most effectively to dispatch your project's tasks. This part also shows you how resources relate to project costs, and how to make resource assignments most effectively.

Chapter 7

Using Your Natural Resources

*P*rojects are like giant water coolers — they're gathering places for people. Projects also utilize equipment and materials. Those people, equipment, and materials are your project *resources.*

Unlike water coolers (you can take an analogy only so far), resources are also the means by which Project tallies up costs in your plan. Assign a resource to work for ten hours on a task, give that resource an hourly rate of $20, and you've just added a $200 cost to your project. Create a resource called *cement,* give it a unit cost of $200, and assign ten units (for example, ten tons of cement), and you've added a whopping $2,000 to the bottom line.

Using resources wisely in Project doesn't involve only assigning them a cost. Rather, it's a delicate art of combining the right resource with the right skills and assigning that resource to put in the right amount of time (or units) for tasks. And you have to do this all without overbooking anyone at any point in your schedule.

Because they affect timing and costs, resources are a big deal in Project. For that reason, many tools are available to help you create resources, make settings for how and when they'll work, assign them to tasks, manage costs, and manipulate their workload. The first step in working with resources is to create them and enter certain information about them. That's what this chapter is all about.

Resources: People, Places, and Things

Many people hear the word *resources* and think of people. Well, people are indeed a frequently used project resource, but they're not the whole story. Resources can also be equipment that you rent or buy as well as materials, such as paper clips or scrap iron. You can even create resources that represent facilities you have to rent by the hour, such as a laboratory or a meeting space. For example, you could create a resource named Plant Visit and assign it a unit cost of $400, which covers the average cost for a trip to your plant, including airfare, hotel, and rental car.

Here are some typical and not-so-typical project resources:

- Engineers
- Trade show booth
- Office supplies
- Hotel ballroom
- Administrative assistants
- Rocket fuel
- Speaker fees
- Furniture
- Computer software
- Printing services
- Graphic designers
- Prototype design

You get the picture. Resources can be practically anything or anyone that you use to complete your project.

Becoming Resource-full

After you create and organize the tasks in your project, the next typical step is to create resources. You can also borrow resources that have been created by others and assign them to your project. Before you start creating resources willy-nilly, though, you must understand how they affect your project.

Understanding resources

The key to understanding resources is to realize that resources in Project equal costs. If you want to account for costs in your project — such as a person putting in hours working on a task, computers that you have to buy, or monthly rent — you must create resources and assign them to one or more tasks. When you do, you can see the resulting costs in the Total Cost column of the Gantt Chart spreadsheet, as shown in Figure 7-1.

One other way to add costs to a project is to use a fixed cost. Fixed costs are not assigned through resources because they don't accumulate costs by hours of work or units used. Instead, a *fixed cost* is a set cost applied directly to individual tasks. (For more on fixed costs, see Chapter 8.)

If a cost is not task-specific — such as a flat $10,000 consulting fee to a firm that's advising you on an overall project — you can create and assign a resource or fixed cost to the summary task for the entire project.

Figure 7-1:
Tasks with assigned resources show the associated total costs in the Total Cost column.

	Task Name	Fixed Cost	Fixed Cost Accrual	Total Cost	Baseline
1	**– Infrastructure Deployment Tem|**	**$0.00**	**Prorated**	**$151,539.00**	**$0.0**
2	**– Scope**	**$0.00**	**Prorated**	**$7,659.00**	**$0.0**
3	Determine project scope	$0.00	Prorated	$0.00	$0.0
4	Secure project sponsorship	$5,009.00	Prorated	$7,409.00	$0.0
5	Define preliminary resources	$0.00	Prorated	$0.00	$0.0
6	Secure core resources	$250.00	Prorated	$250.00	$0.0
7	Scope complete	$0.00	Prorated	$0.00	$0.0
8	**– Analysis**	**$0.00**	**Prorated**	**$61,520.00**	**$0.0**
9	**– Review Current Infrastruct**	**$0.00**	**Prorated**	**$21,020.00**	**$0.0**
10	Review hardware environm	$0.00	Prorated	$3,000.00	$0.0
11	Review software environm	$786.00	Prorated	$3,786.00	$0.0
12	Review communications en	$0.00	Prorated	$3,000.00	$0.0
13	Review connectivity LANA	$0.00	Prorated	$3,000.00	$0.0
14	Review support environmer	$0.00	Prorated	$3,000.00	$0.0
15	Review geographic factors	$2,234.00	Prorated	$5,234.00	$0.0
16	Review current infrastructu	$0.00	Prorated	$0.00	$0.0
17	Review business goals/directi	$0.00	Prorated	$4,000.00	$0.0
18	**– Identify Target Areas for In**	**$4,500.00**	**Prorated**	**$22,500.00**	**$0.0**
19	Identify hardware improven	$0.00	Prorated	$3,000.00	$0.0
20	Identify software improvem	$0.00	Prorated	$3,000.00	$0.0
21	Identify communications cor	$0.00	Prorated	$3,000.00	$0.0
22	Identify connectivity LANA	$0.00	Prorated	$3,000.00	$0.0

After you create the resources that Project uses to tally your project costs, you need to manage the workflow for any resource that has limited time availability for your project. You create resources that are available so many hours per day and so many days per week. For example, one person might be available 50% of the time, or 20 hours in a 40 hour workweek, while another might be available full time (40 hours). When you assign those kinds of resources to your project, you can use various views, reports, and tools to see whether any resource is overbooked at any point during your project. You can also see whether people are sitting around twiddling their thumbs when they might be available to help out on another task. You can even account for resources that work on multiple projects across your organization and make sure that they're being used efficiently. Views such as Resource Usage view (as shown in Figure 7-2) help you visualize resource working time in your project.

Finally, you need to understand that the number of resources you assign to work on a task will usually have an effect on the duration of that task. In other words, if you have a certain amount of work to perform but few people to do that work, a typical task takes longer to finish than if you had scads of folks.

The task type determines whether a task's duration changes based on the number of resources assigned to it. Take a look at Chapter 4 for more about task types.

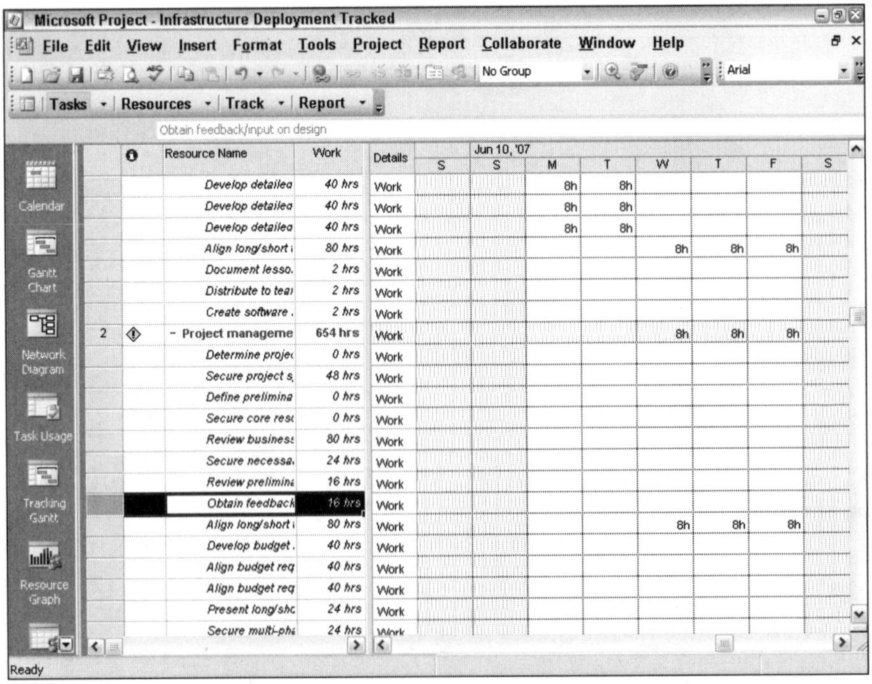

Figure 7-2:
You can see total hours on the project by resource and an itemization of the hours assigned task-by-task for that resource.

Enterprise or local?

If your organization has you choose resources from an organization-wide group, you can assign *enterprise resources* to your project. To assign resources created for your enterprise in Project Server, you use the Build Team from Enterprise command, located on the Tools menu; this command is available to you only if you are nicely set up on a network with Project Server in place. (See Chapter 18 for more about Project Server.)

To set up so-called *local* or *non-enterprise* resources, you simply create your own resource list in your projects; these resources are not available to other project managers.

Resource types: Work, material, and cost

Although people and things come in all shapes and sizes, only three types of resources exist as far as Project is concerned: work resources, material resources, and cost resources:

- ✔ **Work resources** are typically (but not always) people. They can't be depleted but can be reassigned. Their costs are associated with the amount of work time they put in, usually at an hourly rate. Work resources are assigned to tasks based on a Working Time calendar (as shown in Figure 7-3), where you specify their working and nonworking hours. You can select one of three base calendars and then modify specific working hours.

- ✔ **Material resources** can have an hourly rate or a unit cost, and they also have an unlimited working time. This type of resource has no calendar, and you make no settings for working and nonworking time.

- ✔ **Cost resources** have a set cost associated with them. Calendars and units of work or unit costs have nothing to do with the amount such resources deduct from the bottom line of your project.

A typical work resource is a person working eight hours a day at a standard rate of $20 per hour and an overtime rate of $30 per hour. Another example of a work resource is a meeting facility available only eight hours a day at an hourly rate. Even though it's not a person, the meeting facility would probably be created as a working resource because it has limited "working" hours.

The three kinds of calendars are Project, Task, and Resource. Calendars, their settings, and how those settings interact are discussed at some length in Chapter 3.

A typical material resource is any material — such as steel, rubber, paper or books, chairs, and shoes — assigned to a task with an associated unit cost.

For example, a resource called *Books* with a unit price of $12.95, assigned to a task called *Computer Training* at ten units, accrues a cost of $129.50 to the task. Another example of a material cost is anyone performing a service for a fee where working time is not an issue. A speaker who presents at a conference for a fee of $1,000 but whose working calendar and time are not your concerns might be created as a material resource with a unit cost of $1,000.

An example of a cost resource is a consultant working for a set fee. The cost might be $2,500, for example, and would not change based on the length of the project, nor is it based on a volume of units used.

How resources affect task timing

For a fixed-unit or fixed-work task type, the addition or removal of resources assigned to the task has an impact on the time it takes to complete the task. In essence, the old saying that "two heads are better than one" might be modified to "two heads are faster than one."

Here's an example: Suppose that one person is assigned to the Dig Ditch task, which should take four hours of effort. Two people assigned to the Dig Ditch task will finish the job in two hours because two hours are being worked by each resource simultaneously, which achieves four hours of effort in half the time.

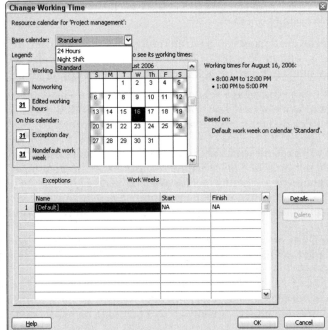

Figure 7-3:
Work resources are assigned to tasks based on a Working Time calendar.

One BIG word of warning here: Assigning additional people to tasks doesn't always cut work time down proportionately even though that's how Project calculates it. When you have more people, you have more meetings, memos, duplicated effort, conflicts, and so on. If you add more resources to a task, you might consider upping the amount of effort required to complete that task to account for inevitable workgroup inefficiencies.

Estimating resource requirements

You usually know how many material resources it takes to complete a task: In most cases, you can calculate the number of pounds, tons, yards, and so on with a standard formula. But how do you know how much effort it will take on the part of work resources to complete the tasks in your project?

As with many aspects of information you put into a Project plan, this judgment rests to a great degree on your own experience with similar tasks and resources. Still, remember these guidelines:

- ✓ **Skill counts.** A less skilled or experienced resource is likely to take more time to finish something.

- ✓ **History repeats itself.** Look at previous projects and tasks. If you've tracked people's time, you can probably see how much effort was required to complete various types of tasks on other projects and draw parallels to your project.

- ✓ **Ask and you shall receive.** Ask the resources themselves how long they think it will take. Then add 10 percent to that time to cover yourself!

Committed versus proposed resources

If you've ever asked somebody to work on your project and gotten a half-hearted, "Well, maybe, if I have time, if my manager says it's okay, if it falls on a Leap Year . . ." in response, you may well ask: So is that resource available or not? It's not always easy to tell. How can Project help? One feature that was new in Project 2003 is the capability to designate a resource as either *proposed* or *committed*. You can use the Booking Type field in the Resource Information dialog box to make this setting.

What does this setting do? Well, if you're not quite sure about a resource's commitment to your project, you call that resource *proposed*. Then you can display the booking type column in a resource view (such as the Resource Sheet), and keep track of resources you might have to firm up as you get closer to finalizing your project plan.

The Birth of a Resource

When a person is born, someone fills out a birth certificate. Creating a resource in Project involves filling out a form, too. On the Resource Information form, you enter information, such as the resource name, rate per hour or cost per use, and availability. You can also enter optional information, such as the work-group the resource belongs to or the resource's e-mail address.

You can create a resource as a single person or thing, a generic resource (that is, a skill set with no person attached, such as Assistant or Engineer), and even a group of several resources that work together.

Creating one at a time

On the simplest level, you create a resource — whether it's a person, a piece of equipment, or a material — as a single entity. In this case, you're thinking of a particular person, or meeting room, or piece of equipment. You create the resource by entering information in the Resource Information dialog box.

Another method for entering resource information is to display Resource Sheet view and enter information in the columns included there. This is often a faster way to create several resources at once.

When you create a resource, you must at a minimum type the Resource Name, but you can also include as much information as you want. Some people prefer to create all the resources first and deal with contact and cost information at a later stage.

To create a resource, follow these steps:

1. **Click Resource Sheet view in the View bar.**

2. **Double-click a blank Resource Name cell.**

   The Resource Information dialog box appears, as shown in Figure 7-4.

3. **In the Resource Name box, type a name.**

4. **From the Type box, choose Work, Material, or Cost.**

   The settings available to you differ slightly depending on what you choose. For example, a material resource won't have the Email box available, and a work or cost resource won't have the Material Label box available.

5. **In the Initials box, type an abbreviation or initials for the resource.**

   If you don't enter anything here, the first letter of the resource name is inserted when you save the resource.

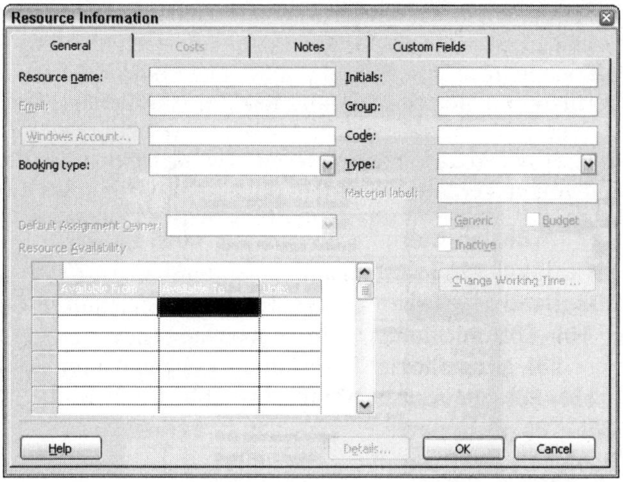

Resource Information

General	Costs	Notes	Custom Fields

Resource name: _____ Initials: _____

Email: _____ Group: _____

Windows Account... _____ Code: _____

Booking type: _____ ▾ Type: _____ ▾

Material label: _____

Default Assignment Owner: _____ ▾   ☐ Generic   ☐ Budget

Resource Availability   ☐ Inactive

_____   Change Working Time ...

Available From	Available To	Units

[Help]   [Details...]   [OK]   [Cancel]

Figure 7-4:
These four tabs can hold a wealth of information about any resource.

6. **Continue to enter any information you want to include for the resource.**

   That information might include an e-mail address, the group (a department, division, or workgroup, for example), Material Label (for example, pounds for food coloring or tons for steel), Booking Type (Proposed or Committed), or Code (such as a cost center code).

   If you enter information in the Group box, you can then use filters, sort features, and the Group feature to look at sets of resources. See Chapter 10 for more about filtering and working with groups.

7. **Click OK to save the new resource.**

If you use Project Server (a feature of Project Professional used along with SharePoint for online collaboration, covered in Chapter 18), you can choose the Microsoft Project Server option in the Workgroup box. You can also use the Windows Account option in the Resource Information dialog box to specify how you'll communicate with the team.

Identifying resources before you know their names

In the planning stages of a project, you'll often find that all your resources aren't assembled. Sometimes even well into the project, you don't know what resource you'll be using; you know only that you need a resource with a certain skill set to complete upcoming tasks. In that case, you might be better off creating some resources as generic resources.

If you want to create a generic resource, you should give it a name that describes its skill, such as Engineer, or Designer, or even Meeting Space (as opposed to a specific resource named Conference Room B). Then, in the Resource Information dialog box, be sure to select the Generic check box.

You can then display a Yes/No column titled *Generic* to identify these resources, and you can create a resource filter to filter for a Yes or No entry in the Generic column to filter resources by this characteristic.

No formula takes the Generic setting into account in recalculating your schedule based on resource availability. However, many people find this setting useful in long-range planning and in situations where they aren't responsible for specific resource assignments (for example, assigning a temporary worker to a task when the specific worker will be chosen by the temp agency).

Resources that hang out in groups

Although you'll probably have little use for chain gangs in your project, they exemplify the principle of a resource that represents multiple resources. Rather than assigning people one by one to some tasks, you'll want to assign a group of people who typically work together. Being able to make one assignment of a *consolidated resource* rather than several separate resources and assignments can be a timesaver in larger projects.

Here's an example of a consolidated resource: Suppose that you're managing a project to get a new Web site up and running. You have four Web designers of equal skill at your disposal, so you create a resource named Web Designers. You can assign Web Designers to a task at 400 percent, and have all four designers working at once. Or you can assign the Web Designer resource to work on a task at 100 percent, thereby assigning one resource to it.

There is no special setting to designate a multiple resource: However, you might want to include some indication of the number of resources in the resource name. For example, you could name your designer resource *Four Web Designers* (if you know the Web design group consists of four people) or *Web Design Group*. What really defines this type of resource is the maximum assignment units; 400 percent would indicate four resources in the group.

Sharing Resources

Many organizations have lots of projects going on at the same time. Some, such as a project to organize an office move, are the only project of its type happening in a company. Others, such as a building design project in an architectural firm, will happen simultaneously with several other similar projects and draw on many of the same resources, such as architects and draftspeople.

When an organization has projects of a similar nature going on at the same time, creating centralized resources is useful. This can save you time because you don't have to create resources when they already exist. It can also help to track resources across projects.

Another timesaving Project feature allows you to pull existing resources from a company address book or your own Address Book in Outlook.

In the swim: Drawing on resource pools

If you use Project throughout your company, it can be beneficial to create a centralized repository of common resources and allow project managers to assign those resources to their various projects. This collection of enterprise resources is a *resource pool.* By using a resource pool, you can get a more realistic idea of how busy resources are across all projects at any point in time.

Don't confuse a resource pool with *enterprise resources,* which require that you have Project 2007 Professional, Project Server 2007, and Microsoft Office Project Web Access set up. With all this in place (see Chapters 18 and 19 for more about enterprise projects), you can track and assign resources across an entire enterprise. A *resource pool,* on the other hand, is simply a list of resources, saved on your company server, that several people can assign to projects. A resource pool saves everybody the trouble of creating these resources again and again in their individual projects.

Both individual resources and consolidated resources can be created in a blank project as a resource pool and saved to an accessible location on your company server. Then, any project manager can call on those resources for his or her own projects; those projects are then referred to as *sharer files* because they share resources with the resource pool. For example, if you have a pool of maintenance people that everyone in your manufacturing company assigns to projects, create a project called *Resource Pools* and then create all your enterprise resources in this project. Or you could create a resource called *CEO* and let all the people managing projects that require the CEO's involvement assign him or her from that central location. Then use the resource-sharing tools in Project to assign these resources to your plan.

When anyone makes resource assignments in a sharer file, that information is also saved in the resource pool file. Then, anyone can use that file to look at resource allocations across all projects in the organization.

To access a resource that's available to your entire organization, follow this procedure:

1. **Choose Tools⇨Resource Sharing⇨Share Resources.**

   The Share Resources dialog box appears, as shown in Figure 7-5.

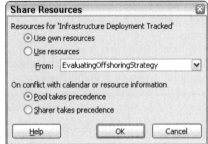

Figure 7-5:
When many
people pull
on the same
resources in
a company,
sharing
resources
becomes a
good idea.

2. **Specify the resources for the project.**

   If you want to specify that a project will use only its own resources (the default), select the Use Own Resources option. If you want to share resources, select the Use Resources option and then choose a project in the From list.

3. **Specify what Project should do when a conflicting resource setting, such as the resource base calendar, exists.**

   If your project's setting will take precedence, select the Sharer Takes Precedence option. If you want the pool setting to rule, select Pool Takes Precedence.

4. **Click OK to complete the process.**

   All resources in the specified resource pool are added to your own project's resource list, ready to be assigned to tasks.

After you add a shared resource to your project, you can update shared resource information. You would want to do this in case the person who maintains those shared resources has made a change, such as upping the resource's rate per hour. To do this, choose Tools⇨Resource Sharing⇨ Refresh Resource Pool.

If you combine separate projects into one master project at any point, Project allows you to have duplicated resources. If you link the combined projects and then delete a duplicate resource in the master project, it's deleted in the subproject as well.

Importing resources from Outlook

If you're like me, you've spent months or years building up your list of e-mail contacts in Outlook. You might as well have a way to leverage all that work: Project supplies this in its capability to pull resources from Outlook.

Drowning in the resource pool

Drawing resources from resource pools saves you time because you don't have to re-create those resources again and again. However, should you track your resource's time in the resource pool file to see whether the resource is overbooked? Most projects in the real world use resources that are not solely dedicated to a single project. New users of Project often get confused because almost every person working on their projects puts in time on other work, from general communication with co-workers and clients to efforts put in on other projects. Should they build resource pools to account for time shared among several projects at one time?

Generally speaking, it would be chaos to try to track every minute of all your resources' days to see whether they're working 100 percent or 50 percent on your tasks or are being shared among multiple projects. Ask yourself this question: When this resource works on a task in your project, "Will he or she put his entire focus on that task at that time?" If so, you might not need to fool around with tracking shared resources across many projects. Especially on shorter tasks, not trying to micromanage the efforts of your resources outside of your own project usually works just fine. If, on the other hand, you have resources who work only half time or split their time between two projects routinely, consider using shared resource tools to keep track of those resources across projects.

You must have Outlook specified as your default e-mail program in order for this to work. Do that by opening Outlook; when you're asked whether you want it to be your default program, say yes.

When you insert one or more Outlook resources in your project, they're added to your project list, taking the resource name and e-mail address as they exist in the Outlook Address Book. The default first-letter initial and work type is also preassigned. You can then add any details you like to the resource.

To insert resources from your Outlook Address Book, display Resource view and then follow these steps:

1. **Choose Insert⇨New Resource From⇨Address Book.**

   The Choose Profile dialog box appears.

2. **Select Outlook.**

   The Select Resources dialog box appears.

3. **Specify a name.**

   You can type a name in the Type Name or Select from List box, or you can click a contact name in the Name list.

4. **Click Add to place the selected name in the Resources list.**

5. **Repeat Steps 2 and 3 to add all the resource names that you want to import to your project.**

6. **When you're finished, click OK.**

The names now appear in your project resource list, ready for you to add additional information.

Say, When Do These Guys Work?

In Chapter 3, you can read all about calendars, including Project, Task, and Resource calendars. Now that you're working with resources, it's worth a closer look at how Resource calendars work.

First you create your Resource calendar based on a base calendar template that can be Standard, Night Shift, or 24 Hours. (You can also create custom calendars.)

- ✓ **Standard** is a typical 9-to-5 workday and five-day workweek.

- ✓ **Night Shift** is an eight-hour work day, scheduled between 11 p.m. and 8 a.m., with an hour off for a meal, from Monday through Friday.

- ✓ The **24 Hours** base calendar shows just what it says: 24 hours per day, 7 days per week.

After you specify a base template for your Resource calendar, you can specify working hours, such as 9 a.m. to 12 p.m. and 1 p.m. to 5 p.m. for a standard eight-hour day, or 8 a.m. to 12 p.m. and 1 p.m. to 4 p.m. for a variation on that eight-hour day. Finally, you can select specific days when a resource is not available (for example, when someone will be on vacation, at an off-site seminar, or busy with another commitment) and mark them as nonworking.

Avoid micromanaging nonworking time for your resources because it could leave you no time to manage anything. For example, if someone is taking off half a day to go to a doctor's appointment, it's probably not necessary to block a day off. However, if a resource is taking a two-week vacation or a three-month sabbatical, it's probably useful to modify that resource's Working Time calendar.

To make all these settings, you can click the Change Working Time button on the General tab of the Resource Information dialog box (refer to Figure 7-4). The Change Working Time dialog box opens, which is shown in Figure 7-6.

To make changes to a resource's calendar, follow these steps:

1. **Display the Resource sheet.**

2. **Double-click a resource name.**

   The Resource Information dialog box appears.

3. **Click the Change Working Time button on the General tab.**

   The Change Working Time dialog box opens.

Change Working Time

Resource calendar for 'Project management':

Base calendar: Standard

Legend:

☐ Working

▨ Nonworking

31 Edited working hours

On this calendar:

31 Exception day

31 Nondefault work week

Click on a day to see its working times:

August 2006

S	M	T	W	Th	F	S
		1	2	3	4	5
6	7	8	9	10	11	12
13	14	15	16	17	18	19
20	21	22	23	24	25	26
27	28	29	30	31		

August 18, 2006 is nonworking.

Based on:

Exception 'Vacation' on calendar 'Project management'.

Exceptions | Work Weeks

	Name	Start	Finish
1	Vacation	8/18/2006	8/31/2006

Details...

Delete

Help | OK | Cancel

Figure 7-6: The legend on the left explains how nonworking and working days appear.

4. **In the Base Calendar box, select a base calendar.**

5. **If there will be an exception to the default base calendar hours, enter the Name, Start, and Finish for the exception on the Exceptions tab, and then click the Details button.**

   The Details for [Exception] dialog box opens (see Figure 7-7).

6. **Select a day. Then click in the From and To boxes and type new times.**

   Note that to build in a break or lunch hour, you must enter two sets of numbers.

7. **Click OK when you're finished, and then click OK twice more to close the remaining dialog boxes.**

To change a day to nonworking time, select it in the Change Working Times dialog box and click the Details button. Click the Set Day(s) to These Specific Working Times radio button, and then clear any working times from the From and To fields and click OK. To change all instances of a particular day (for example, all Wednesdays) as nonworking, choose the day in the Details dialog box and then click Set Days to Nonworking Times and click OK.

To find out more about calendars or to create a custom Resource calendar, see Chapter 3.

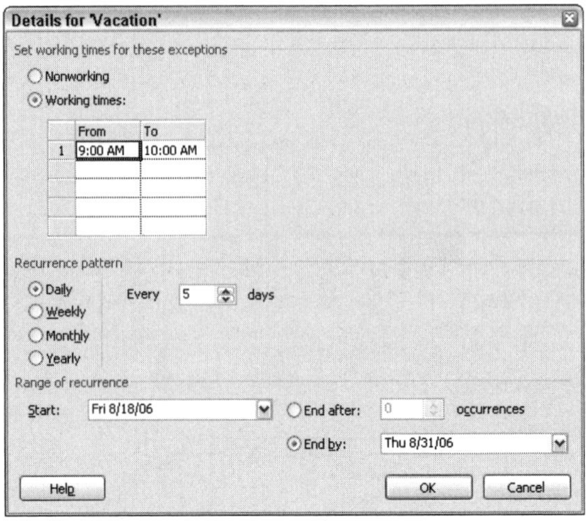

Figure 7-7:
You can set
the details
for a
working
time
exception
here.

Now That I've Got 'Em, How Do I Manage 'Em?

Before I leave the topic of resources, I'd be remiss if I didn't tell you a bit about the vital project management skill of *resource management*. Here, in a nutshell, is your nickel tour of the art of managing the people who will make your project happen.

Acquiring the right resources

Just like an award-winning performance in a movie begins with casting the right actor, resource management starts with finding the right resources for your tasks. What makes a resource is a combination of factors. The right resource for a task is somebody who has

- ✔ The right skills for the task at hand (or who is trainable, if training is part of your budget)
- ✔ Enough time available to complete the task according to your schedule
- ✔ The ability to commit to the project (This sometimes involves getting another manager's buy-in.)
- ✔ A cost that fits in your budget

Although the above list covers the basic requirements, consider other details, such as whether the resource is set up to work with the project team, and whether the technology to communicate and share documents is available (see Chapters 18 and 19 for more about this). Also, give some thought to how well each resource you choose will work as part of the team, and whether the resource can be considered dependable.

In Project, you have several ways to flag and find resources, categorizing them by skill or other criteria:

- ✔ **Use the Resource Notes area** to record information about a resource's skills and abilities. Then use the Find feature to search note fields for words such as *highly skilled, dependable,* and *trainable.*

- ✔ Use the **Code field** in the Resource Information form to rank resources by skill, cost, or ability to work well with others.

- ✔ Create **Custom Fields** for resources to note specific skills and search for resources by those skills.

Sometimes it's worthwhile to consider using a less-experienced, cheaper resource to save money — just be sure to factor in the time and money needed for any training required.

Balancing workload

Another important part of resource management is managing the assignment of resources so that nobody is as overbooked as a CPA at tax time. Although occasional overtime is expected of most workers, constant overtime causes burnout and poor work quality. Keep in mind that a less skilled worker will take longer to do a task than a skilled worker. Take that into account when scheduling the time that resource might need to complete his or her work.

You get the scoop about making resource assignments in Chapter 9, and more about resolving resource overallocation in Chapter 10.

You can do three main things to stay aware of resource workload when working with Project:

- ✔ **Keep an eye on your Project plan.** Various tools such as a Resource Graph view (as shown in Figure 7-8) allow you to spot overbooking on tasks.

- ✔ **Track the workload of individual resources.** When tracking activity on tasks, you will receive an accounting from resources (see Chapter 13 for how to gather this accounting) about the actual time they're spending on tasks. Notice the people who have to constantly put in overtime to keep their heads above water.

- ✔ *Ask* **people.** That's right. This isn't a feature of Project, but it's an old-fashioned communications device that works amazingly well. Check in with resources often and ask whether things are going okay — including whether your human resources are being run ragged. Then help those who are overworked by modifying your schedule or adding other resources to help.

Managing conflict gracefully

Although the fine art of managing people and the conflicts they seem to get into is beyond the scope of a book on Microsoft Project, this topic is worth a word to the wise. *Conflict resolution* is a necessary skill for project managers. It involves creating an environment of cooperation and respect, building consensus (agreement) among team members, and encouraging honest communication.

As a project manager, you can set up well-designed communications tools (such as frequent status meetings or reports) so people stay in touch throughout your project. You can also make a point of staying alert to conflict — and nipping it in the bud. (A conflict ignored will only fester and become something worse.) Try to keep the focus of discussions on the project goal, not on personalities.

In Chapter 16, I tell you all about designing and generating reports in Project that help you keep your resources in the loop. Chapter 18 provides several tools to help resources communicate clearly with each other, which can help you avoid misunderstandings.

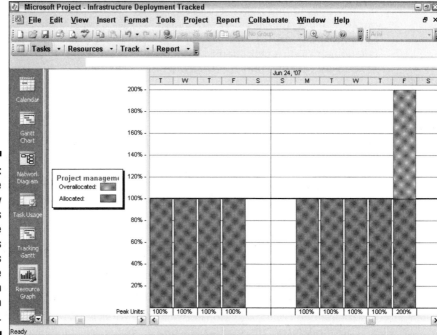

Figure 7-8:
Resource
Graph view
shows
resource
assignments
and helps
you see
problem
times in
your project.

Chapter 8

What's All This Gonna Cost?

There's no such thing as a free lunch — and if you use Project to track costs, there's no such thing as a free resource because Project uses resources working on tasks as a way of calculating most of the costs of your project.

When you create a resource, you specify a work resource rate (by default, this rate is tallied up per hour) or a material resource per use cost. You can also create *cost resources:* that is, a set cost for a task that isn't calculated using a per-use or hourly rate, such as a trade show fee.

Some other factors come into play as well, such as how many hours a day a resource is available to work and any overtime rates. At the end of the day, all these settings come together to put you over — or under — budget.

In this chapter, you explore the relationship between resources and costs and also find out how to set resource standard and overtime rates, create fixed costs, and set the availability of resources on individual tasks in your project.

Mary, Mary, How Do Your Costs Accrue?

Project helps to account for costs on your various tasks with a combination of costs per hour, costs per unit, and fixed costs. Before you begin to flesh out cost information about your resources, you have to understand how these calculations work.

You'll have two main pictures of the budget in your project: one at the moment you freeze your original plan (a *baseline plan*) and the ongoing picture of actual costs that comes from the activity and material usage you record as your project moves along. You record a certain amount of work effort on tasks, and tasks with resources assigned to them then run up costs based on the effort expended or units of materials used.

It all adds up

The best way to understand how costs add up in your project is to look at an example. John Smith (that's not his real name) is managing a project involving the building of a new gourmet ice-cream packaging plant. John has created a task called *Install Ice-Cream Mixers*. Here are the costs John anticipates for that task:

✔ About ten person-hours of effort to do the installation

✔ A fixed cost of $500 paid to the mixer manufacturer to oversee the installation and train workers on the machine

✔ Twenty pounds of ice-cream ingredients to test the mixers

The ten hours of effort will be expended by work resources. The total cost for the ten hours is a calculation: 10 × the resource rate. If the resource rate is $20, this cost totals $200. If two resources work on the task, one at a rate of $20 and one at a rate of $30, then (by default) Project splits the ten hours of effort between them, and the resulting cost is $250.

The fixed cost of $500 for a fee to the manufacturer is created as a cost resource. When you assign this resource to a task, you enter a cost for that resource on that task. This cost won't change based on the number of resources or the time involved.

Finally, the cost for 20 pounds of ice cream (any flavor you like) is calculated as 20 × the unit cost of the ice-cream ingredients. If the unit cost is $2, this cost would be $40.

And that's how costs are assigned and how they add up on your projects.

You can create and assign resources that have no associated costs. For example, if you want your boss to be available to review status reports but your company doesn't require that your boss be charged to your project, you can simply use those resource assignments to remind you about the need for your boss's availability on that day or at that time.

When will this hit the bottom line?

In business, you rarely get to choose when you pay your own bills. In Project, however, you can choose when your costs hit your budget.

Resources can be set to accrue at the start or end of the task that they're associated with or to be prorated throughout the life of the task. So, if a three-month-long task begins April 1, a $90 cost resource could be added to your actual costs to date on day 1, on day 90, or at a dollar per day until the end of the task.

This isn't exactly a purely realistic reflection of how you have to pay for costs, because face it: Most bills come due 30 days after they hit your desk. It's more a factor of when you want that cost to show up for the purposes of tracking costs and reporting expenses on your project.

Pay Day: Assigning Resources to Your Project

Most projects involve a combination of cost types: cost, work, and material. You have to do your homework before you can enter the information at the task or resource level. You have to find out the fixed costs as well as the hourly or unit rates for all your resources.

During the planning stages, you might not be able to anticipate exactly what a particular cost will be or know every resource's rates. If you have to, build the resource or fixed cost with your best estimate. That way, at least some cost will be reflected in your plan, and you can go back to enter more accurate information as soon as you know it.

Use a field in your Resource Sheet, such as Code, to designate resources as having estimated rates or costs so you can easily go back to those tasks and update the estimates as your plan progresses.

There's no avoiding fixed costs

Maybe it's that huge fee for the consulting company your boss insisted you use, even though you knew that the report wouldn't tell you a thing you didn't already know. Or perhaps it's the $2,000 for a laptop computer you talked your boss into getting you so you could manage your project when you're on the road. Whatever it is, it's a cost that won't change no matter how many hours the task goes on or how many people work on the task. It has no unit cost or rate per hour. It's a *fixed cost.*

You can specify fixed costs by creating a resource with a Cost type. Every time you assign the resource to a task, you specify the cost associated with it.

You can also simply enter a fixed cost associated with a task without having to create and assign a cost resource to it. To do so, you can use the Cost Table.

Tables are preset column combinations that make entering certain information in a sheet pane easier.

Follow these steps to enter a fixed cost for a task:

1. **Display the project in Gantt Chart view.**

2. **Choose View⇨Table⇨Cost.**

   The table of columns appears, as shown in Figure 8-1.

3. **Click the Fixed Cost column for the task to which you want to assign the cost and then enter the amount.**

That's all there is to it, but because you can enter only one fixed-cost amount for a task, you should also enter a task note where you can itemize fixed costs if you have more than one. Note also that the default fixed-cost accrual method is prorated; if you prefer to have your fixed costs hit your budget at the start or end of a task, use the Fixed Cost Accrual column in this table to select another option.

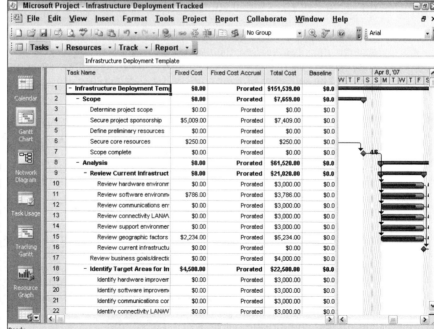

Figure 8-1: You can insert the Fixed Cost column in any sheet, but the Cost table is ready for you to use.

When resources get paid per hour

Whether it's minimum wage or the astronomical fees your lawyer charges you every time you sneeze, most people get paid something per hour. To represent most people involved in your project, you create work resources and charge them to your project at an hourly rate.

After a resource has an hourly rate, when you then enter the estimate of how many hours that person will work on each task that he's assigned to, Project totals his estimated costs in your plan. When you track actual effort expended on tasks, a calculation of actual effort times the hourly rate returns actual costs.

By comparing estimated costs and actual costs, you get an ongoing picture of whether your project is on track.

To set resource rates per hour, follow these steps:

1. **Display Resource Sheet view.**

2. **Click the Std. Rate column for the resource to which you want to assign a cost.**

3. **Type a dollar amount.**

   If you're entering a rate for a unit other than hours, type a slash (/) and then the unit (for example, **minute** or **month**).

4. **Press Enter.**

   The entry is saved.

Note that you can also make cost-rate entries in the Resource Information dialog box. The Costs tab of this dialog box, which is shown in Figure 8-2, offers a Standard Rate, an Overtime Rate, and a Per Use Cost.

In addition, five tabs labeled A through E allow you to enter different rates for the resource. By using the Effective Date column, a resource could work for several months at one rate and then start working at a different rate on a preset date. This helps you account for periodic raises or seasonal shifts in rates (for example, paying a premium for construction resources in months with better weather when they are more in demand).

If you use ten gallons at $2 per gallon . . .

This one might feel like a problem from your high school algebra class. (*So many gallons of water in a bathtub with a leak. . . .*) Well, if you weren't that great at algebra, you'll be glad to hear that there is a pretty straightforward calculation Project makes to arrive at *cost per use.*

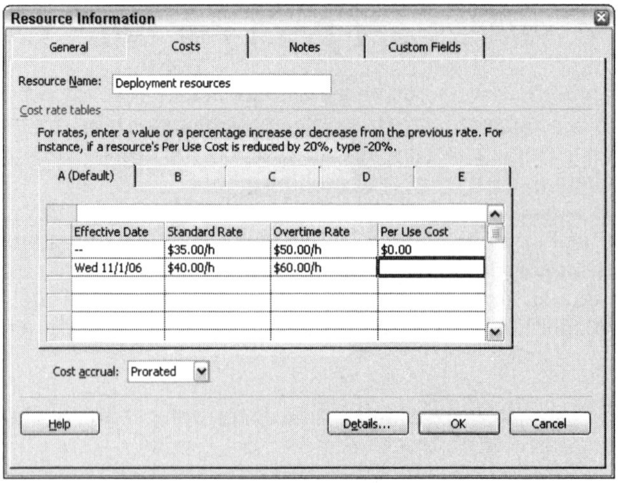

Resource Information

| General | Costs | Notes | Custom Fields |

Resource Name: Deployment resources

Cost rate tables

For rates, enter a value or a percentage increase or decrease from the previous rate. For instance, if a resource's Per Use Cost is reduced by 20%, type -20%.

| A (Default) | B | C | D | E |

Effective Date	Standard Rate	Overtime Rate	Per Use Cost
--	$35.00/h	$50.00/h	$0.00
Wed 11/1/06	$40.00/h	$60.00/h	

Cost accrual: Prorated

Help   Details...   OK   Cancel

Figure 8-2:
You can set
several
rates for a
resource.

Technically speaking, you can have a cost per use for either a work or material resource. You could, for example, have a consultant who costs $500 per use (that is, each time you use him to consult on a task, you get hit with a $500 fee). More commonly, you use a cost per use for a material resource such as rubber or milk, assign a cost for a single unit (per yard, or ton, or gallon, for example), and assign so many units to each task. The cost is tallied by the number of units times the cost per use.

To assign a cost per use, follow these steps:

1. **Display Resource Sheet view.**

2. **Click the Cost/Use column for the resource you want to set and then type an amount for the per-use cost.**

3. **Click the Material Label column for that resource and then type a unit name (such as gallon).**

4. **Press Enter to accept your entry.**

Note that you can use the Resource Information dialog box also to enter up to five per-use costs with effective dates to account for fluctuations in unit cost over the life of your project.

Making allowances for overtime

Overtime is a fact of life: It's great for people who earn it, albeit hard on the project manager with a budget. If you have resources that shift into earning overdrive after so many working hours, you can enter an overtime rate for them. Overtime kicks in when their calendar indicates that their regular day is over. For example, a resource with a standard eight-hour-day calendar who puts in ten hours on a one-day task will be charged by Project with eight hours at the standard rate and two hours at the overtime rate.

To enter an overtime rate for a resource, follow this procedure:

1. **Display Resource Sheet view.**
2. **Click the Ovt. Rate column for the resource.**
3. **Type an amount.**
4. **Press Enter.**

   The entry is saved.

It's an Availability Thing

Lots of Project features deal with resources — in particular, helping you spot resource overallocation. *Overallocation* is a calculation involving the resource's calendar and availability.

So, consider Monica Melendez, an engineer who works a standard, eight-hour day based on her calendar. Monica is assigned to the Write Final Report task at 50 percent of her availability and to the Create Design Specs task — which occurs at the same time as the report task — at 100 percent of her availability. Monica is now working at 150 percent of her availability, or 12 hours per day. Poor Monica is overbooked.

By default, a resource is assigned to a task at 100 percent availability, but you can modify that if you know a resource will be assigned to several tasks and is likely to put in only part of that person's time over the course of a task.

Setting availability

Availability is easier to estimate for some resources than for others. A manager isn't likely to give an entire day over to any single task because he has to deal with all the people who report to him, or she has to sign authorizations, go to meetings concerning various projects, work on budgets, and so on. With a production worker, it might be simpler to pin down availability to a single task: If one manufacturing job is going through the line for three days and one person is working on the line all that time, it's closer to the mark to say that he or she is working on that task full-time.

One big mistake that new users of Project make is to micro-think availability. Of course, no one actually spends eight hours every day on a single task in one project. People spend part of their days reading e-mail about company holidays, chatting with co-workers, and answering phone calls about non-project-related stuff (you know — J Lo's love life, UFOs landing at the UN, the usual). A resource might spend seven hours on a task one day but only three the next. Don't get hung up on a day-by-day resource schedule in estimating availability. If over the life of a task, the person is pretty much devoted to it, 100 percent availability is a good setting. If that person will put in only, say, five days of work on a ten-day task, that's 50 percent availability whether she works four hours per day for ten days or five full days at any point.

The Availability setting is there to help you spot overbooking of a resource who might work on multiple tasks at the same time in a project schedule.

To set resource availability, follow these steps:

1. **Display Resource Sheet view.**

2. **Double-click a resource.**

   The General tab of the Resource Information dialog box appears, as shown in Figure 8-3.

3. **In the Units column (in the Resource Availability area), either click the arrows to raise or lower the availability in 50 percent increments or type a number.**

   For example, type **33** for a resource available one-third of the time, or 400% for a pool of four resources all available full-time. The most common entry here (the default entry) is 100% for a single resource working full-time on the task.

4. **Click OK to save the setting.**

When a resource comes and goes

In addition to being available only a certain percentage of the time on any task or project, a resource might be available for only a certain period of time during the life of the task or project. Another scenario might be a resource that's available half-time for the first few days of the project and then full-time for the rest of the project. In that case, you enter a date range in the Available From and Available To columns of the Resource Availability area in the Resource Information dialog box (refer to Figure 8-3) to specify varying availability.

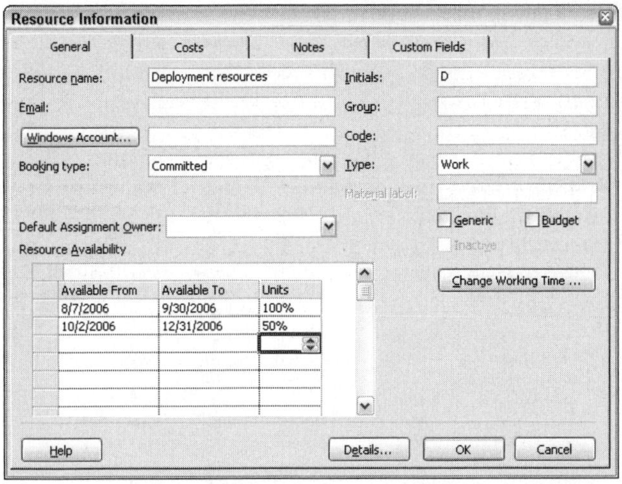

Figure 8-3:
You can
enter any
number you
like in the
Units box.

Adding It Up: How Your Settings Affect Your Budget

In Chapter 9, you explore assigning resources to tasks. But to help round out this discussion of costs, you should know that in addition to a resource cost per hour and a resource base calendar and availability, you assign resources to tasks at certain percentages. All these factors work together in calculating the cost of the resource when assigned to tasks.

Don't worry about the calculations — Project does those for you. That's the beauty of entering information in Project: After you make settings for your resources, Project does the work of tallying and showing total costs to you in views, such as the Cost table of Gantt Chart view shown in Figure 8-4.

For example, suppose you want to assign a mechanic to a task. Here are the specifics:

Base calendar: Night Shift (eight hours, six days per week, between 11 p.m. and 8 a.m.)

Cost per hour: $20

Overtime cost: $30

Availability: 100 percent

Assigned to a two-day task: 50 percent

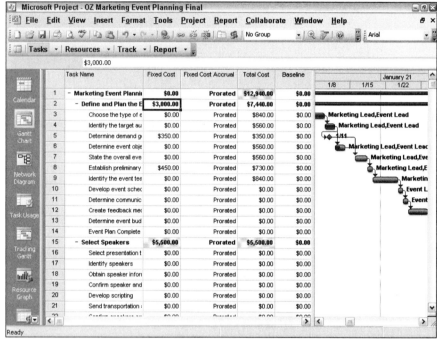

Figure 8-4:
Total costs
at the
summary-
task level
give you a
quick idea
of your total
budget and
costs in this
table.

What is the cost of this resource? Here's how it works: two days at half-time availability based on an eight-hour calendar is a total of eight hours (four hours per day). The resource incurs no overtime, so the cost is 8 × $20, or $160.

Change one setting for the same resource, and see what you get:

Assigned to a two-day task: 150 percent

Now the resource is working 12 hours per day (150 percent of 8 hours) over two days. With 16 total hours at the standard rate ($20) and 8 hours of over-time ($30), this person will cost $560.

Customizing Cost Fields

When you display the Cost table with fields, such as the Standard Resource Rate, you can click in any cost column and enter a rate for each resource. A neat shortcut is to customize those fields with a lookup table.

A *lookup table* allows you to create a drop-down list of values in a field to select from. So, if your company has a few standard hourly rates or per-use costs for materials, customizing these fields can make your information entry faster and also help prevent data-entry mistakes that can occur when you enter all rates manually.

To customize a field, follow these steps:

1. **Display a table with the column you want to customize.**

   You display tables by choosing View⇨Table and selecting one from the list that appears.

2. **Right-click the column heading and choose Customize Fields from the shortcut menu that appears.**

   The Custom Fields dialog box appears, as shown in Figure 8-5.

3. **Click the Lookup button.**

   The Edit Lookup Table dialog box appears, as shown in Figure 8-6.

4. **Enter a value (if you're filling in a cost field, this would be a dollar amount) in the Value column.**

5. **Enter a description (for example, plant worker or engineer for the category of resource charged at this rate) in the Description column.**

Figure 8-5:
You can use the Rename button in this dialog box to rename a cost field if you like.

Figure 8-6:
Create
preset
values for
the field by
building a
Value list.

6. **Repeat Steps 4 and 5 to enter additional values for this field.**

7. **If you want to restrict the field to accept only the values in this list, make sure the Data Entry option Allow Additional Items to be Entered into the Fields check box is not selected.**

   You may have to click the plus symbol to the left of Data Entry Options to see this check box.

8. **Click a radio button to select an order for the list (you may have to click the plus sign to the left of Display Order for Lookup Table to see these options):**

   - *By Row Number:* Lists the items as you've listed them in this dialog box

   - *Ascending:* Lists them in ascending value order, lowest value first

   - *Descending:* Lists them in descending value order with the highest value first

9. **Click Close and then click OK to save the list and close all dialog boxes.**

TIP

A good view to use if you want to see all of a resource's work assignment information is Resource Allocation view. You can display it by clicking the Resource Allocation View button on the Resource Management toolbar, or you can select it from the More Views dialog box. (Read more about the Resource Management toolbar function in Chapter 9.)

Working with Budgets

You can specify a resource as a budget resource by selecting the Budget check box in the Resource Information dialog box (see Figure 8-7). You then assign these resources to the project's single summary task. Using budget resources, you can display fields that allow you to compare budgeted work with planned work. (Believe me, there is often a difference.) For example, you might have $10,000 budgeted for computer programmer time, and you might have planned to use $11,450 of resource work for programming. The budget setting can help you compare these amounts as you add and delete resources from various tasks.

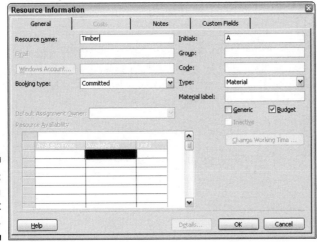

Figure 8-7:
Creating a
budget
resource.

If you assign a budget resource, you use Task Usage view or Resource Usage view to enter a work amount for that resource. You can view budgeted work by displaying the Budget Work field. Note that this field reflects only material and work resource type costs. You can use the Budget Cost field to view the budgeted amount for cost resource types.

Chapter 9

Assigning Resources to Get Things Done

*Y*ou might have entered a cost per hour (or per use) for every resource in your project, but those resources won't cost you a thing — or, for that matter, get anything done — until you assign them to tasks.

When you do begin making assignments, several interesting things happen. Not only will your budget start to swell, but also some of your tasks may actually change duration. You may also start to see evidence of people who are overbooked on several tasks that happen around the same time. Understanding how those results occur is key to making intelligent assignments.

However, your work won't be over even when everything about your assignments looks hunky-dory. That's when you have to communicate the assignments to your team and make sure that each resource agrees to take them on. If they don't, it's back to the assignment drawing board.

In fact, assigning resources is something of an ongoing process throughout your project. As usual, Project provides the tools to help you manage this entire process relatively painlessly.

You'd Be Surprised What Assignments Can Do to Your Timing

The three task types (as described in Chapter 4) are *fixed units, fixed work,* and *fixed duration.* Each defines the relationship that balances a task's duration, the work required to complete the task, and resource availability. This is known as *the golden triangle.*

Your selection of task type — in combination with a setting that determines whether a task is effort-driven — has an effect on the timing of your tasks relative to your resource assignments.

Pinning down your type

Essentially, task types specify what will remain constant in a task when you add or remove work resources to it after making the initial resource assignment. Although this whole work and duration and resource assignment percentage calculation can be complicated, you need to understand it if you want Project to accurately determine task durations in your plan according to resource assignments.

The default task type is fixed units. With a fixed-units task, the task duration you enter and the resource effort (work) assigned to that task jointly determine the timing of the task. With this task type, the assignment units you specify for your resources won't change even if the number of hours required to complete the task shrinks or grows.

With a fixed-units task, if you increase the duration of Task A from two to three days, your resources will continue to work on it at the assigned units for the specified duration; Project increases the Work amount accordingly. When you add or take away resources, Project changes the task duration accordingly, based on the assignment units you specify.

The fixed-work task type, on the other hand, takes a specified number of work units to be completed. A one-day task requires eight hours to be completed (assuming a Standard calendar). This type of task changes its duration in response to the number of resource units you assign.

With a fixed-work task, resource assignments may change in response to a work change. For example, suppose Task A takes four days to complete when one person is assigned; with a fixed-work task, the same task takes only two days when two people are assigned. Project doesn't modify the hours of work required to complete the task, but it does modify resource assignment units to complete that work within the specified timeframe. Thus, if you up the duration of Task A, resource assignment units shrink in response. If you reduce the time to complete Task A, resource assignments increase to complete the unchanged amount of work hours in less time.

A fixed-duration task does not vary its length, no matter what resource assignments you make.

With a fixed-duration task, Task A will take four days. If you assign additional resources or remove resources, the task still takes four days, but the resource-assignment units will change.

Figure 9-1 shows the same task with the three different types specified. Each task was created with a four-day duration and one resource at 100 percent. Then an additional resource was added at 100 percent. Note the resulting change — or lack of change — with each type. The fixed-duration task didn't change duration but *did* reduce resource assignments. The fixed-units task kept resource assignments constant at 100 percent — but reduced the task duration. Fixed work was accomplished faster, and the work (32 hours) stayed constant.

When effort is in the driver's seat

Project's complex calculation of work, task duration, and assignment units involves not only task types but also the effort-driven setting. (In Figure 9-1, the effort-driven setting is active for all tasks.)

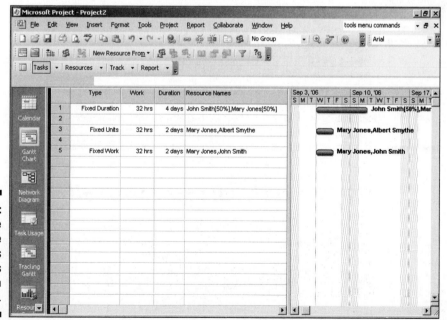

Figure 9-1:
Select the
task type
that reflects
what is
variable on
your task.

With the *effort-driven* setting active, if you add resources to a task, Project distributes the specified work equally among them and may change the task duration according to the total resource effort, depending on the task type.

With all three task types, Project assumes (by default) that each task is effort-driven. You can turn on the effort-driven setting or turn it off if you choose the fixed-duration or fixed-units task type. With the fixed-work task type selected, the effort-driven setting is turned on automatically and can't bc turned off.

Follow these steps to change the settings for an effort-driven task:

1. **Double-click a task.**

   The Task Information dialog box appears.

2. **Click the Advanced tab, as shown in Figure 9-2.**

3. **To turn off the effort-driven setting, select the Effort Driven check box to remove the check mark.**

   The effort-driven setting is on by default.

4. **Click OK to save the new setting.**

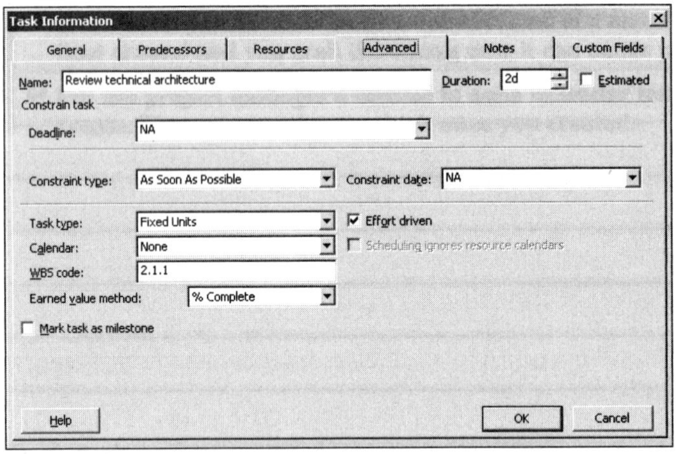

Figure 9-2: The effort-driven setting is selected and unavailable to you if you select a fixed-work task.

Task Information						
General	Predecessors	Resources	Advanced	Notes	Custom Fields	

Name: Review technical architecture   Duration: 2d   ☐ Estimated

Constrain task

Deadline: NA

Constraint type: As Soon As Possible   Constraint date: NA

Task type: Fixed Units   ☑ Effort driven
Calendar: None   ☐ Scheduling ignores resource calendars
WBS code: 2.1.1
Earned value method: % Complete

☐ Mark task as milestone

Help   OK   Cancel

Suppose task calendars prevail?

One other setting on the Advanced tab of the Task Information dialog box, Scheduling Ignores Resource Calendars, has an effect on how resources are scheduled when you make task assignments. You can instruct Project to let the Task calendar override any Resource calendar setting for resources assigned to it. Then, for example, if a task is set to use the Standard calendar and a resource assigned to it uses a Night Shift calendar, that resource will work standard hours on that task.

In some situations, certain calendar settings won't be available. Chapters 3 and 7 provide details about how all kinds of Resource calendar settings work if you need a refresher course about this.

Use this setting to provide some timing flexibility in your task: for example, if someone who normally works the night shift will be called on to attend a two-day seminar that takes place during standard working hours.

Finding the Right Resource

Sometimes there's no one in the world who can perform a certain task like Albert, and you'll get Albert to do that job if it kills you. Other times, just about anyone could handle the work.

If any Tom, Dick, or Mary with a certain skill level (or a certain rate per hour) will do, you can use Project features to find the right resource and make sure he or she has enough time to take on just one more task.

Needed: One good resource willing to work

You've probably used the Find feature in other software to find a word or phrase or number. That's child's play compared with Project's Find feature, which can find you a backhoe, a corporate jet, or even a person! You can use Project's Find feature to look for resources with certain rates or in a certain workgroup. You can search for resources by their initials, their maximum assignment units, their standard or overtime rate, and so on.

For example, you might need to find a resource whose standard rate is less than $50. Or you might want to find someone who can put in extra work on a task, so you search for any resource whose maximum units are greater than 100 percent. (In other words, the resource can put in a longer than usual day before he or she is considered *overallocated*.) Perhaps you need to find a material resource that is a chemical measured in gallons, but you can't remember the exact chemical name. In that case, you can search for resources whose material label includes the word *gallons*.

First display any resource view and then follow these steps to find resources in Project:

1. **Choose Edit⇨Find.**

   The Find dialog box appears, as shown in Figure 9-3.

2. **In the Find What box, type the text you want to find.**

   For example, type **50** if you want to search for a resource with a standard rate of $50 or less, or **laboratory** if you want to find a resource whose material label contains that word.

3. **From the Look In Field list, choose the name of the field you want to search in.**

   For example, to search for resources that have a maximum unit assignment percentage of more than 100 percent, choose the Max Units field here.

4. **In the Test box, select a criterion.**

   For maximum units of more than 100 percent, for example, this choice would be Is Greater Than.

5. **If you prefer to search backward from your current location (that is, the currently selected cell in the task list) instead of forward, choose Up from the Search box.**

6. **If you want to match the case of the text, select the Match Case check box.**

7. **To begin the search, click Find Next.**

8. **Continue to click Find Next until you find the instance you're looking for.**

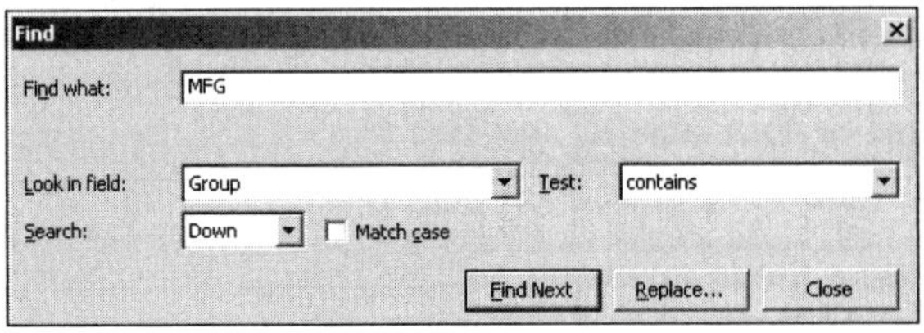

Figure 9-3:
Searching combines looking for some element in a particular field that meets a certain criterion.

You can use the Find feature also to find and replace an entry. For example, if your Manufacturing department (MFG) changes its name to Production (PDTN), you can search the Group field for the code *MFG.* In the Replace dialog box that appears, click the Replace button, and type the words *PDTN,* as shown in Figure 9-4. Then click the Replace button to replace each instance one by one or click the Replace All button to replace every instance of that entry in that field, wherever it occurs in your project.

Figure 9-4:
Use
Replace
With to
quickly
change
every
instance of
specified
text in your
project field
by field.

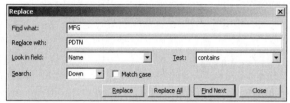

Custom fields: It's a skill

When assigning resources, you often need to take a person's skills into account. If a person with less skill or experience could work on a particular task (and save you money because he or she has a lower rate per hour), wouldn't it be nice to be able to find such resources easily?

Well, Project doesn't include a Skill field, but it does allow you to add fields of your own. You can use these fields for anything, but one great way to use them is to code your resources by skill level. You can use a rating system such as A, B, and C, or use terms such as *Exp* for an experienced worker and *Beg* for a beginning-level worker.

Here's how to add a custom field:

1. **Display the Resource sheet (or whatever sheet you want to view the custom field in).**

2. **Right-click a column heading and choose Insert Column.**

   The column is inserted to the left of the column you clicked.

3. **In the Field name box, select one of the custom fields, designated as Text 1 through Text 30.**

4. **In the Title box, type a name for the field.**

5. **Click OK to insert the column.**

You can enter whatever you like in this column for each resource in your project. Then you can search for specific entries in that field using the Find feature, or turn on a filter to display only resources with a certain skill level in that field. (Read more about filters in Chapter 10.)

Some organizations designate custom fields for certain company information such as an accounting code or vendor rating. If you have a Project administrator who is in charge of these enterprise-wide standards, check with him or her before you choose a custom field to designate skill level.

A Useful Assignation

If you understand how task types and effort-driven scheduling can affect your tasks' timing, you've fought 95 percent of the battle in assigning resources. The rest is just the software equivalent of paperwork. First, you have to create resources before you can assign them. (If you haven't, wander to Chapters 7 and 8 for a refresher course.) After you create resources, you can use a couple of methods to assign them to tasks and also specify the resource assignment units. These assignment units differ slightly between work resources and material resources, however, so read on.

Determining work material and cost-resource assignment units

Work resources, which are typically people, are assigned to a task using a percentage: for example, 100 percent, 50 percent, or 150 percent. When you assign a resource at a percentage, the assignment is based on the Resource calendar. A resource with a Standard calendar will put in eight hours a day if you assign it at 100 percent assignment units. Theoretically, a resource with a 24-hour calendar will work a grueling 24 hours a day at 100 percent (and probably fall right over) or 12 hours at 50 percent.

A *material resource* is assigned in units, such as gallons, consulting sessions, yards, or tons. When you assign a material resource to a task, you designate how many units of that resource will go to that task.

A *cost resource* is one that incurs a certain cost every time you assign it. For example, if you create a cost resource called Permit Fee and assign a cost of $100, every time you assign a permit fee to a task, it is assigned at $100.

 Note that material resource units are part of the entire work-unit-duration calculation that can cause work resource assignments to change task durations.

Making your assignments

You have four methods of making resource assignments in Project. You can select resources from the Resources tab of the Task Information dialog box, enter resource information in the Resource column in the Entry table (displayed in Gantt Chart view), split the window and use the Resources and Predecessors form in a pane, or use the Assign Resources dialog box.

Which method you use depends to some extent on your own preferences, but generally speaking, here are some parameters for using each method:

✔ When you use the Resource column, you're assigning at a default 100 percent assignment. If you want to assign a different percentage, don't use this method.

✔ Use the Assign Resources dialog box if you may want to replace one resource with another (there's a handy Replace feature in this dialog box) or if you want to filter the list of available resources by a criterion (for example, resources with a cost of less than a specified amount). This is very useful for making multiple resource assignments.

✔ Work in the Task Information dialog box if it's helpful to have task details (such as task type or the constraints contained on other tabs of this dialog box) handy when you make the assignment.

Picking resources from the Resource column

You can use this method to add resources in a resource column, whether from Gantt Chart view or Tracking Gantt view.

Even though it lists tasks in its sheet pane and can even display a Resource column, Task Usage view cannot be used to add resource assignments.

Follow these steps to assign resources at a default percentage:

1. **Display Gantt Chart view by clicking it in the View bar.**

2. **Choose View⇨Table⇨Entry.**

3. **Click in the Resource Names column for the task on which you want to make a resource assignment.**

   An arrow appears at the end of the cell.

4. **Click the arrow to display a list of resources.**

5. **Click the resource you want to assign.**

   The resource name appears in the Resource column, assigned at 100 percent.

You can always change the assignment units later by opening the Task Information dialog box and changing the assignment units on the Resources tab.

Using the Assign Resources dialog box

To assign a work or material resource to a task, you can select a task and then use the Assign Resources dialog box to make assignments. To do so, follow these steps:

1. **Click a task to select it.**

2. **Click the Assign Resources button on the Standard toolbar.**

   The Assign Resources dialog box appears, as shown in Figure 9-5.

3. **Click a resource to select it and then click the Assign button.**

   A check mark appears next to the assigned resource in the Resource Name column.

4. **Click the Units column for the resource you just assigned.**

   If it's a work resource, the default assignment of 100% appears. If it's a material resource, the default is one unit.

5. **Specify a percentage of assignment units for the resource.**

   Click the spinner arrows in the box to increase or decrease the setting. For a work resource, change the percentage units in 50-percent increments by clicking the arrows; or, you can simply type a percentage. For a material resource, use the spinner arrows in the Units column to increase or decrease the unit assignment, or type in a number of units.

6. **Repeat Steps 3–5 to add all resources.**

7. **If you want to replace one resource with another, click an assigned resource (indicated with a check mark), click Replace, select another name on the list, set its units, and click OK.**

8. **Click the Close button to save all the assignments.**

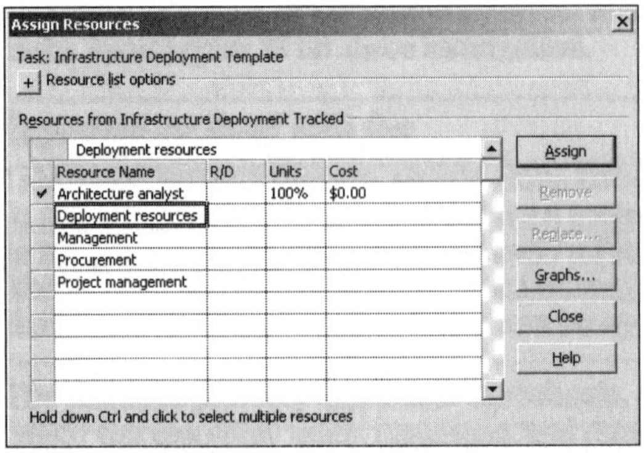

Figure 9-5: Every resource you've created is shown in this list.

You can also get to the Assign Resources dialog box from the Resource Management toolbar. This toolbar also offers handy tools for adding resources to your project from sources such as your Outlook Address Book and managing overallocated resources.

Adding assignments in the Task Information dialog box

Finally, you can assign resources on the Resources tab of any Task Information dialog box by following these steps:

1. **Double-click a task name in Gantt Chart view.**

   The Task Information dialog box appears.

2. **Click the Resources tab to display it.**

3. **Click in a blank Resource Name box and then click the arrow that appears at the right side of the box.**

   A drop-down list of resources appears.

4. **Click the resource you want to assign.**

5. **Click the Units column and use the spinner arrows to set an assignment percentage.**

6. **Repeat Steps 3–5 to assign additional resources.**

7. **Click OK.**

If assigning a material resource, the Units default is a single unit. (If your units are pounds, the default assignment is 1 lb.) Use the spinner arrows in the Unit field to assign additional material units.

Getting the contour that's right for you

When you make a work resource assignment, Project spreads the work out evenly over the life of the task. However, you can modify the level of work that goes on during the life of the task — called a *work contour* — so that more work takes place near the beginning, middle, or end of the task.

For example, if you know that the people on a task to install a new computer network will have to spend some time up front studying the manuals and reviewing the schematics for the wiring before they can begin to make measurable progress on the installation, you might use a late-peaking contour. Or, if you know that people are likely to put in a lot of work up front on a survey — and then sit back and wait for the results to come in — you might choose an early-peaking contour.

Using a different contour on a particular resource's task assignment could free up that resource to work on a second task that occurs during the life of the first task. This can help you resolve a resource conflict.

The contour you select will have slightly different effects depending on the task type. Trust me: Most project managers don't even want to try to understand this complex equation. Simply try a different contour and see whether it solves your problem and doesn't make too dramatic a change to your task duration or other resource assignments.

To set a task's contour, follow these steps:

1. **Display Task Usage view.**

   This view shows resource assignments by task.

2. **Double-click a resource.**

   The Assignment Information dialog box appears, as shown in Figure 9-6.

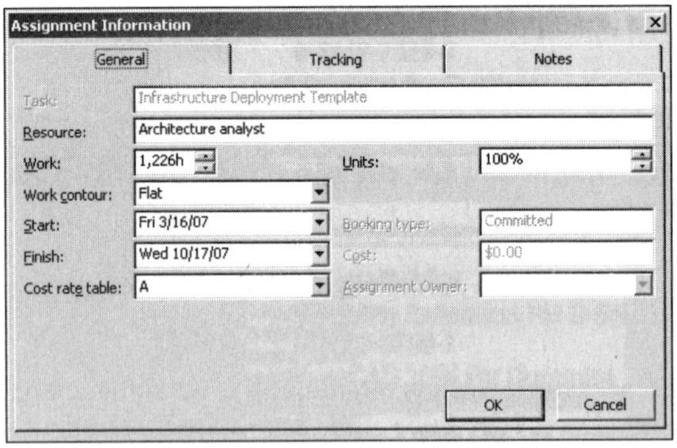

Figure 9-6: This is a handy summary of all assignment information for a resource on a task.

Assignment Information			✕
General	Tracking	Notes	

Task: Infrastructure Deployment Template
Resource: Architecture analyst
Work: 1,226h   Units: 100%
Work contour: Flat
Start: Fri 3/16/07   Booking type: Committed
Finish: Wed 10/17/07   Cost: $0.00
Cost rate table: A   Assignment Owner:

OK   Cancel

3. **From the Work Contour box, choose one of the preset patterns.**

4. **Click OK to save the setting.**

   A symbol for the contour pattern is displayed in the Indicator column for the resource.

   If none of these patterns fits your situation, you can manually modify a resource's work by changing the number of hours the resource puts in day by day on a task in Task Usage view.

Before you save, make sure your modifications add up to the number of hours you want, or you could inadvertently change the resource's assignment.

Resource Allocation view is useful for reviewing resource assignments at this stage. This view gives a side-by-side comparison between a single resource's workload and all the tasks going on during a particular time period in your project.

Communicating an Assignment to Your Team

After you work out all your resource assignments on paper, see whether your ideas will work for your resources' schedules.

Of course, you should check to see who is available for your project. And because things can change in the time it takes to work out your plan and make assignments, make sure that your resources are committed to you before you commit yourself to a final plan.

 If you use Project Server and Project Web Access with Project, you can use collaborative tools to publish assignments to a server, where people can review them and accept or decline. For more on Project Web Access, see Chapters 18 and 19.

You can send your entire project plan to resources as an e-mail attachment or just send selected tasks. You can also generate a resource assignment report and send that to people so that they can review their assignments in detail.

It's in the e-mail

E-mail can be a project manager's best friend. You can use it to communicate throughout the life of your project and to send your project plan for review at various stages. One of those stages is the point at which you want your resources to commit to their task assignments.

You can send your project as an e-mail attachment or as a *schedule note,* which is an e-mail with only updated tasks attached. You also have the choice of sending an entire plan or just selected tasks from it.

To send a project as an e-mail attachment, follow these steps:

1. **Choose File⇨Send To⇨Mail Recipient (as Attachment).**

   An e-mail form is displayed.

2. **Fill in a subject and your e-mail message.**

3. **Click Send to send the message.**

If you want to send a schedule note, follow these steps:

1. **Choose File⇨Send To⇨Mail Recipient (as Schedule Note).**

   The Send Schedule Note dialog box, as shown in Figure 9-7, appears.

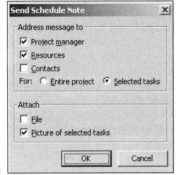

Figure 9-7:
Use this
dialog box
to specify
who will
receive your
note.

2. **Choose any intended recipients of the message from among Project Manager, Resources, and Contacts.**

3. **Select either Entire Project or Selected Tasks to specify what to include in the schedule note.**

4. **In the Attach area, select what to attach to the e-mail message.**

   If you select the File option, the entire file will be attached. If you instead select the Picture of Selected Tasks option, Project will attach a bitmap picture of the selected tasks in the view you had active when you started the Send procedure.

   Note: If you were in a Resource view when you began this process, this option will read Picture of Selected Resources, and the resources you had selected will be sent.

5. **Click OK.**

   An e-mail form is displayed.

6. **Fill in a subject and your e-mail message.**

7. **Click Send to send the message.**

To help you track e-mails to resources on your project, set your e-mail program to provide return receipts when messages are received or read.

Report your findings

Remember the days when you read a report on paper, instead of on your computer screen? Those days aren't gone: In lots of situations, a printed report is your best bet for clear communication about your project.

Going the Project Web Access route

Project Web Access allows you to do a lot of communicating and interacting with your team online, including notifying people of assignments, allowing them to see your Project plan (even if they don't have Project installed), and requesting status reports. You can also use features of Project Web Access to view resource availability, build a resource team from an enterprise resource pool, and review resource assignments across projects. Chapters 18 and 19 give you an overview of Project Web Access, which requires that your organization have Project Server installed. If your organization decides to implement this enterprise approach to project management, it can make your life much easier!

You can use several assignment reports to inform your human resources of their assignments on projects. To help you out, the four assignment report types provide the following information:

- ✔ **Who Does What report:** Provides a list of tasks organized by resource with total work hours, number of days delay from the original schedule, and start and finish dates. It also reflects a total number of work hours for a resource on all tasks in the project.

- ✔ **Who Does What When report:** Shows a calendar listing tasks organized by time period with resource assignment totals.

- ✔ **To-Do List report:** Generated for a single resource (not all resources, as with the other report types) week by week in a project. It lists the task names, durations, start and finish dates, and predecessor tasks by task number.

- ✔ **Overallocated Resources report:** Shows resource assignments for human resources who are overbooked on tasks during the project, including total hours, unit assignments, total hours of work on each task, and any delay from the original schedule.

Follow these steps to generate an assignment report:

1. **Choose Report⇨Reports.**

2. **Click Assignments and then click Select.**

   The Assignment Reports dialog box appears, as shown in Figure 9-8.

3. **Click one of the four reports.**

4. **Click Select.**

   A preview of the report appears. Figure 9-9 shows a sample Who Does What report.

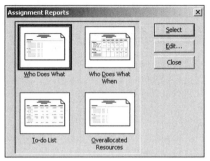

Figure 9-8:
Assignment reports deal with resource assignments to individual tasks.

5. **If you need to modify the Page Setup, click Page Setup.**

   For example, you might want to modify the margins or set the document to print landscape or portrait.

6. **To print the report, click Print.**

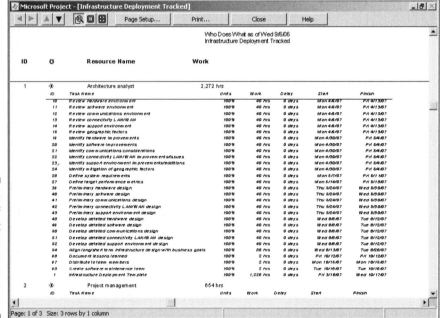

Figure 9-9:
A wealth of assignment information can be contained in these reports.

See Chapter 16 for much more about reporting options in Project 2007, including the new Visual Reports feature.

Part III
Well, It Looks Good on Paper

The 5th Wave   By Rich Tennant

"Our customer survey indicates 30% of our customers think our service is inconsistent, 40% would like a change in procedures, and 50% think it would be real cute if we all wore matching colored vests."

In this part . . .

When you've charted a course for your project, it's time for the critical eye: Does your project plan pass muster in terms of budget and timing? If not, you can use the built-in Project tools to tinker with resource assignments, adjust task timing, trim costs, and meet deadlines. Result: a better final plan. You also get a look at modifying how items in your project are formatted. (After all, a polished presentation, whether on-screen or in print, is invaluable.)

Chapter 10

Fine-Tuning Your Plan

As they say, the best-laid schemes of mice and project managers go oft awry (or is that "gang aft agley?"), and your plans are no different. After you take your best shot at laying out your project plan, creating every task, and assigning every resource — and you think you're ready to start your project — think again.

A close look at almost any plan will reveal some issues that you should resolve before you begin working on your first task. These might include a schedule that ends a month after your deadline, human resources who are assigned to work 36-hour days, or a budget that exceeds the national debt. (Details, details. . . .)

But even if you don't see any glaring problems in the areas of time, workload, or money, you should do a few things to make sure that your project is as realistic as possible before you commit to it. So take a moment to give your project the once-over.

Everything Filters to the Bottom Line

A first step in making sure that your plan is solid is simply looking at it from a few different perspectives. It's like walking around a car to see all its features before you fork over the down payment. Filters help you get that kind of perspective.

Two major problem areas that filters can help you examine at this stage are

- ✔ **Overallocated resources:** These are resources working more than the number of hours you specified.
- ✔ **Tasks on a critical path:** A *critical path* consists of the series of tasks in your project that must happen on time for the project to meet its final deadline.

Any task that has *slack* — that is, any length of time that it could be delayed without delaying the entire project's timing — is not on the critical path. If your project has little in the way of slack, any delays that occur are likely to derail your project.

Predesigned filters

Filters are like the Zoom feature in your word processor: They give you a closer look at various aspects of your plan and help you spot clues about problems (such as overallocated resources). You can set a filter to highlight tasks or resources that meet certain criteria or to remove any tasks or resources from view that don't meet such criteria.

Project provides predesigned filters that you can simply turn on for tasks or resources, using criteria such as

- ✔ Tasks with a cost greater than a specified amount
- ✔ Tasks on the critical path
- ✔ Tasks that occur within a certain date range
- ✔ Milestone tasks
- ✔ Tasks that use resources in a resource group
- ✔ Tasks with overallocated resources

Several filters, such as Slipping Tasks and Overbudget Work, help you spot problems after you've finalized your plan and are tracking actual progress. (See Chapter 13 for more about tracking.)

You can access filters in a couple of ways. When you use the Filter button, you choose from a list of built-in filters. The filters act to remove any tasks from view that don't meet specified criteria.

To turn on such filters from the Formatting toolbar, follow these steps:

1. **Display a resource view (such as Resource Sheet view) to filter for resources or a task view (such as Gantt Chart view) to filter for tasks.**

2. **Click the Filter list on the Formatting toolbar and then choose a criterion.**

    The Filter list is a drop-down list; when no filter is applied, All Tasks or All Resources appear in the list. If you choose a filter that requires input, you'll see a dialog box such as the one in Figure 10-1. Otherwise, the filter is applied immediately and removes from view any resources or tasks that don't match your criteria.

3. **If a dialog box is displayed, fill in the information and then click OK.**

    The filter is applied.

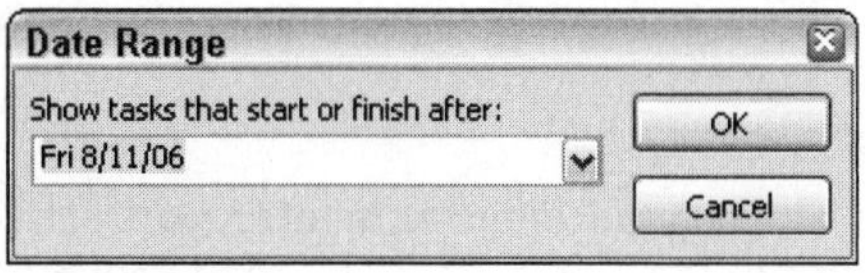

Figure 10-1: Some filters require that you enter parameters.

Date Range

Show tasks that start or finish after:

Fri 8/11/06

OK

Cancel

To redisplay all tasks or resources, click Filter on the Formatting toolbar and then click either All Resources or All Tasks (depending on whether a Resource or Task filter is currently applied).

Putting AutoFilters to work

You can also use the AutoFilter button on the Formatting toolbar to turn on an AutoFilter feature. When you click the AutoFilter button, arrows appear at the head of columns in the currently displayed sheet. Click the arrow for the Task Name column (for example), and the name of every task in your project is listed in alphabetical order. Click a task name, and all tasks but that task and any parent tasks for it are removed from view. You can also choose a Custom setting from each of these menus (as shown in Figure 10-2) to customize AutoFilter with certain criteria.

Follow these steps to activate and use AutoFilter:

1. **Display the view that contains the fields (columns) you want to filter.**

2. **Click the AutoFilter button.**

    Arrows appear at the top of each column.

3. **Click the arrow on the column that you want to filter.**

4. **Click the criterion you want for your filter.**

   For example, if you are filtering for task duration, in the Duration column, you can choose >1 day, >1 week, or a specific number of days (such as 5 days or 100 days). All tasks or resources that don't meet your criteria disappear.

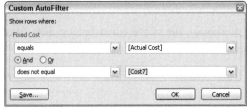

Figure 10-2:
AutoFilter
choices are
specific to
each field of
information
in your
sheet.

TIP

If you want to apply a highlight to each item that meets your filter criteria rather than remove nonmatching items from view, choose Project⇨Filtered For⇨More Filters. Click the filter you want and then click Highlight.

Do-it-yourself filters

You don't have to use predesigned filters: You can get creative and design your own filters. To define a new filter, you specify a field name, a test, and a value.

For example, the following filters for any task on the critical path:

> **Critical** (field name) **Equals** (test) **Yes** (value)

You can also include additional qualifiers to the filter. The following filters for tasks that are both on the critical path and have a baseline cost of more than $5,000:

> **Critical** (field name) **Equals** (test) **Yes** (value)
>
> and
>
> **Baseline Cost** (field name) **Is Greater Than** (test) **5000** (value)

Here's how to build your own filter definition:

1. **Choose Project⇨Filtered For⇨More Filters.**

   The More Filters dialog box appears, as shown in Figure 10-3.

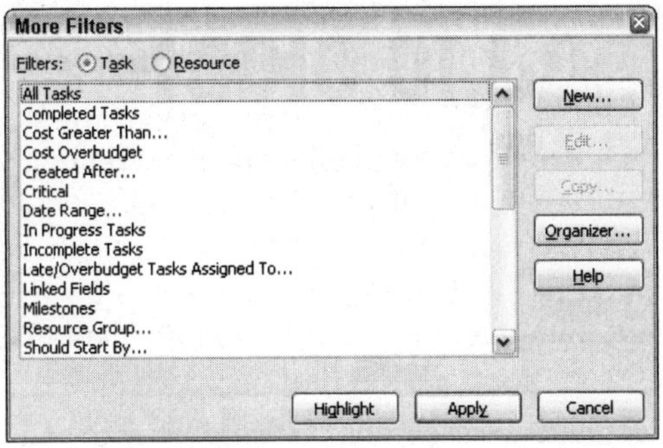

Figure 10-3:
This dialog box lists all available filters, built-in and custom.

2. **Select either the Task or Resource option to specify which list of filters you want the new filter to be included in.**

3. **Click New.**

   The Filter Definition dialog box appears.

4. **In the Name field, type a name for the filter.**

5. **Click the first line of the Field Name column, and then click the down arrow that appears to display the list of choices, as shown in Figure 10-4.**

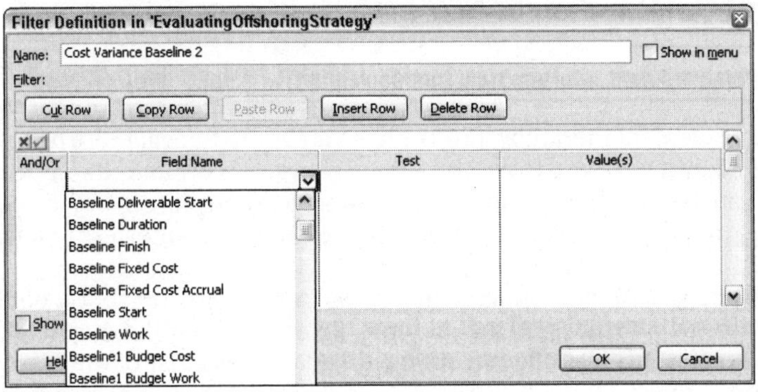

Figure 10-4:
Give your new filter a name that describes what it does.

6. **Click a field name to select it.**

7. **Repeat Steps 5 and 6 for the Test and Value(s) columns.**

   - *Test* is a condition that must be met, such as does not equal or is greater than.

   - *Value(s)* is either a value you enter (such as a specific date or cost) or a predetermined value (such as baseline cost).

8. **If you want to enter a qualifier, such as a dollar amount, click the entry box above the column headings and then type the amount at the end of the filter definition.**

   For example, if you choose Cost for the field name and Equals for the test, you might enter the number **5000** at the end of the definition in the entry box.

9. **If you want to add another condition, choose And or Or from the And/Or column, and then make choices for the next set of Field Name, Test, and Value(s) boxes.**

   Note that you can cut and paste rows of settings you've made to rearrange them in the list, or use the Copy Row or Delete Row button to perform those actions for filters with several lines of criteria.

10. **If you want the new filter to be shown in the list when you click the Filter box on the Formatting toolbar, select the Show in Menu check box.**

11. **Click OK to save the new filter and then click Apply to apply the filter to your plan.**

You can click the Organizer button in the More Filters dialog box to copy filters you've created in one Project file to another file.

Hanging Out in Groups

Remember those groups you used to hang out with in high school? (I'm sure *you* were part of the *cool* group!) Groups helped you see the underlying order of your adolescent hierarchy. Project lets you group things, too. The Group feature essentially allows you to organize information by certain criteria. For example, you can use the Group feature if you want to see resources organized by work group, or you might organize tasks by their duration, shortest to longest.

Organizing tasks or resources in this way may help you spot a potential problem in your project: for example, if you find that the majority of your resources at project startup are unskilled or that most of the tasks at the end of your project are on the critical path. Like filters, groups come predefined or you can create custom groups.

Applying predefined groups

Predefined groups are quick and easy to apply and cover a host of common requirements in projects. Follow these steps to apply a predefined group structure to your project:

1. **Display either a resource view (such as Resource Sheet view) to group resources, or a task view (such as Gantt Chart view) to group tasks.**

2. **On the Standard toolbar, click the Group By list and then choose a criterion.**

   The information is organized according to your selection. Figure 10-5 shows an example.

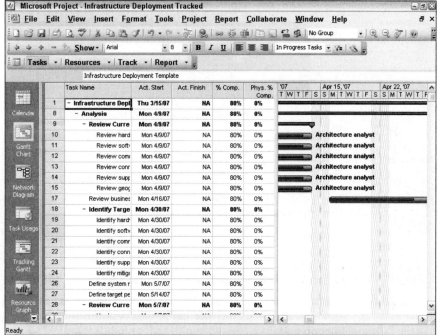

Figure 10-5:
Organizing
tasks to
show only
tasks in
progress
provides
this view of
your project.

To redisplay all tasks or resources in their original order, click the arrow in the Group box on the toolbar to display the list and click No Group. (When no group is applied, the Group box displays No Group.)

Devising your own groups

Custom groups include three elements: a field name, a field type, and an order. For example, you might create a group that shows the field name (such as Baseline Work) and a field type (such as Tasks, Resources, or Assignments) in a certain order (Descending or Ascending). A group that shows Baseline Work for Tasks in Descending order, for example, would list tasks in order from the most work hours required to the least. Other settings you can make for groups control the format of the group's appearance, such as the font used or a font color applied.

Follow these steps to create a custom group:

1. Choose Project⇨Group By⇨More Groups.

The More Groups dialog box appears, as shown in Figure 10-6.

Figure 10-6:
This dialog box is organized by task- or resource-oriented groups.

2. Select either Task or Resource to specify in which list of groups you want the new group to be included.

3. Click New.

The Group Definition dialog box appears, as shown in Figure 10-7.

4. In the Name field, type a name for the group.

5. Click the first line of the Field Name column, click the down arrow that appears to display the list of choices, and then click a field name to choose it.

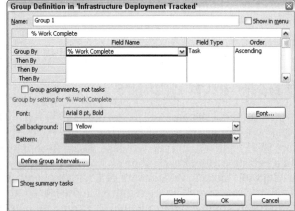

Figure 10-7:
Use your own groups to organize data.

6. Repeat Step 5 for the Field Type and Order columns.

Note that if you want the Field Type option of grouping by assignment rather than by resource or task, you must first select the Group Assignments, Not Tasks check box to make that field available to you. Otherwise the Field Type of Task or Resource appears by default.

7. **If you want to add another sorting criteria, click a row titled Then By, and make choices for the Field Name, Field Type, and Order columns.**

8. **If you want the new group to be shown in the list when you click the Group box on the Formatting toolbar, select the Show in Menu check box.**

9. **Depending on the field name you've chosen, you can make settings for the font, cell background, and pattern to format your group.**

   For example, the font and color of each duration group heading in Figure 10-5 was determined by making choices from these three lists.

10. **If you want to define intervals for the groups to be organized in, click the Define Group Intervals button.**

   This displays the Define Group Interval dialog box; use the settings here to set a starting time and an interval. For example, if the Group By criterion is Standard Rate and you select a Group Interval of 10.00, groupings would be in $10 intervals (those making 0–$10 an hour in one grouping, those making $11–$20 in another, and so on).

11. **Click OK to save the new group and then click Apply to apply the group to your plan.**

If you want to make changes to an existing predefined group, apply the group and then choose Project➪Group By➪Customize Group By. This takes you to the Customize Group By dialog box for that group. This dialog box — whose options are identical to the Group Definition dialog box — allows you to edit all those settings for an existing group.

Figuring Out What's Driving Your Project

With all the things going on in a project — perhaps hundreds of tasks, thousands of dependencies, calendars, and so on — it can be hard to see why your project plan has turned out the way it has. Three new features in Project 2007 can help you to see what's driving your project and make those all-important tweaks before you finalize your project plan:

✔ **Task Drivers** is a powerful feature that tells you what is driving the timing of tasks in your project.

✔ **Multiple Undo** allows you to try out different approaches and then undo several changes in a row (in previous versions of Project, you could undo only the last action).

✔ **Change Highlighting** helps you see the results of any change you make to your plan.

Spotting Task Drivers

When you play a game of golf, several factors affect your game. You might be getting a cold, the weather could be bad, or you could have been handed a defective club. (These are the reasons I give myself.) Likewise, the timing of every task in your project is affected by certain conditions. The Task Drivers feature will help you recognize these conditions, which could include

✔ **Actual Start Date or Assignments:** You have entered an actual start date, or you have made a resource assignment to a task and the resource is not available.

✔ **Leveling Delay:** If you turned on leveling to deal with resource overallocations, it may have caused a delay on a task.

✔ **Constraints:** You apply a constraint to a task, such as forcing it to finish on a certain date.

✔ **Summary Tasks:** Summary tasks' timing are driven by the timing of their child tasks or subtasks.

✔ **Dependency Relationships:** A predecessor task can cause changes in a task's timing.

To display task driver information, simply click the Task Drivers button on the Standard toolbar (it looks like a taskbar with an arrow and question mark above it). The Task Drivers pane appears (see Figure 10-8), explaining the various conditions driving a task's timing. You can click another task to display its drivers; click the Close button in the Task Drivers pane to close it when you're done.

Undo, undo, undo

When Microsoft held a prerelease conference announcing new features in Project 2007, it touted Multiple Undo as the most requested feature and announced with glee that it had finally arrived.

Why is this feature such a big deal? Individual changes to anything in your project plan can have several effects. For that reason, undoing several actions in a row was a major technology challenge. If you want to try out different scenarios that involve several changes to your project, you used to have to do an action and then undo it, then do the next action and undo it, and so on, which is time-consuming and doesn't allow you to see cumulative affects. Now, you can try out several changes and then undo the whole list of changes or a portion of them at once. Because you often want to try out several changes when finalizing or making adjustments to a project — for example, changing the timing of several tasks or the hourly rates of several resources — Multiple Undo is very handy.

TIP

You do have to undo all changes in order. For example, if you made five changes and you want to undo the fourth change, you have to undo changes one through four. To undo a change, click the down arrow of the Undo button on the Standard toolbar and then choose the change you want to undo (see Figure 10-9). That change and all others you performed subsequent to it are undone.

Highlighting changes

Another useful tool you can use to see how changes you make to fine-tune your project schedule have an impact on your project is Change Highlighting. You can toggle this feature on and off by clicking the Show Change Highlighting/Hide Change Highlighting button on the Standard toolbar. When you turn Change Highlighting on and take any action to change your project's schedule, a highlight appears on every task that the change has had an impact on (see Figure 10-10).

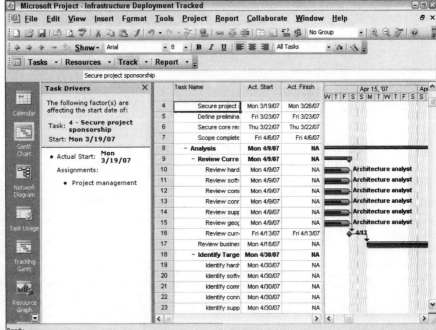

Figure 10-8:
The Task
Drivers
pane shows
you the
influences
on your
task's
timing.

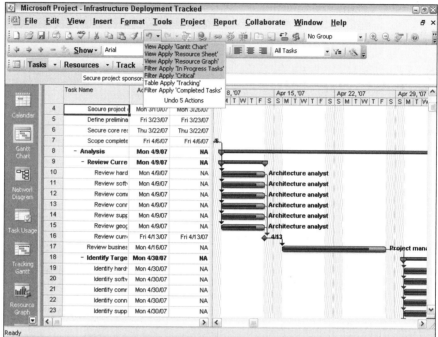

Figure 10-9:
Undo
more than
one task,
sequentially.

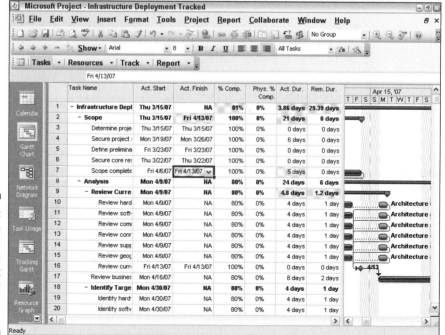

Figure 10-10:
Change
Highlighting
lets you see
just what
effect your
changes will
have.

Change Highlighting shows you only the results of the last change you made and works only on scheduling changes.

It's About Time

We've all had this experience: Your boss asks you to commit to getting a project finished by a certain date. Your palms sweat, you get a sick feeling in the pit of your stomach, you add a week onto the deadline the boss suggests to cover yourself, and then you promise to deliver the impossible. You hope you can do it. You want to do it. But *can* you do it?

Project allows you to feel much more confident about committing to a timeframe because you can see how long all your tasks will take to complete. Before you go to your boss and make any promises, make sure you're comfortable with two things: the total time it takes to complete the project and the critical path (the longest series of tasks that must be completed on time in order for you to meet the overall project deadline).

The timing data for your project summary task tells you how long the entire project will take. Just display Gantt Chart view and look at the Duration, Start, and Finish columns. If your finish date doesn't work, you'll have to go back and modify some tasks.

You should also make sure that there's room for error. You can use filters and groups to identify the critical path in, for example, Gantt Chart view or Network Diagram view. If you judge that too many tasks are on the critical path, it's wise to add some slack to the plan to allow for inevitable delays.

Giving yourself some slack

How many tasks should be on the critical path in your project, and how many should have some slack — that is, some time that they could be delayed without delaying the entire project? I wish I could give you a formula, but sadly, it's not a science. Ideally, every task in your project *should* have slack because things can come up that you never expected (shortages of vital materials, asteroid strikes, management turnover that places you in an entirely different department). If you add slack to each and every task, however, your project is probably going to go on into the next millennium. Figure 10-11 shows a more typical scenario, with a mix of noncritical and critical tasks.

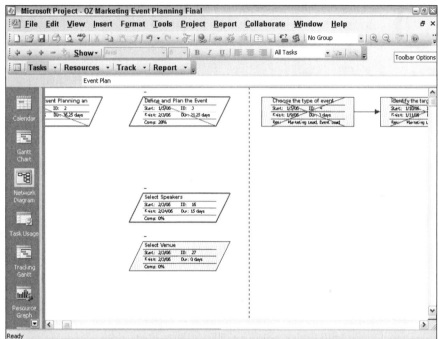

Figure 10-11:
Follow the
critical path
in Network
Diagram
view.

Some tasks have slack naturally because they occur during the life of a longer task with which they share a dependency. The shorter task could actually be delayed until the end of the longer task without delaying the project.

Think about this example: You can start installing the plumbing and electrical elements of a new office building as soon as the framing inspection is complete. The plumbing takes two weeks, and the electrical work takes one week. The next task, mechanical inspection, can't happen until both the plumbing and electrical tasks are finished. The shorter of the two (electrical) has a week of slack because nothing else can happen until the dependent task, plumbing, is finished (as in Figure 10-12). However, if electrical runs one week late, the electrical task becomes critical.

These natural cases of slack occur in any project. In many cases, though, you have to build in slack. Slack can be added in a few ways.

First, you can simply inflate task durations. Add two days to the duration of all the tasks in your project, or go in and examine each task to figure out the risk of delay and pad each duration accordingly. This method is a little problematic, however, because when changes occur, you may have to go into many tasks and adjust durations to deal with a schedule that's ahead or behind. You also have to keep track of exactly how much slack you built into each task.

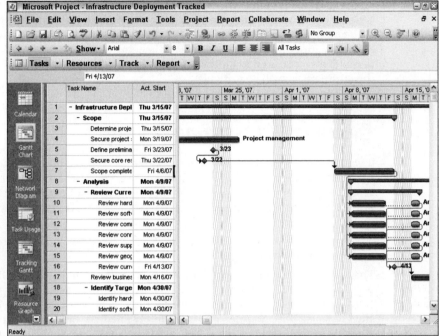

Figure 10-12:
Taskbars
help you
visualize
slack
available to
tasks not on
the critical
path of your
project.

The second method of building in slack is the one I like best. You build one slack task or several slack tasks that occur throughout your project — say, one at the end of each phase of the project.

Now, there's one must-do here, even if it seems obvious: Don't call this task *Slack.* Nobody in a position of responsibility would be caught dead approving slack time for anybody. Give slack tasks appropriately respectable names that reflect useful (but admittedly, somewhat generic) activities — say, *Engineering Analysis,* or *Debriefing,* or *CYA Meeting.* Then give the task a duration that provides breathing space for the other tasks in that phase. For example, at the end of a two-month phase of designing a new product package, you might add a task called *Design Debriefing* and make it one week long. (That way, if a sudden mandate for design tweaks comes out of nowhere, you're covered.) Then create a dependency between that task and the last "real" task in the phase.

I'm not talking dishonesty here — just reality. In the real world, slack is indispensable.

As things slide in your project (and they will, trust me), you'll spot that slack is being eaten up because the slack task is suddenly ending later than the date you'd wanted the phase to end. You can change the duration of the slack task, reflecting the fact that your slack is being used up. The duration of that task will give you a good indication of how much more time you have before the entire phase will go critical.

Doing it in less time

If you do your homework and add slack to tasks, you're making your plan realistic, but the price you pay is that you're adding time to your project. What happens when your project finish date just won't cut it with the powers-that-be? That's when you have to try a few tactics to chop your timing down to size.

Check your dependencies

The timing of your plan is determined, to a great extent, by the timing relationships you build among tasks: that is, by dependencies. So ask yourself, *Did I build all my dependencies in the best way I could?* Perhaps you didn't start one task until another was completely finished, but you could actually start the second task two days before the end of its predecessor. Building in that kind of overlap will save you time.

Use the Task Drivers feature, covered in the earlier section of this chapter, "Spotting Task Drivers," to help you scope out dependencies.

Here's an example: You created a finish-to-start relationship for the *Do Research* and *Write Speech* tasks, such that you could not start writing the speech until your research was finished. But is that true? Couldn't you do a first draft of the speech starting three-fourths of the way through the research? Especially when you have two different resources working on those tasks, getting the second task going before the first is complete can save you time.

Over the life of a project with hundreds of tasks, adding that kind of overlap to even a few dozen tasks could save you a month of time or more!

You can take a refresher course in creating and changing dependencies in Chapter 6.

We could use some help here!

Another factor that drives timing is the availability of resources. Sometimes you set a dependency relationship where one task can't start before another is over simply because the resources aren't available until the predecessor task is over. Here are a few things to look for with resource-dependent timing:

✔ Maybe you delayed the start of a task because a resource wasn't available. But could some other resource do the work? If so, switch resources and let the task start sooner.

✔ Project calculates the duration of some tasks (fixed work and fixed units with effort-driven scheduling) according to the number of resources available to do the work. If you add resources to those tasks, Project shortens their duration.

✔ If you assign a more skilled resource to some tasks, you might be able to shorten the hours of work required to complete the task because the skilled person will finish the work more quickly.

✔ Could you hire an outside vendor to handle the work? If you have money but no time or resources, that's sometimes a viable option.

Chapter 9 covers the mechanics of making and changing resource assignments.

Cut to the chase: Deleting some tasks and slashing slack

When all else fails, it's time to cut some very specific corners. Can you skip some tasks, such as that final quality check, the one that occurs after the other three you already built in? Or should you pull back on some of the slack you've allowed yourself?

Never, I repeat, *never* get rid of all the slack in your schedule. Otherwise, it will come back and haunt you like the Ghost of Christmas Past. Just tell your boss I said so.

Could you get some other project manager to handle some of your tasks for you with different sets of resources? If your buddy has a project that involves writing specs for a new product, could you convince him to also write the user's manual, which was your responsibility in designing product packaging? It's worth a shot.

Getting It for Less

After you assign all your resources to tasks and set all your fixed costs, it's time for sticker shock. Project will tally all those costs and show you the project's budget. But what if those numbers just won't work? Here are some tips for trimming that bottom line:

✔ **Use cheaper resources.** Do you have a high-priced engineer on a task that could be performed by a junior engineer? Did you assign a high-priced manager to supervise a task that could be handled by a lower-priced line supervisor?

✔ **Lower fixed costs.** If you allowed for the travel costs associated with four plant visits, could you manage with only three? Could you book flights ahead of time and get cheaper airfares? Could you find a cheaper vendor for that piece of equipment you allocated $4,000 to buy? Or could you make do with the old equipment for just one more project?

✔ **Cut down on the overtime.** Are resources that earn overtime overallocated? Try cutting down their hours or using resources on straight salary for those 14-hour days.

✔ **Do it in less time.** Resource costs are a factor of task durations, hourly wages, or number of units. If you change tasks so that fewer work hours are required to complete them, they'll cost less. However, don't be unrealistic about the time it will *really* take to get the work done.

Your Resource Recourse

Before you finalize your plan, you should consider one final area: resource workload. As you went about assigning resources to tasks in your project, you probably created some situations where resources are working round the clock for days on end. It may look okay on paper, but in reality, it's just not going to work.

Your first step is to see how to spot those overallocations. Then you have to give those poor folks some help!

Checking resource availability

To resolve issues with resource assignments, you have to first figure out where the problems lie. You can do that by taking a look at a few views that focus on resource assignments.

You can use some collaboration features of Project Web Access to get resource availability information online. See Chapters 18 and 19 for more about working with Project Web Access.

Resource Usage view (shown in Figure 10-13) and Resource Graph view (shown in Figure 10-14) are useful in helping you spot overbooked resources.

First, keep in mind that resources are flagged as overallocated in these Resource views based on their assignment percentage and calendars. A resource based on a standard eight-hour-day calendar, assigned at 100 percent to a task, will work eight hours a day on it. If you assign that same resource at 50 percent to another task that happens at the same time, the resource will put in 12-hour days (8 plus 4) and be marked as overallocated.

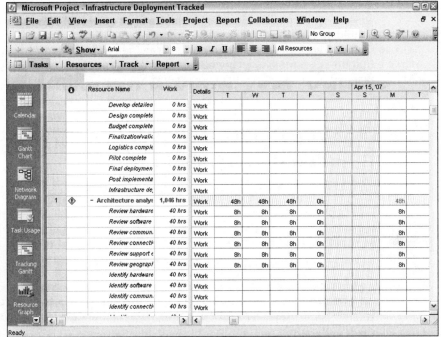

Figure 10-13:
Resource
Usage view
spells out
workflow,
resource by
resource.

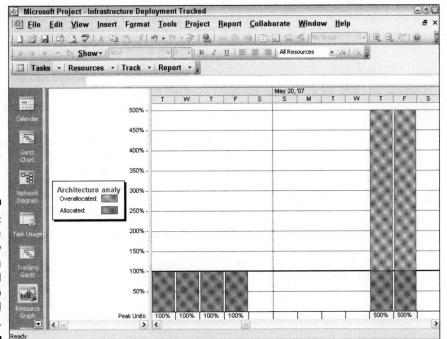

Figure 10-14:
Resource
Graph view
gives you
a visual
clue to
overworked
resources.

In Resource Graph view, work is summarized in the Peak Units row, and all work in the part of the bar graphic that's above the 100 percent mark is highlighted. In the Resource Usage view, any overallocated resource has a yellow diamond with an exclamation point in the Indicator column. The total hours that the resource is working each day on his or her combined tasks is summarized on the line that lists the resource's name.

Deleting or modifying a resource assignment

So, you discover that poor Henrietta is working 42 hours on Tuesday and 83 hours on Friday. What to do?

You have a few options:

- ✔ **Remove Henrietta from a few tasks to free up some time.**

- ✔ **Change Henrietta's Resource calendar to allow for a longer workday: for example, 12 hours.** Keep in mind that this means a 100-percent assignment will have Henrietta working 12 hours on any one task in a day. If you stretch a resource's workday, you should probably reduce the resource's assignments. For example, if someone frequently puts in 16 hours on two tasks in one day (based on an 8-hour calendar) and two 100-percent assignments, try changing to a 12-hour calendar and 50-percent assignments (6 hours on each of the two tasks, totaling 12 hours a day). However, if the person typically works an 8-hour day and 12- or 16-hour days *are the exception,* you shouldn't change the resource's base calendar because that will have an effect on *all* assignments for that resource.

  Keep in mind that the two previous options may lengthen the tasks that the resource is assigned to, regardless of whether you remove the resource or reduce the resource's assignment.

- ✔ **Change Henrietta's availability by upping her assignment units to more than 100 percent in the Resource Information dialog box.** For example, if you enter 150% as her available units, you're saying it's okay for her to work 12 hours a day, and Project will then consider her fair game and not overallocated until she exceeds that 12 hours.

- ✔ **Ignore the problem.** I don't mean this facetiously: Sometimes someone working 14 hours *for a day or two* during the life of a project is acceptable, and there's no need to change the resource's usual working allocation to make that overwork indicator go away. (However, consider telling Henrietta it's okay to order pizza on the company on those long workdays — and make sure you don't let them become the norm.)

Getting some help

When one person is overworked, it's time to look for help. You can free up resources in several ways.

One way is to assign someone to help out on a task and thus reduce the overbooked resource assignment now that he or she is not needed for as many hours. Reduce the resource's work assignment on one or more tasks — say, reducing 100 percent assignments to 50 percent. You do this in the Task Information dialog box on the Resources tab, shown in Figure 10-15, or by selecting the task and clicking the Assign Resources tool to open the Assign Resources dialog box.

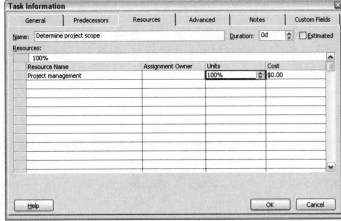

Note that you can quickly check a work graph for any resource by clicking the Graphs button in the Assign Resources dialog box.

You'll also find that by adding resources to some tasks, you'll shorten the task duration. That means you might free up your resource in time to eliminate a conflict with a later task in the project.

Try changing the work contour for the resource. By default, Project has a resource work on a task at the same level for the life of the task. You can modify the work contour, for example, so that a resource puts in the most effort at the start of a task, which frees up the resource's workload later when a conflict with another assignment might occur. See Chapter 9 for information about how to apply a work contour to a resource assignment.

Getting your resources level

Resource leveling sounds something like the St. Valentine's Day massacre, but it's not. It's a calculation that Project goes through to try to resolve resource overallocation in your project. The feature works in two ways: by delaying a task until the overbooked resource frees up, or by splitting tasks. Splitting a task involves (essentially) stopping it at some point, thereby freeing up the resource, and then resuming it at a later time when the resource is available.

You can make such changes yourself or let Project do the calculation. Project will first delay tasks that involve overallocated resources to use up any available slack. When no more slack is available on these tasks, Project makes changes based on any priorities you've entered for tasks, dependency relationships that are affected, and task constraints (such as a Finish No Later Than constraint).

But don't worry: You can turn on leveling to see what changes Project would make, and then clear the leveling to reverse those actions if you don't like the results.

To level the resources in your project, follow these steps:

1. **Choose Tools⬄Level Resources.**

   The Resource Leveling dialog box appears, as shown in Figure 10-16.

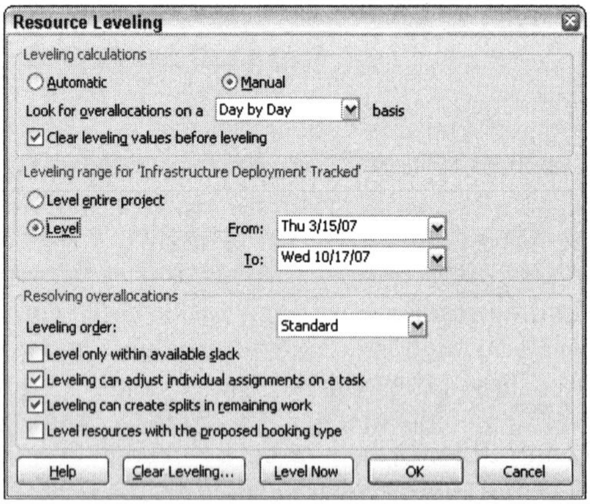

Figure 10-16: You can control some aspects of the resource-leveling calculation.

2. **Make a choice between allowing Project to do Automatic or Manual leveling:**

- *Automatic* tells Project to level every time you change your plan.

- *Manual* requires that you go to the Resource Leveling dialog box and click Level Now.

3. **If you choose to level automatically, be sure to enable the Clear Leveling Values Before Leveling check box, if you want previous leveling actions reversed before you level the next time.**

4. **Set the leveling range to either:**

- *Level Entire Project.*

- *Level: <a date range>.* Then fill in a date range by making choices in the From and To boxes.

5. **From the Leveling Order drop-down list, click the down arrow and make a choice:**

- *Standard* considers slack, dependencies, priorities, and constraints.

- *ID Only* delays or splits the task with the highest ID number: in other words, the last task in the project.

- *Priority, Standard* uses task priority as the first criteria in making choices to delay or split tasks (rather than using up slack).

6. **Select any of the four check boxes at the bottom to control how Project will level:**

- *Within available slack:* No critical tasks are delayed, and your current finish date for the project is retained.

- *Adjusting resource assignments:* This allows Project to remove or change assignments.

- *Splitting tasks only for unstarted work in the project:* This can put some tasks on hold for a period of time until resources are freed up for work.

- *Relative to booking type: Booking type* (proposed or committed) relates to how firm you are in using that particular resource. Allowing resource leveling to consider a resource's booking type means that committed resource assignments are considered more sacred when Project goes about making changes than proposed assignments.

7. **Click Level Now to have Project perform the leveling operation.**

To reverse leveling, go to the Resource Leveling dialog box (Tools⇨Level Resources) and click Clear Leveling.

To level or not to level?

As both a process and a program feature, resource leveling has pros and cons. It can make changes that you might not want it to make — for example, taking a resource off a task where you absolutely need that person's unique skills. It frequently delays your project's finish date, which might not be acceptable to you (or your boss).

The safest setting for Resource Leveling — that is, the one that makes the least drastic changes to your timing — is to level only within slack. This setting may delay some tasks, but it won't delay your project completion date.

If you just can't live with everything Resource Leveling did, the capability to turn Resource Leveling on and off is your best ally. You can turn the feature on and look at the things it did to resolve resource problems, and then turn it off and manually institute the portions of the solution that work for you. Also remember that the Multiple Undo feature now allows you to make several changes manually and undo them to get back to where you started.

Mixing Solutions Up

One final word about all the solutions suggested in this chapter to deal with time, cost, and overallocation problems. To be most successful, you'll probably have to use a combination of all these methods. Solving these problems is often a trial-and-error process. Although you might initially look for one quick fix (who doesn't?), in reality, the best solution might come through making a dozen small changes. Take the time to find the best combination for your project.

Chapter 11

Making Your Project Look Good

An old chestnut would have you believe clothes make the man. Well, in the same spirit, sometimes the look of your schedule makes the project. Having a project that looks good serves two purposes. One, it impresses people with your professionalism (sometimes to the point where they'll overlook a little cost overrun); second, it allows people looking at your project both on-screen and on hard copy to easily make out what the different boxes, bars, and lines indicate.

Project uses default formatting that's pretty good in most cases. However, if you have certain company standards for reporting — say, representing baseline data in yellow and actual data in blue, or more frequent gridlines to help your nearsighted CEO read Project reports more easily — Project has you covered.

Whatever you need, Project provides tremendous flexibility in formatting various elements in your plan.

Putting Your Best Foot Forward

Microsoft has decided to capitulate to the artist in all of us by allowing you to modify shapes, colors, patterns, and other graphic elements in your Project plans. This gives you great flexibility in determining how your plan looks.

When you print Project views (covered in Chapter 16), you can print a legend on every page. The legend helps those reading the plan understand the meaning of the various colors and shapes that you set for elements.

One important thing to realize is that all the views and formatting choices that Project offers you aren't confined to the screen. You can print your project or reports. What displays on-screen when you print a view is what will print. So, knowing how to make all kinds of changes to what's on your screen allows you to present information to team members, managers, vendors, and clients in hard copy too.

With all the improved methods of collaborating on projects, such as sharing documents via Project Web Access, a visually appealing schedule can be seen by even more people across the Web.

Printing in color is useful because you can provide the full visual impact and nuance of the various colors used for graphic elements (such as taskbars and indicators). If you print in black and white, you might find that certain colors that look good on-screen aren't as distinct when you print. Being able to modify formatting allows your project to look good in both color *and* black and white, both on-screen and in print.

Formatting Taskbars

Taskbars are the horizontal boxes that represent the timing of a task in the chart pane of Gantt Chart view. You can format each bar individually or change global formatting settings for different types of taskbars.

You can change several things about taskbars:

- ✔ **The shape that appears at the start and end of the bar.** You can change the shape's type and color. Each end can be formatted differently.

- ✔ **The shape, pattern, and color of the middle of the bar.**

- ✔ **The text that you can set to appear in five locations around the bar: left, right, above, below, or inside the bar.** You can include text in any or all of these locations, but keep in mind that too many text items can quickly become impossible to read. As a rule, use just enough text to help readers of your plan identify information, especially on printouts of large schedules where a task might appear far to the right of the Task Name column that identifies it by name in the sheet area.

When you track progress on a task, a progress bar is superimposed on the taskbar. You can format the shape, pattern, and color of the progress bar. The goal is to contrast the progress bar with the baseline taskbar so that you can see both clearly.

By formatting taskbars, you can help readers of your plan identify various elements, such as progress or milestones. If you make changes to individual taskbars, people who are accustomed to Project's standard formatting might have trouble reading your plan.

To create formatting settings for various types of taskbars, follow these steps:

1. **Right-click the chart area outside any single taskbar and then choose Bar Styles.**

   The Bar Styles dialog box appears, as shown in Figure 11-1.

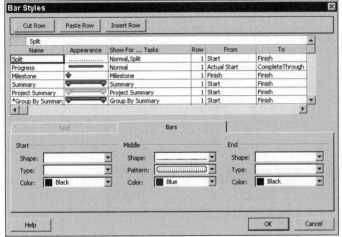

Figure 11-1:
You can modify the look of taskbars and the text you display along with them.

2. **Click the Text tab.**

3. **In the spreadsheet, along the top in the Name column, click the type of task that you want to modify (Split, Progress, Milestone, and so on).**

   For example, if you want to modify the styles used for all summary tasks, click Summary. The choices in the Bars tab in the bottom half of the dialog box change based on the task type that you click.

4. **Click in the Show For . . . Tasks column for the task type you want to modify and then select criteria for the task from the drop down list that appears, such as Critical or Finished.**

5. **Click the Bars tab to display it, if necessary, and then do the following:**

   a. Click any of the Shape lists to modify the shape of either end or the middle of the taskbar.

   Shapes on either end might be an arrow, a diamond, or a circle. The shape in the middle consists of a bar of a certain width.

b. *Click any of the Color lists to modify the color used on either end or in the middle of the taskbar.*

The Automatic choice is the default color for this type of taskbar element.

c. *Click either of the Type lists to modify the type of formatting for the shape on either end of the taskbar.*

This setting controls how such a shape is outlined: framed with a solid line, surrounded by a dashed line, or filled in with a solid color.

d. *Click the Pattern list to select another pattern for the middle of the bar.*

6. **Click the Text tab (as shown in Figure 11-2), and then do the following:**

a. *Click any of the text locations.*

An arrow appears at the end of that line.

b. *Click the arrow to display an alphabetical list of possible data that you can include, and then click a field name to select it.*

c. *Repeat Steps 6a and 6b to choose additional text locations.*

7. **Click OK to accept all new taskbar settings.**

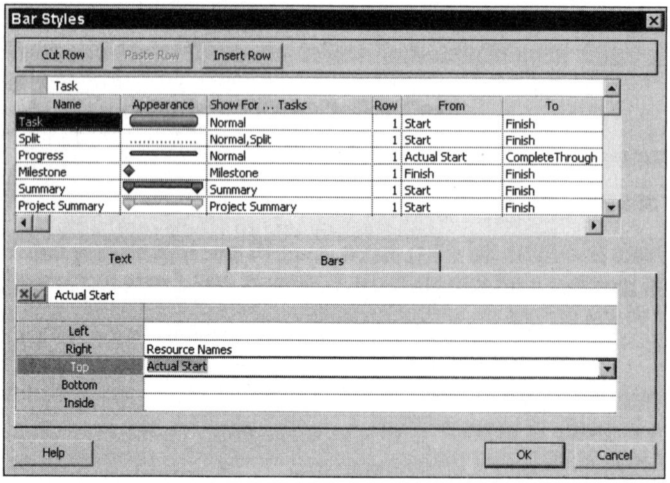

Figure 11-2:
You can place text in up to four locations around your taskbars.

If you want to make the same types of changes to an individual taskbar rather than to all taskbars of a certain type, right-click the taskbar and then choose Format Bar. A Format Bar dialog box appears, offering the same Text and Bar tabs found in the Bar Styles dialog box without the options at the top to select the type of item to format.

The Gantt Chart Wizard

What would formatting be without a wizard to help you make all your settings quickly? The Gantt Chart Wizard allows you to make formatting settings to the entire Gantt chart, including what information to display (standard, critical path, baseline, or several combinations of these), one piece of information to include with your taskbars, and whether you want to display lines to show dependencies among tasks.

If you choose to make custom settings while using the Gantt Chart Wizard, you can specify many of the settings that you see in the Bar Styles dialog box, but those choices affect *all* taskbar elements of that type *in the project,* not just individual taskbars. You access the Gantt Chart Wizard by selecting it from the Format menu.

Formatting Task Boxes

Network Diagram task boxes use different shapes to help you spot different types of tasks:

- ✔ **Summary tasks** use a slightly slanted box shape and include a plus or minus symbol, depending on whether the summary task's subtasks are hidden or displayed. Click the symbol to hide or display subtasks.

- ✔ **Subtasks** show up in simple rectangular boxes.

- ✔ **Milestones** are shown in diamond-shaped boxes with blue shading.

You can change the formatting of each task box individually or by type. To change the formatting of task boxes displayed in Network Diagram view, do this:

1. **Display Network Diagram view.**

2. **Right-click the task box that you want to change and then choose Format Box. Alternatively, right-click anywhere outside the task boxes and then choose Box Styles to change formatting for all boxes of a certain style.**

   The Format Box or Box Styles dialog box appears (as shown in Figure 11-3).

3. **To modify the border style, make your selection in the Shape, Color, and Width lists.**

4. **To modify the background area inside the box, make a selection in the Color list, Pattern list, or both (at the bottom of the dialog box).**

5. **Click OK to save your new settings.**

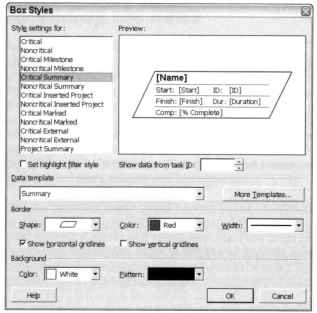

Figure 11-3:
Change
styles for all
boxes in the
Box Styles
dialog box.

When you modify the formatting of individual boxes in Network Diagram
view, the standard settings of slanted summary tasks and shaded milestones
no longer serve as a visual guide to *all* tasks. If you make changes and decide
that you'd like to put a task box back to its default setting, click Reset in the
Format Box dialog box.

Adjusting the Layout

In addition to displaying particular columns and formatting taskbars, you can
make certain changes to the layout of your view. These options vary a great
deal, depending on what view you're working with. The layout of Calendar
and Network Diagram views is quite different than the layout choices offered
in Gantt Chart view, for example.

To display the Layout dialog box for a view, right-click the area (for example,
the chart area of the Gantt Chart view) or anywhere in Calendar view or
Network Diagram view, and then choose Layout from the menu that appears.
The appropriate dialog box appears. Figures 11-4, 11-5, and 11-6 show the various layout choices available in the different views.

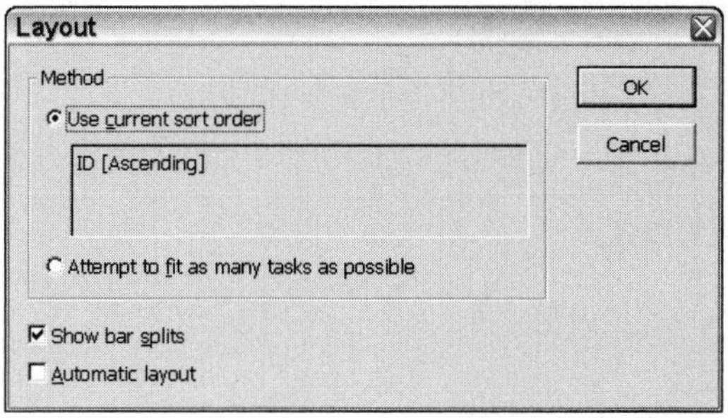

Figure 11-4:
The Layout
dialog box
for Calendar
view.

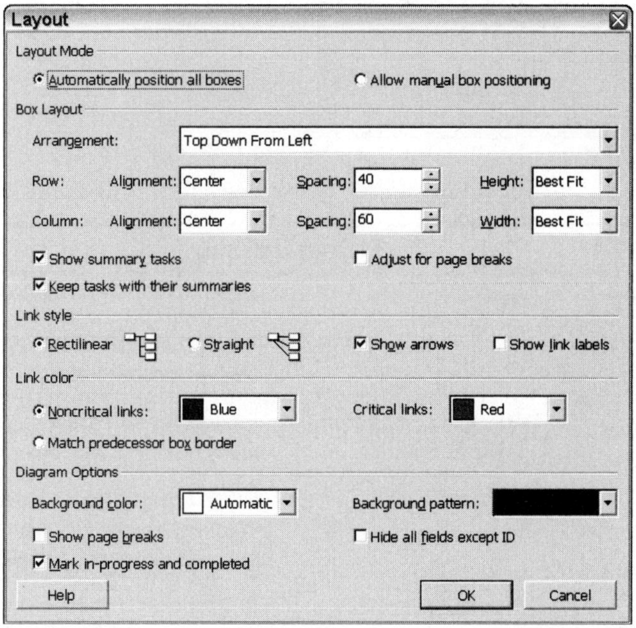

Figure 11-5:
The Layout
dialog box
for Network
Diagram
view.

In general, the settings in these Layout dialog boxes deal with how the
elements on the page are arranged and how dependency link lines are
displayed.

Table 11-1 shows you the layout settings. You could probably spend a week
toying with all of these settings to see what they look like, and I could spend
a few days writing about the various options. The tools that Project offers to
modify the formatting of elements such as taskbars and task boxes provide
wonderful flexibility.

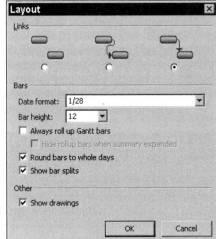

Figure 11-6:
The Layout
dialog box
for Gantt
Chart view.

Table 11-1	Layout Options	
Layout Type	*Option*	*Use*
Calendar view	Use Current Sort Order	Project uses the latest sort order you've applied to tasks.
	Attempt to Fit as Many Tasks as Possible	Ignores the sort order and fits as many tasks in a date box as possible.
	Show Bar Splits	When a task includes a period of inactivity, that task can be shown as split into different parts over time.
	Automatic Layout	Project modifies the layout in response to the insertion of additional tasks.
Network Diagram view	Layout Mode area	Allows automatic or manual positioning.
	Box Layout area	The settings in this section arrange and align boxes, adjusting alignment, spacing, and height, and also modify how summary tasks are displayed.
	Link Style area	Modifies the style for dependency link lines and labels.
	Link Color area	Sets the color for links both on and off the critical path.

Layout Type	Option	Use
	Diagram Options area	Controls the background color and pattern for boxes as well as how page breaks and progress on tasks are indicated.
Gantt Chart view	Links	Style of lines indicating dependency links.
	Date Format	Modifies the format of the date used to label taskbars.
	Bar Height	Sets the height of taskbars in points.
	Always Roll up Gantt Bars	When checked, taskbar details roll up to the highest-level summary task.
	Round Bars to Whole Days	When you have portions of days, allows bars to represent the nearest whole-day increment.
	Show Bar Splits	When a task includes a period of inactivity, that task can be shown as split into different parts over time.
	Show Drawings	When you include drawings, they are displayed on-screen and in the printout.

Now that you've seen the many options available for modifying view layouts, I have some advice: Stick with default settings unless you have a specific reason to make a change (such as when you want to highlight certain types of information for a project presentation). When you don't need that layout change anymore, go right back to the default settings. Or, if you want to make changes, make them globally across your organization and stick to them. That makes it much easier for those reading your project plan to interpret the different kinds of information presented in views. Generally speaking, if you tinker too often with the way Project displays information, it just makes your own learning curve steeper — and confuses those who know Project's default settings.

One other change that you can make to your overall interface is to create a custom Project Guide. You do this by providing an XML file with custom content. For example, you might add to the four Guide sections of Tasks, Resources, Track, and Report another section titled Accounting that provides links to accounting codes and procedures within your organization. See Chapter 17 for more about this procedure.

Modifying Gridlines

Just as phone numbers are broken up into several shorter sets of numbers to help you remember them, visual elements are often broken up to help you understand information in chunks. Tables use lines, calendars use boxes, football fields use yard lines, and so on.

Several views in Project include gridlines to indicate certain things, such as the break between weeks or the status date (that is, the date as of which progress has been tracked on a project). These lines help the reader of your plan discern intervals of time or breaks in information; for example, gridlines can be used to indicate major and minor column breaks. You can modify these gridlines in several ways, including changing the color and style of the lines and the interval at which they appear.

To modify gridlines, use the Gridlines dialog box, as follows:

1. **Right-click any area of a view that contains a grid (for example, the chart area of Gantt Chart view or Calendar view) and then choose Gridlines.**

   The Gridlines dialog box appears, as shown in Figure 11-7.

2. **In the Line to Change list, click the gridline that you want to modify.**

3. **Use the Normal Type and Color lists to select a line style and color.**

4. **If you want to use a contrasting color at various intervals in the grid to make it easier to read, do the following:**

   a. *Select an interval at which to include a contrasting line.*

   This setting is typically used with a different style or color from the Normal line setting to mark minor intervals for a grid. Note that not all types of gridlines can use contrasting intervals.

   b. *Choose the Type and Color of that line from the lists.*

5. **Click OK to save your settings.**

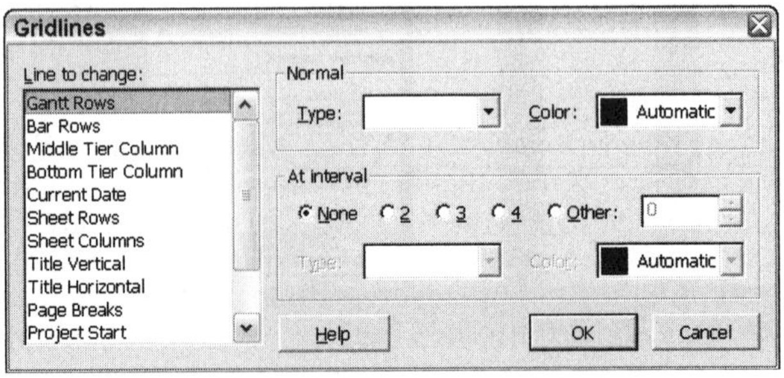

Figure 11-7:
The possible lines you can change vary somewhat from one view to another.

You make choices for modifying gridlines one by one, and there is no Reset button to put these settings back the way they were. Also note that gridlines modified in one view don't affect gridlines in any other view.

When a Picture Can Say It All

Words and numbers and taskbars and task boxes are fine, but what if you want to add something of your own? For example, you might want to draw attention to a task by drawing a circle around it, or you might want to include a simple drawing to show a process or working relationship in your plan.

You can use a Drawing toolbar to draw images in the chart area of Gantt Chart view. Follow these steps to add a drawing:

1. **Display Gantt Chart view.**

2. **Choose Insert⇨Drawing.**

   The Drawing toolbar appears, as shown in Figure 11-8.

3. **Click the drawing tool that represents the type of object you want to draw, such as an oval or a rectangle.**

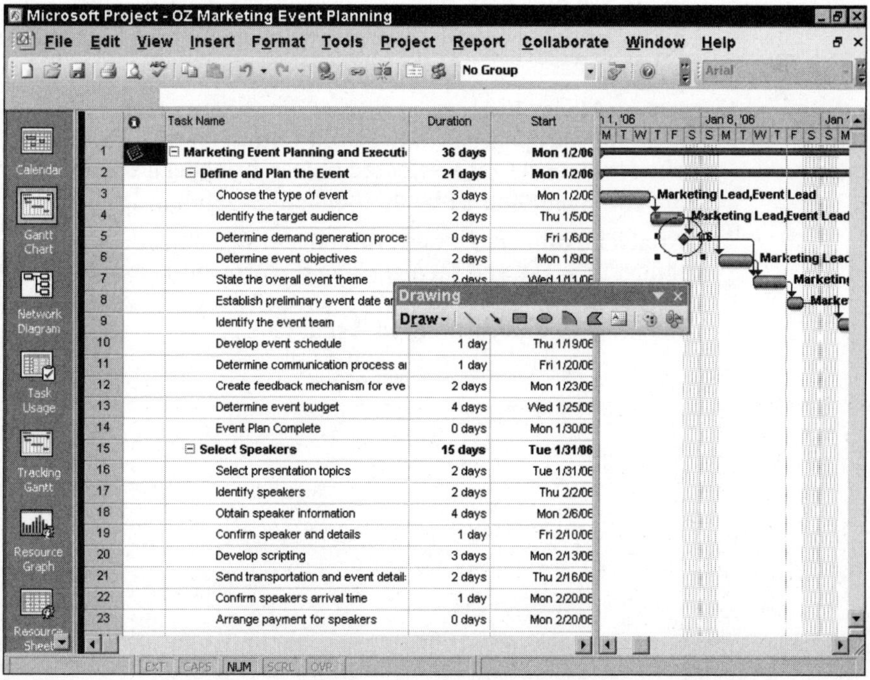

Figure 11-8:
This Drawing toolbar has some tools in common with other Office products you may have used.

4. **Click at the location on the chart where you want to draw the object, and drag your mouse until the item is drawn approximately to the scale you want.**

5. **Release the mouse button.**

When you draw an object over an element such as a taskbar, the drawn object is solid white and covers up what's beneath it. You have a couple of choices if you want the item underneath to show throw:

- ✔ Click the Cycle Fill Color button until you hit the No Fill option.

- ✔ Use the Draw menu to change the order of objects.

At this point, you have a few options:

- ✔ **Add text.** If you drew a text box, you can click in it and then type whatever text you like.

- ✔ **Resize objects.** Resize any object you've drawn by selecting it and then clicking and dragging any of the resize handles (little black boxes) around its edges outward to enlarge it or inward to shrink it.

- ✔ **Move objects.** Move the mouse over the object until the cursor becomes a four-way arrow. Then click the object and drag it elsewhere on the chart.

- ✔ **Use fill color.** You can use the Cycle Fill Color tool to choose a color for a selected object. Each time you click this tool, it displays another color in the available palette. Just keep clicking the tool until the color you want appears.

- ✔ **Layer objects.** If you have several drawings or objects that you want to layer on your page, click the Draw button on the Drawing toolbar and choose an order for a selected object, bringing it to the front of other images or sending it behind them.

- ✔ **Attach an object to a task.** Attach a drawn object to any task by moving it next to a task and then clicking the Attach to Task drawing tool. If you should add or delete tasks to your task list or move the attached task, the drawing moves along with that task.

Part IV
Avoiding Disaster: Staying On Track

The 5th Wave   By Rich Tennant

"It's an electronic wedding planner. It'll create all your check lists and time tables, and after the ceremony it turns all the documents into confetti and throws it in your face."

In this part . . .

And behold, Murphy decreed: No project shall happen the way you thought it would. To head off project manager's frustration, this part shows you how to save a baseline picture of your project and to use it as you track the ongoing struggle between actual activity and your ideal plan. You get a look at tracking and reporting progress, pick up tips on how to get back on track if the project strays from the strait and narrow, and get handy new tools for using past data to make better future project plans.

Chapter 12

It All Begins with a Baseline

*W*hen you go on a diet (and I know you all have at one time or another!), you step on the scale the first day to check your weight. Then, as your diet progresses, you have a benchmark against which you can compare your dieting ups and downs.

Project doesn't have a weight problem, but it does have a method of benchmarking your project data so that you can compare the actual activity that takes place on your tasks against your original plan. This saved version of your plan data is called a *baseline,* and it includes all the information in your project, such as task timing, resource assignments, and costs.

Project also provides something called an *interim plan,* which is essentially a timing checklist. It includes only the actual start and finish dates of tasks as well as the estimated start and finish dates for tasks not yet started.

This chapter shows you when, why, and how to save a baseline and interim plan for your project.

All about Baselines

Saving a baseline is like freezing a mosquito in amber: It's a permanent record of your estimates of time, money, and resource workload for your project at the moment when you consider your plan final and before you begin any activity. A baseline is saved in your original Project file and exists right alongside any actual activity that you record on your tasks.

You can use baselines to debrief yourself or your team at any point in a project. This is especially useful at the end of a project, when you can compare what really happened against your best guesses those many weeks, months, or even years ago. You can then become a much better user of Project, making more accurate estimates up front. You can also use a baseline and the actual activity that you track against it to explain delays or cost overruns to employers or clients by using a wide variety of reports and printed views.

Finally, you can also save and clear baselines for only selected tasks. So, if one task is thrown way off track by a major change, you can modify your estimates for it and leave the rest of your baseline alone. Why throw out the baby with the bathwater?

What does a baseline look like?

After you save a baseline and track some actual activity against it, you get baseline and actual sets of data as well as visual indications of baseline versus actual.

Figure 12-1 shows Gantt Chart view for a project, displaying baseline and actual data. In the sheet area, you can display columns of data to compare baseline estimates and actual activity: for example, baseline finish and actual finish. In the chart area, the black line superimposed on the taskbar represents your baseline estimate. This black line indicates actual activity on that task.

Figure 12-2 shows Network Diagram view. Here, the progress of tasks is represented by

- ✓ **A single slash:** This indicates tasks where some activity has been recorded.
- ✓ **An X:** This indicates tasks that are complete.

A notation of percent completed is included in each task box not marked as complete.

You can change how different graphic elements are represented by reformatting. See Chapter 11 for more about formatting taskbars and task boxes.

How do I save a baseline?

You can save a baseline at any time by displaying the Set Baseline dialog box. One setting here — how Project *rolls up* data to summary tasks when you set a baseline — requires a little explanation.

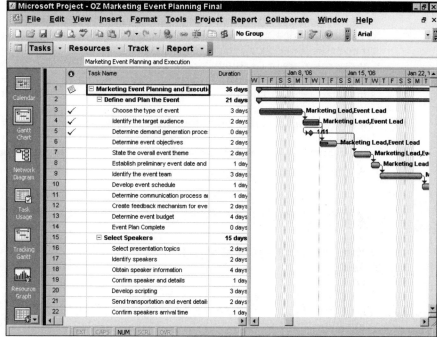

Figure 12-1:
You can stay constantly aware of variations between your plan and reality with both data and graphics.

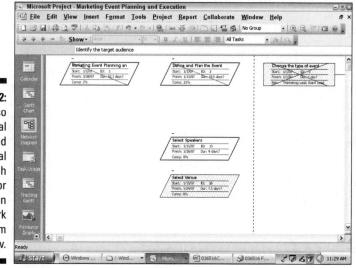

Figure 12-2:
You can also spot critical and noncritical tasks, which are color coded in Network Diagram view.

By default, after you save a baseline the first time, a summary task's baseline data isn't updated if you make changes to a subtask below it, even if you delete a subtask. However, you can change that functionality by making a choice about how the baseline rolls up data. You can choose to have modifications rolled up to all summary tasks or only from subtasks for any summary tasks that you select. This second option works only if you've selected summary tasks but not selected their subtasks.

You can save a baseline by following these steps:

1. **If you want to save a baseline for only certain tasks, select them.**

2. **Choose Tools⇨Tracking⇨Set Baseline.**

   The Set Baseline dialog box appears with the Set Baseline option selected, as shown in Figure 12-3.

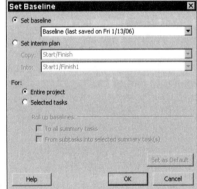

Figure 12-3:
This dialog box is used for baselines and interim plans.

3. **Select the Entire Project or the Selected Tasks radio button.**

4. **Make selections for how the baseline rolls up, or summarizes, changes to task data.**

   You can have changed data summarized in all summary tasks or only for the summary tasks that you select.

5. **Click OK to set the baseline.**

What if 1 want more than one baseline?

I know you love to hear about features in Project 2007 that you might never take full advantage of. (Who doesn't?) Here's one: You can save your baseline up to 11 times during the life of your project. That's 11 potentially catastrophic events you can adjust for by resaving your baseline!

Although you might never use all 11 possible baselines, the ability to save multiple baselines can help you see the progress of your planning over the life of a longer project. They are also a sneaky but effective way of showing your boss that, yes, you really did anticipate that budget overrun, even though you didn't include it in your original saved plan. (I'm not advocating this, but it works as long as your boss didn't keep a copy of the original plan.)

The Set Baseline dialog box includes a list of these baselines, with the last date each was saved, as shown in Figure 12-4. When you save a baseline, you can save without overwriting an existing baseline by simply selecting another one of the baselines in this list before saving.

Figure 12-4:
Each
baseline to
which
you've
saved
something
includes the
last saved
date in this
list.

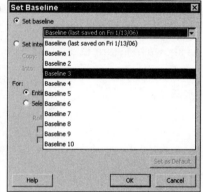

If you save multiple baselines or interim plans, you can view them by displaying columns in any sheet view for those plans. For example, if you want to display information for a baseline you saved with the name Baseline 7, you would insert the column named Baseline 7 in your Gantt Chart view sheet.

You can view multiple baselines at one time by displaying the Multiple Baselines Gantt view.

How do I clear and reset a baseline?

Okay, if you read the first part of this chapter, you know that I said that a baseline is intended to be a frozen picture of your project plan that you keep sacrosanct and never change. Well, that's the theory. In practice, things can happen that make an original baseline so obsolete that it's less than useful. It's not even worth keeping as one of your 11 possible baselines.

For example, if you have a project that takes four years from beginning to end, you might want to save a new baseline every year because costs go up or resources change. Then you can see incremental versions of your estimates that reflect the changes you made based on changes in the real world. Or, perhaps you start your project with a wonderful, well-thought-out baseline plan, but a week later, the entire industry shuts down with a massive strike that goes on for three months. All your original estimates of timing would be bogus, so it's better to make adjustments to your plan, save a new baseline, and move ahead after the strike is resolved.

To clear an existing baseline, follow these steps:

1. **If you want to clear the baseline for only certain tasks, select them.**

2. **Choose Tools⇨Tracking⇨Clear Baseline.**

    The Clear Baseline dialog box appears with the Clear Baseline Plan option selected by default, as shown in Figure 12-5.

Figure 12-5:
Use this to clear the baseline or interim plan.

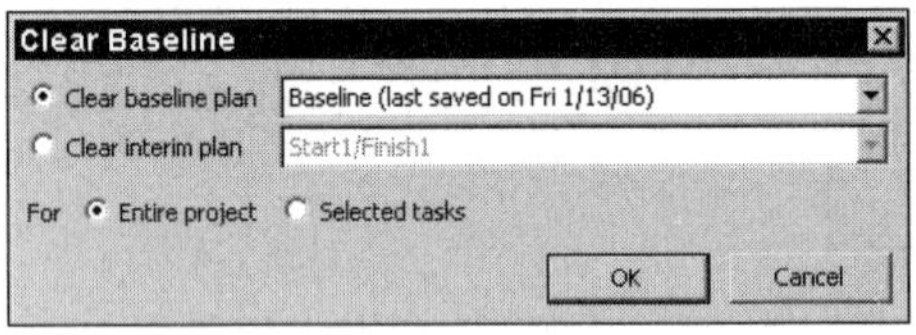

Clear Baseline

- ● Clear baseline plan   Baseline (last saved on Fri 1/13/06)
- ○ Clear interim plan   Start1/Finish1

For ● Entire project ○ Selected tasks

[OK] [Cancel]

3. **From the Clear Baseline Plan drop-down list, choose the baseline that you want to clear.**

4. **Select either the Entire Project radio button to clear the baseline for the entire project or the Selected Tasks radio button for selected tasks.**

5. **Click OK.**

    The project baseline or selected tasks are cleared.

In the Interim

An interim plan is sort of like Baseline Lite. With an interim plan, you save only the actual start and finish dates of tasks that have had activity tracked on them as well as the baseline start and finish dates for all unstarted tasks.

Why save an interim plan rather than a baseline? An interim plan saves only timing information. If that's all you need, why save all the data about resource assignments and costs and so on? (Keep in mind that you'll end up with a huge file if you save a large number of baselines.)

Another issue with a baseline is that because there's so much data, the baseline can become obsolete at some point. An interim plan can be saved to record date changes but not overwrite your original baseline cost data.

Finally, although you're allowed to save up to 11 baseline plans, if you need more than that, consider using some interim and some baseline data to expand the number of sets of data that you can save.

Do not go baseline and interim plan crazy. Even in a long project, saving too many sets of plans can get confusing. When you do save a plan, print a copy for your records and make a notation of when and why the plan was saved to help you keep track.

Saving an interim plan

Interim plans and baselines are saved via the same dialog box. The difference is that with an interim plan, you have to specify where the data is coming from. For example, if you want to save the start and finish dates from your Baseline2 plan into the third interim plan, you copy from Baseline2 to Start/Finish3. If you want the current scheduled start and finish dates for all tasks, choose to copy from Start/Finish.

If you want to change currently scheduled start and finish dates in a baseline but you don't want to change all the other data typically saved in a baseline, you can copy from Start/Finish to the baseline plan that you want to change.

To save an interim plan, do this:

1. **If you want to save an interim plan for only certain tasks, select them.**

2. **Choose Tools⇨Tracking⇨Set Baseline.**

   The Save Baseline dialog box appears, as shown in Figure 12-6.

Figure 12-6:
You can copy settings from any saved baseline to an interim plan.

3. Select the Save Interim Plan radio button.

4. From the Copy drop-down list box, select the set of data that you want to copy to the interim plan.

5. From the Into drop-down list box, select the fields in which you want to store the interim plan data.

6. Select the appropriate radio buttons to save the plan for the entire project or selected tasks.

7. If you choose to save the plan for selected tasks, use the check boxes to indicate how Roll Up Baseline options should work.

8. Click OK to save the plan.

By using the Copy and Into fields in the Set Baseline dialog box, you can save up to ten interim plans based on baseline or actual data.

Clearing and resetting a plan

Ten interim plans might seem like a lot now, but in the thick of a busy and ever-changing project, it might actually end up falling short of what you need. Because you can save only ten interim plans, you might need to clear one at some point and resave it.

Project piggybacks baseline and interim plan settings, so you actually choose a Clear Baseline menu command to clear an interim plan. This can be frightening to those who think that clicking a Clear Baseline command will send their baseline into oblivion. Don't worry — it won't!

To clear an interim plan, follow these steps:

1. If you want to clear only some tasks in an interim plan, select them.

2. Choose Tools⇨Tracking⇨Clear Baseline.

   The Clear Baseline dialog box appears, as shown in Figure 12-7.

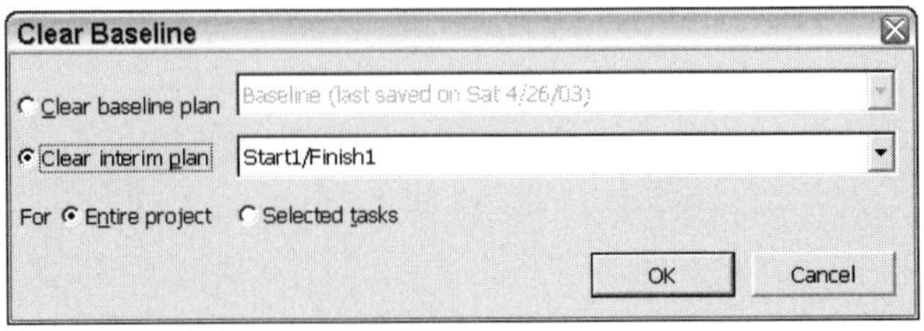

Figure 12-7:
Clear and
reset interim
plans as
often as you
like.

Clear Baseline

C Clear baseline plan   Baseline (last saved on Sat 4/26/03)

⊙ Clear interim plan   Start1/Finish1

For ⊙ Entire project   C Selected tasks

OK   Cancel

3. **Select the Clear Interim Plan option, and then choose the plan that you want to clear from the accompanying list.**

4. **Click to clear the specified interim plan for the entire project or for any tasks you have selected.**

5. **Click OK to clear the plan.**

You can now save a new set of information to that interim plan, if you like.

You might want to save a backup of various versions of your file with interim and baseline data. If you clear a baseline or an interim plan, that data is gone forever!

Chapter 13

On the Right Track

*A*fter a project moves out of the planning stage and into action, it's like a constantly changing game in which there are rules, goals, and a general timeframe, but no one really knows which team will win (and sometimes where the ball is) until it's over.

Whether a task happens as planned or wanders off in an unexpected direction, your job at this stage of the game is to record that activity, an activity referred to as *tracking*.

Tracking starts when your team reports their activity on the project. Then you (or someone else assigned to deal with tracking) must manage inputting that activity task by task.

When you track activity, you'll be amazed at what data Project returns to you. Some of it will be good news, some bad, but all of it is useful in managing your project throughout its lifetime.

Gathering Your Data

The first step in tracking progress on your project is to get information about what's been going on. The amount of data you collect will be determined by what you need to track and at what level of detail. For example, some people don't even create and assign resources to tasks because they use Project only to create a timeline for their activities, not to manage resource time or tally costs. Others use resources and want to track their total work on tasks, just not to the level of detail that scrutinizes hourly work performed. For some people, simply marking one task 50 percent complete and another 100 percent complete — and letting Project assume all resources put in their estimated amount of work — is fine. Your tracking method is determined by the amount and type of information you need to monitor.

Therefore, the first thing you have to do is identify the best tracking method for you.

A method to your tracking madness

Microsoft has identified four tracking methods:

- ✔ **Task-total method**
- ✔ **Task-timephased method**
- ✔ **Assignment-total method**
- ✔ **Assignment-timephased method**

You can begin to understand these by looking at the difference between task and assignment tracking. You can track information at the *task* level, indicating total work or costs for the task up to the present or as of a status date you select. Or you can track costs by *resource assignment,* which is the more detailed way of tracking.

For example, suppose that the Test Electrical Components task is estimated to take 12 hours of work, according to your project baseline. Three human resources — Engineer, Electrician, and Assistant — are assigned at 100 percent of their time. Tracking by task, you can simply note that the task is 75 percent complete, which translates into nine hours of work finished.

Project assumes that the three resources split that work up equally. In reality, however, the Engineer put in one hour, the Electrician put in six, and the Assistant put in two. If you want more detailed tracking that shows you totals of work for each resource assignment and accurately tracks them, you would track the work at the resource-assignment level.

But here's where the timephased variable comes in: Whether you choose to track work on a task or the work done by individual resources on the task, you can also track by specific time increments — which Microsoft calls *timephased* tracking.

So, with the Test Electrical Components task, you can use a task approach of tracking nine hours of work to date or use a timephased approach to record those hours on a day-by-day basis. With a resource assignment approach, you can go to the very deepest level of tracking detail by tracking each and every resource's work hour by hour, day by day.

Let your project make the rounds

You can use the Send To feature on the File menu of Project to send your project to others and have them update their own activity. You can do this by either e-mailing a file or selected tasks as a file attachment, or you can route one file and have people make their changes in one place.

The challenge with the first method is that you need to manually incorporate the changes in the various files into a single file.

The challenge with the second approach is getting people to do the updating accurately and forward the file to the next person on the routing slip in a timely fashion. Generally, the best use of e-mail for updating projects is simply to have team members send an e-mail with their activity to the person updating the project and then let that person make all the changes in one central location.

Finally, if you want Project to keep an eye on costs, be sure to track fixed costs and material used on each task.

Going door to door

How do you get all the information about what work has been performed, by whom, and when? Well, the first method is the one you've probably been using for years: Hunt down the people on your project and ask them. Ask them in the hallway, in your weekly one-on-one meeting, or over lunch. Give each person a call or have everyone turn in a form.

This isn't rocket science, but you still have to determine upfront what information you want, when you want it, and what form it should be in. The simpler you can keep manual reporting of progress on a project, the better, because people will actually do it. The more routine you can make it — such as every Friday, on a set form turned into the same person, and so on — the easier it will be.

If you need only a summary of where the task stands — say 25, 50, 75, or 100 percent complete — have the person in charge of the task give you that informed estimate. If you need total hours put into a task to date, resources can summarize their hours for you. If you need a blow-by-blow, hour-by-hour, day-by-day report, you're likely to collect some form of timesheet from resources.

If your company is set up to use the Project Server feature, you can use Project Web Access to gather resource timesheets in one convenient location. (See Chapter 19 for more about how to do this.)

You can probably get information about fixed costs that have been incurred if you ask your accounting department for it, or by getting a copy of a purchase order or receipt from the human who spent the money.

Consider a third-party add-on product such as Timesheet Professional (`http://timesheetprofessional.com`) for reporting resource activity. You make Timesheet available to every resource on the project. The resources record their work time on it, and you can use Timesheet's tools to automatically update your project. If you're using Project Professional edition, Timesheet's features are incorporated into Project Web Access.

Where Does All This Information Go?

After you gather information about task progress, fixed costs, and resource hours, you can input that information in several ways. You can use various views and tables to enter information in sheets of data; you can input information in the Task Information dialog box; or you can use the Tracking toolbar.

Doing things with the Tracking toolbar

Sometimes it seems like Microsoft provides a toolbar for everything, so why should tracking be any different? You can use the Tracking toolbar to perform updates on selected tasks in any sheet view. Figure 13-1 shows the Tracking toolbar and the tools it has to offer.

Figure 13-1:
Select a task and click one of these tools to update it.

The Tracking toolbar allows you to open the Project Statistics dialog box or display the Collaborate toolbar. (The tools on the Collaborate toolbar only become available to you if your organization has implemented Project Server.) You can use other tools to make specific updates to selected tasks:

✔ Selecting a task and clicking the **Update as Scheduled tool** automatically records activity to date as you anticipated in your baseline.

- The **Reschedule Work tool** reschedules all tasks that begin after the status date you set or the current date if you didn't set a status date.

- The **Add Progress Line tool** turns on a kind of drawing tool. When you select the tool and then click the mouse cursor over a spot on the chart area, a progress line is placed at that point on the timescale. A progress line indicates which tasks are ahead of schedule as well as which ones are behind schedule, by means of a line that connects in-progress tasks.

- By clicking a **Percentage Complete tool** (0% to 100%), you can quickly mark a task's progress using a calculation of the percentage of work completed based on the type of activity (fixed units, work, or duration).

- The **Update Tasks tool** displays a dialog box containing tracking fields that you might recognize from the Task Information dialog box as well as some other fields you can use for updating your project.

You can also choose Tools⇨Tracking⇨Update Tasks to display the tracking fields from the Update Tasks dialog box; this is the same dialog box that the Update Tasks button on the Tracking toolbar displays.

For everything there is a view

By now, you probably know that Project has a view for everything you want to do. For example, Task Sheet view and Task Usage view (as shown in Figures 13-2 and 13-3, respectively) allow you to update either task or resource information easily. So many variations are available, you might think that Microsoft charged by the view!

Depending on the method of tracking you need (see "A method to your tracking madness," earlier in this chapter), different views serve different purposes. Table 13-1 shows the best view to use for each tracking method.

Table 13-1	Tracking Views	
Tracking Method	*Best View to Use*	*Table or Column Displayed*
Task	Task Sheet	Tracking table
Task timephased	Task Usage	Actual Work column
Assignment	Task Usage	Tracking table
Assignment timephased	Task Usage	Actual Work column

When you find the right view with the right columns displayed, entering tracking information is as simple as typing a number of hours, a dollar amount for fixed costs, or a start or finish date in the appropriate column for the task you're updating.

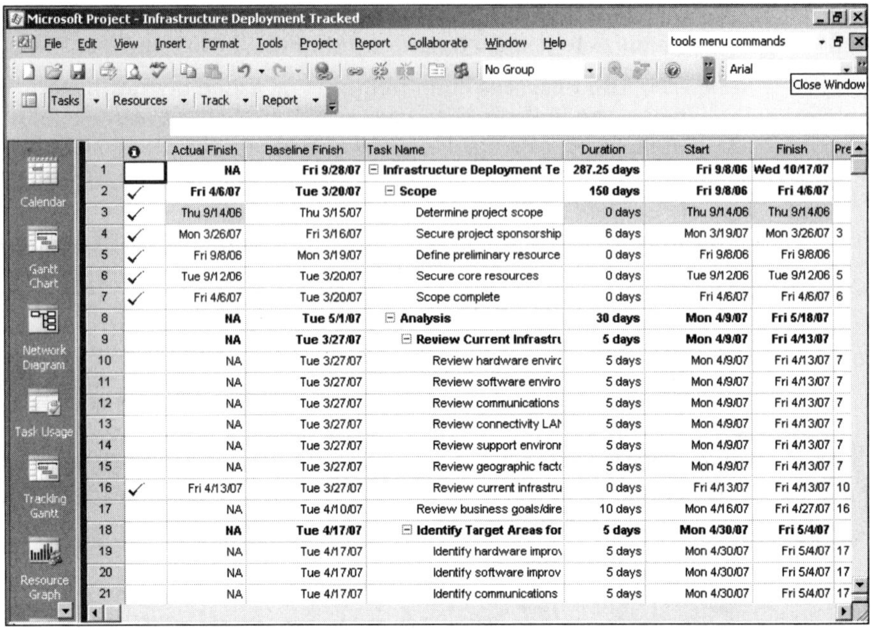

Figure 13-2: Task Sheet view is a great place for tracking work, start, and finish dates.

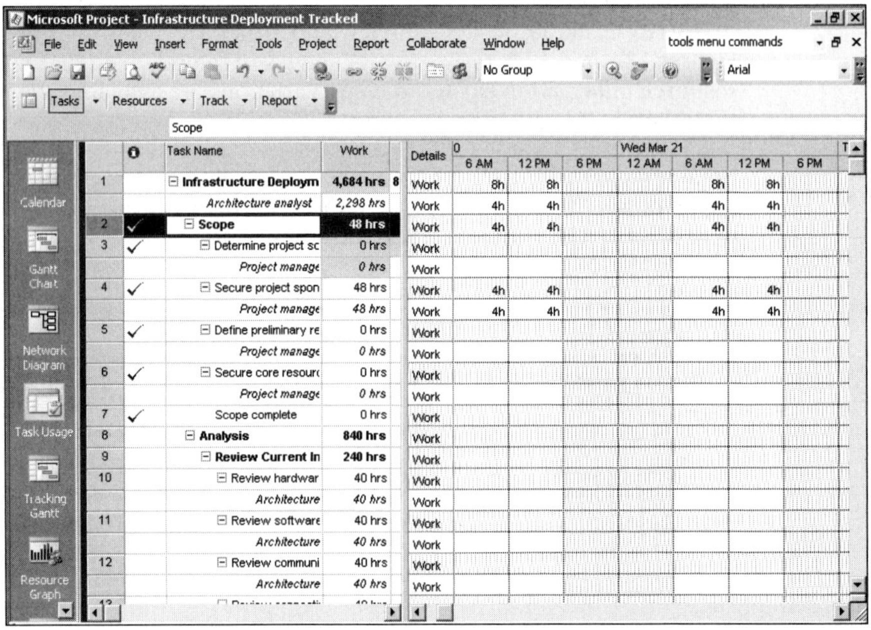

Figure 13-3: Task Usage view allows you to enter specific resource hours on task day-by-day on your project.

Tracking your work for the record

You need to input several types of information to track progress on your project. First, you have to tell Project as of when you want to track progress: By default, it records information as of the current date based on your computer's calendar settings. However, if you want to record progress as of, say, the end of your company's quarter, you can do that, too.

You can record actual start and finish dates for tasks, the percentage of a task that is complete (for example, a task might be 75 percent complete), and actual work performed (that is, the number of hours that resources put in on each task). If you think that the task will take less or more time than you anticipated, based on progress to date, you can modify the remaining duration for the task. You can also enter units of materials used, and fixed-cost information for expenditures incurred, such as equipment rental or consulting fees.

Progress as of when?

If you don't know what day of the week it is, you can't very well gauge whether you're making the right amount of headway through your week's work. Well, tracking is like that: The first thing you have to do is establish a *status date:* that is, the date as of which you are tracking progress.

By default, Project uses the calendar setting of your computer as the current date when you enter actual activity information. However, sometimes you'll want to time-travel. For example, suppose that your boss asks for a report showing the status of the project as of the last day of the quarter, December 31. You gathered all your resources' timesheets up through that date, but you didn't get around to inputting those updates until three days after the end of the quarter. You can deal with this situation by setting the status date in Project to December 31 and then entering your tracking data.

After you set the status date and enter information, Project uses that date to make calculations such as *earned value* (the value of work completed to date). Also, any task-complete or percentage-complete information records as of that date and progress lines in the chart area reflect that timing. Any reports or printouts of views that you generate give a picture of the status of your project as of that date.

Here's how to set the status date:

1. **Choose Project➪Project Information.**

   The Project Information dialog box appears, as shown in Figure 13-4. When you first open this dialog box, the status date is not set; your project is controlled by the current date.

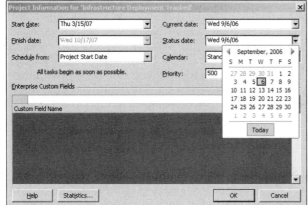

Figure 13-4: Set the status date here.

2. **In the Status Date field, click the down arrow to display the calendar.**

3. **If you want to set the status date in another month, use the right or left arrow at the top of the calendar to navigate to that month.**

4. **Click the date you want.**

5. **Click OK.**

Now you're ready to start inputting tracking data.

Percentage complete: How to tell?

When people ask me how to figure out whether a task is 25 percent, 50 percent, or even 36.5 percent complete, I usually refer them to their own intuition. If your boss asks you how things are coming on that report, you typically go through a quick internal calculation and come back with a rough estimate with no problem. A rough estimate, based on your experience and the information your resources provide you about their progress, is often good enough.

Can tracking get too detailed?

Does it make sense to track 2.25 percent of progress every other day on a two-month task? Probably not. Except on the lengthiest tasks, entering a percentage more finely broken down than 25, 50, 75, and 100 percent complete probably isn't worth it. That's partly because tasks longer than a few weeks should probably be broken down into subtasks for ease of tracking, and partly because one of the main purposes of tracking is reporting. If your boss or board or client could really care less about when you hit your exact 33.75 percent-complete point, why track it?

On the other hand, if (for some reason known only to you) your project must include a six-month task and you can't break it into subtasks, you might use percentages such as 10, 20, 30, 40, 50, and so on to prevent having to wait a month between updates with (apparently) no progress to show.

You can also calculate percentage complete in more precise ways. For example, if you estimate that a task should take ten hours of effort and your resources report performing five hours of effort, you could say you're 50 percent there. But be careful. Just because people have spent half the allocated time doesn't mean that they have accomplished half the work.

You could go by costs: If your original estimates said that your four resources assigned to a four-day task would tally $4,000 of costs and the time your resources report spending on the task add up to $3,000, you could *guess* that the task is 75 percent finished. But again, just because you've spent three quarters of the money doesn't mean you've accomplished three quarters of what you set out to do.

When a task's deliverable is measurable, that helps a lot. For example, if you have a task to produce 100 cars on the assembly line in four days and you've produced 25 cars, you might be about 25 percent finished with the task. Or if you were supposed to install software on ten computers in a computer lab and you've installed it on five of them, that's an easy 50 percent.

But not every task can be calculated so neatly. The best rule of thumb is to trust your instincts and review what your team is telling you about their progress.

The simplest and quickest way to update percent complete on a task is to click the task to select it in any view, and then click the 0%, 25%, 50%, 75%, or 100% button on the Tracking toolbar. Alternatively, you can double-click any task to open the Task Information dialog box and then enter the percent complete there. You can also select a task and click the Update Tasks button on the Tracking toolbar to open the Update Tasks dialog box and make the change there. If you want to enter a percentage in increments other than 25 percent, you'll have to enter it in the Task Information or Update Tasks dialog box or the Percent Complete column in any sheet view.

When did you start? When did you finish?

If you note that a task is complete and don't enter an Actual Start date, Project (ever the optimist) assumes you started on time. If you didn't start on time and you want to reflect the actual timing, you should modify the Actual Start date. If you finished late, you should enter the Actual Finish date. However, be aware that if you don't modify the task duration and enter an earlier finish date, the start date will be calculated to have occurred earlier.

You have several options of where to track this information. You can use the Update Tasks dialog box (shown in Figure 13-5), which appears when you click the Update Tasks button on the Tracking toolbar. You can also display a sheet view with Actual Start and Actual Finish columns, such as Tracking Gantt or Gantt Chart view with the Tracking table displayed. Then use the drop-down calendar in the Actual Start or Actual Finish dates columns to specify a date.

Figure 13-5:
Click the arrow of the Start or Finish fields and choose a date from a drop-down calendar.

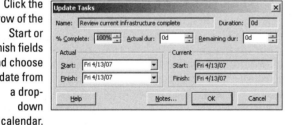

A few conditions could cause a warning message to appear when you enter an actual start or finish date: for example, if the actual start date falls before the start date for the project, or if it causes a conflict with a dependent task. When this warning message appears, you have the following options:

✔ Cancel the operation.

✔ Force the conflict to exist (or the task to start) before the project starts.

If you want to cancel the change, correct what's causing the problem (for example, by modifying the project start date), and then go back and enter the actual information, you can. Or you can force the conflict, and let it stand.

John worked three hours, Maisie worked ten

If you want to get to the blow-by-blow level of tracking, you need to record exactly how many hours each resource put in on your tasks. This can be about as much fun as typing the New York City phone book into a database, but it has some benefits. After you track actual hours, you can get tallies of total hours put in by each resource in your project by day, week, or month. If you have to bill clients based on resource hours (for example, if you're a lawyer), you have a clear record to refer to. If you're tracking a budget in detail, resource hours multiplied by their individual rates will tally an accurate accounting of costs as finely as day by day.

If you don't enter specific hours, Project just averages the work done on the task according to the total duration. For many people, that's fine; for others, more detail is better. If you're in the detail camp, specify actual resource hours as a total by task or day-by-day through the life of each task.

To enter resource hours, follow these steps:

1. **Display Resource Usage view, which is shown in Figure 13-6.**

2. **In the Resource Name column, scroll down to locate the resource you want to track.**

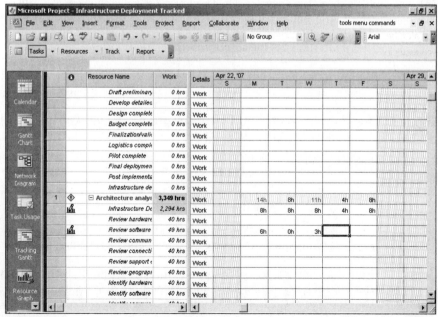

Figure 13-6: Track resource activity day by day in this view.

Automating updates via Project Web Access

If your organization uses Project Server with Project Web Access to handle projects across your enterprise, you can use tools from the Collaborate menu to help automate your tracking. By using the Request Progress Information command, you can notify your resources to update their progress with a status report, or they can enter their specific hours worked in an online timesheet. By using the Update Project Progress command, you can access those timesheet updates and accept or reject the data there as updates to your project plan.

Improvements to timesheets in Project 2007 include the ability to track billable and non-billable hours as well as future time reporting, which is required by some organizations.

Note: If you have Project Standard, you will not see the Collaborate menu. Additionally, if you don't have Project Server and Project Web Access set up, most of the Collaborate menu commands are not available. See Chapters 18 and 19 for more about using Project Web Access.

The tasks that each resource is assigned to are listed underneath the resource name.

3. **Enter the hours put in by the resource:**

   • *If you want to enter only total hours:* Locate the task name under the resource listing. Display the Actual Work column and enter the total hours there.

   • *If you want to enter hours on the task day by day:* Scroll in the chart pane to locate the timeframe for the task. Click the cell for a day that the resource worked and enter a number. Repeat this for each day that the resource worked on that task.

If the hours you enter for a resource total more or less than the baseline estimate for that resource on that task, here's what happens:

✔ When you enter an amount and press Enter, the Work column total recalculates to reflect the total hours worked on that task.

✔ The hour notation on that date is displayed in red, showing some variation from baseline hours.

✔ A little pencil symbol appears in the ID column for that task, indicating that the assignment has been edited.

✔ A yellow box with an exclamation point appears in the ID column to the left of the task's summary task, indicating a resource overallocation.

Note that you can easily look up the total hours put in by each resource on the project by checking the summary number of work hours listed next to the resource in the Resource Name column of Resource Usage view.

Uh-oh, we're into overtime

When you enter 16 hours of work on a single day for a resource, even though that resource is based on a calendar with an 8-hour day, Project doesn't recognize any of those hours as overtime. This is one case where you have to lead Project by the hand and actually tell it to specify overtime work.

When you enter hours in the Overtime Work field, Project interprets that as the number of total Work hours that are overtime hours. So, if you enter 16 hours of work on a task in the Work column and then enter 4 in the Overtime Work column, Project assumes that there were 12 hours of work at the standard resource rate and 4 hours at the overtime rate.

To enter overtime hours, follow these steps:

1. **Display Resource Usage view.**

2. **Right-click a column heading and then click Insert Column.**

   The Column Definition dialog box appears.

3. **In the Field Name box, click Overtime Work.**

4. **Click OK to display the column.**

5. **Click in the Overtime Work column for the resource and task you want to modify, and then use the spinner arrows to specify the overtime hours.**

Note that if you specify overtime, Project assumes that effort-driven tasks are happening in less time. After all, if the task was to take three 8-hour days (24 hours of work) to complete and you recorded that the resource worked 12 hours for two days in a row, Project figures that all the effort got accomplished in less time. The duration for the task will actually shrink. If that's not what happened, you have to go in and modify the task duration yourself.

Specifying remaining durations

A lot of tracking information has a weird and wonderful relationship in Project. For example, Project tries to help you out by calculating durations based on other entries you make, such as actual start and finish dates. In that particular case, Project figures out task duration according to those dates. (This works in reverse, too: If you enter the task duration, Project recalculates the finish date to reflect it.)

Sometimes you want to enter a duration rather than have Project base it on other information you input. For example, you might have entered a start date and 20 hours of work on a task that had a baseline of 16 hours of work. What Project can't know is that the scope of the task changed, and now the task is not complete and will also take another 20 hours of work. You have to tell Project about that.

The way in which Project calculates task duration has changed in Project 2007. Previously, if you marked an assignment as 100% complete and then extended the task duration, Project automatically extended the assignment and work. In Project 2007, if you mark work as complete and then extend the task duration, Project extends the duration but doesn't extend the work.

To modify the duration on a task in progress or completed, follow these steps:

1. **Display Gantt Chart view.**

2. **Choose View⇨Table⇨Tracking.**

   The Tracking table is displayed.

3. **Click in the Actual Duration column for the task you want to modify and then use the arrows to adjust the actual duration up or down.**

4. **If you want to enter a remaining duration, click in the Remaining Duration column and type a number as well as an increment symbol.**

   For example, you might type **25d** (where *d* is the increment symbol for days).

If you enter a percentage-of-completion for a task and then modify the duration to differ from the baseline, Project automatically recalculates the percentage considered complete to reflect the new duration. So, if you enter *50% complete* on a 10-hour task and then modify the actual duration to 20 hours, Project considers that 5 hours (50% of 10 hours) as only 25% of the 20 hours.

Entering fixed-cost updates

Fixed costs are costs that aren't influenced by time, such as equipment purchases and consulting fees. Compared with the calculations and interactions of percentage completions and start and finish dates for hourly resources, fixed-cost tracking will seem like simplicity itself!

Here's how to do it:

1. **Display Gantt Chart view.**

2. **Right-click in a column heading and then click Insert Column.**

   The Column Definition dialog box appears.

3. **In the Field Name box, select Fixed Cost.**

4. **Click OK.**

5. **Click in the Fixed Cost column for the task you want to update.**

6. **Type the fixed cost, or a total of several fixed costs, for the task.**

That's it! However, because Project lets you enter only one fixed-cost amount per task, consider adding a note to the task itemizing the costs you've included in the total. Also, there is no baseline fixed cost column, so to compare how your actual fixed costs outstripped your baseline estimates, you have to do a little math to find the difference between baseline costs and actual costs: Deduct non-fixed costs to get the variation in fixed costs.

Consider using some of the 30 customizable Text columns for itemized fixed-cost entry. Rename one Equipment Purchase, another Facility Rental, and so on, and then enter those costs in those columns. Of course, these columns of data won't perform calculations such as rolling up total costs to the summary tasks in your project, but they'll serve as a reminder about itemized fixed costs.

In Project 2007, you can designate a resource type as Cost and assign a cost to that resource. The Cost column then reflects the amount spent for Cost resources on tasks. See Chapter 7 for more about resource types.

Update Project: Sweeping Changes for Dummies

If it's been a while since you tracked activity and you want to update your schedule, Update Project might be for you. It allows you to track chunks of activity for a period of time. Update Project works best, however, if most tasks happened pretty much on schedule.

This is not fine-tuned tracking: It's akin to getting your bank balance, drawing a line in your checkbook, and writing down that balance as gospel rather than accounting for your balance check by check. (If you're like most of us, you've done this at least once.) Doing so assumes that all your checks and deposits probably tally with what the bank says as of that date; thus, going forward, you're back on track.

Here are the setting choices Update Project offers you:

✔ **Update Work as Complete Through:** You can update your project through the date you specify in this box in one of two ways. The Set 0% – 100% Complete setting lets Project figure out the percent complete on every task that should have begun by that time. By making this choice, you tell Project to assume that the tasks started and progressed exactly on time. The Set 0% or 100% Complete Only setting works a little differently. This setting says to Project, just record 100% complete on tasks that the baseline said would be complete by now, but leave all other tasks at 0% complete.

✔ **Reschedule Uncompleted Work to Start After:** This setting reschedules the portions of tasks that aren't yet complete to start after the date you specify in this dialog box.

To use Update Project, do this:

1. **Display Gantt Chart view.**

2. **If you want to update only certain tasks, select them.**

3. **Choose Tools➪Tracking➪Update Project.**

    The Update Project dialog box appears, as shown in Figure 13-7.

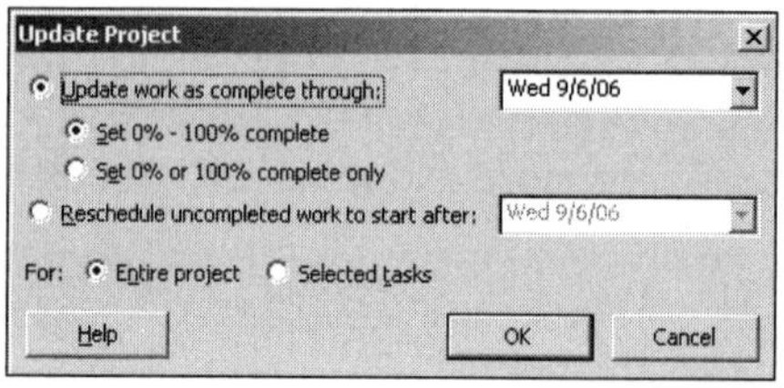

Figure 13-7:
You can update only selected tasks or the entire project.

4. **Choose the Update method you prefer: Set 0% – 100% Complete or Set 0% or 100% Complete Only.**

5. **If you want a status date other than the current date, set it in the field in the upper-right corner.**

6. **If you want Project to reschedule any work rather than updating work as complete, select the Reschedule Uncompleted Work to Start After option and then select a date from the list.**

7. **Choose whether you want these changes to apply to the entire project or only to selected tasks.**

8. **Click OK to save the settings and have Project make updates.**

If you want, you can use Update Project to make some global changes, such as marking all tasks that should be complete according to baseline as 100 percent complete. Then go in and perform more detailed task-by-task tracking on individual tasks that are only partially complete.

Materials Usage

...aterials used on tasks involves tracking actual units ...evel. So, if you create a resource called *rubber* and ...facture Tires at 500 tons, but you actually used only ...you made 450 tons of rubber streeeetch) you would ...units used.

...e way you track work resource hours on tasks. To ...these steps:

...ge view (see Figure 13-8).

...source in the list and scroll in the right pane ...meframe appears.

...used on each task to which you assigned that

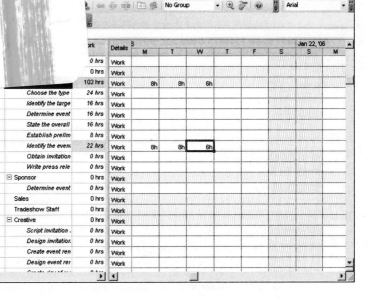

Figure 13-8:
Change the baseline units here and the actual usage will change in the Work column.

Just keep in mind that if you assign the material resource of, say, 500 tons to a five-day task, Resource Usage view reflects that Project spread the usage out — 100 tons for each of the five days of the task. If you don't care on what day of the task the materials were used, you can simply modify one of the settings to be higher or lower to make up for any difference in actual usage.

Tracking More Than One: Consolidated Projects

Often you'll have either projects that are related in some fashion (such as sharing resources or having timing dependencies between them) or a series of smaller projects that make up a larger project. In that case, you can consolidate those separate projects into one file, either as a series of summary tasks or with all summary and subtasks included.

When you consolidate projects, you can choose to link to the source file. When you do, any changes to the source file are represented in the consolidated file.

If it's your job to keep track of the big picture, you have to understand how consolidated projects get updated.

Consolidating projects

Creating a consolidated project is sort of like going to a Chinese restaurant — one from Column A, one from Column B, and so on, until you build yourself a tasty meal. In Project, you open a blank file and then insert existing projects to build a satisfying master project plan.

The neat thing about consolidated projects is that you have some choices about how the consolidated project and the source files you insert in it interact. For example, you can link to a source file so that changes made in the source file will be reflected in the consolidated project. This is a great tool for somebody who has to keep his or her eye on multiple phases or many smaller projects.

 You can also create dependencies between inserted projects in the consolidated file. If you have (for example) one project that can't start until another one finishes, you can clearly see in the consolidated file how various separate projects in your organization have an impact on each other.

The other thing you can do to relate consolidated projects to their source files is to make your consolidated project a two-way street, allowing changes in it to be reflected in the source files. You can also make the choice to have the source files be read-only so your changes won't go mucking around with other people's files — whichever suits your purposes.

To create a consolidated file, follow these steps:

1. **Open a blank Project file and display Gantt Chart view.**

2. **Click in the Task Name column.**

   If you're inserting multiple projects, click the row in which you want the inserted file(s) to appear. If you want to insert a project between existing tasks, click the task beneath where you want the project to be inserted.

3. **Choose Insert⇨Project.**

   The Insert Project dialog box, shown in Figure 13-9, appears.

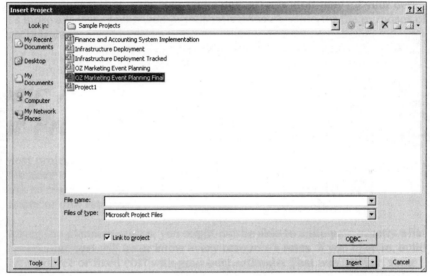

Figure 13-9:
Make choices about how your projects interact in this dialog box.

4. **Using the Look In list, locate the Project file you want to insert and select it.**

5. **(Optional) Click the down arrow on the Insert button if you want to change the default Insert setting to Insert Read Only.**

6. **If you want to link the project in this file to the source file so that whenever you open the consolidated file it updates automatically, make sure the Link to Project check box is selected.**

7. **Click OK.**

   The project is inserted in your file with the summary task showing and all subtasks hidden. To display all tasks in the inserted project, just click the plus sign to the left of the summary task.

Updating consolidated projects

There are two ways to skin the cat called *updating a consolidated project,* and the one you use depends on whether you linked to the source files when you inserted them. If you linked the files and you inserted them without the read-only setting, changes in source files are reflected in the consolidated file (and vice versa). Updating is simply a matter of making sure all the files are available in their original linked locations (for example, in a folder on your network), and then Project updates automatically.

If you haven't linked the files, changes in source files won't be reflected in consolidated files, and the consolidated file information will have no effect on the source information. You might create such an unlinked consolidated file if you simply want to see a snapshot of how all projects are going at the moment, and you don't want to run the risk of having your settings changing the source information. In this case, however, if you want to track progress, you have to create a new consolidated project, or manually enter all updates.

After you insert projects in a file, you can move them around using Cut and Paste tools. When you do, the Planning Wizard may appear, offering you options to resolve any conflicts that may occur because of dependency links you've created between inserted projects.

Changing linking settings

Changing your mind is a project manager's prerogative. So, if, after you have inserted a source file in a consolidated file, you find you didn't initially establish a link, you can go in and change that setting so the files update each other automatically.

Follow these steps to make changes to the inserted project:

1. **Open the consolidated file.**
2. **Display Gantt Chart view.**
3. **Click the Task Name of the inserted project you want to update.**
4. **Click the Task Information button on the Standard toolbar.**

   The Inserted Project Information dialog box (as shown in Figure 13-10) appears.

5. **Display the Advanced tab.**
6. **Select the Link to Project check box and then click the Browse button.**

   The Inserted Project dialog box appears.

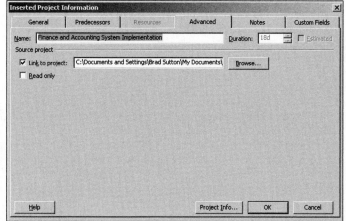

Figure 13-10:
Data on the
source file
is displayed
in this
dialog box.

7. **Use the Look In feature to locate the file you want to link to and select the file.**

8. **Click OK.**

9. **If you want the source file to be Read Only, select that check box.**

10. **Click OK to save the link.**

Chapter 14

A Project with a View: Observing Progress

In This Chapter

▶ Seeing what your progress looks like with indicators and taskbars

▶ Seeing progress from various Project views

▶ Examining cost and time variances

▶ Understanding earned value

▶ Modifying calculation options

Some people use Project just to paint a pretty picture of what their project will entail and then put the plan in a drawer. That's a mistake. After you enter all your project data, save a baseline, and then track actual activity on your project, you get an amazing array of information back from Project that helps you to stay on time and on budget.

After you track some actual activity on tasks, Project allows you to view baseline estimates right alongside your real-time plan. Project alerts you to tasks that are running late and also shows how the critical path shifts over time.

Project also provides detailed budget information. In fact, the information that you can get about your costs might just make your accounting department's heart sing. The information is detailed and uses terms that accountants love (such as *earned value, cost variance,* and *budgeted cost of work performed,* all translated in a later section of this chapter).

So keep that project file close at hand — and take a look at how Project can make you the most informed project manager in town.

Look at What Tracking Did!

You diligently entered resource work hours on tasks, recorded the percentage of progress on tasks, and entered fixed costs. Now what? Well, all that information has caused several calculations to go on — and updates to be reflected — in your project. Time to take a quick look at the changes all your tracking has produced in your Project plan.

Getting an indication

A lot of information in Project just sits there waiting for you to hunt it down in obscure views or tables, but one tool that Project uses to practically jump up and down and say, "Look at this!" is *indicator icons.* You've seen these icons in the Indicator column and probably wondered what the heck they were for. Well, these little symbols give you a clue to important facts about each task, sometimes alerting you to problems or potential challenges.

Figure 14-1 shows several of these indicators, some of which relate to the results of tracking your project.

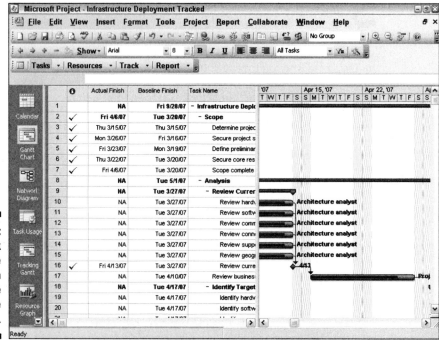

Figure 14-1: The check marks here mean that the tasks are complete.

If you see an unfamiliar indicator icon crop up in your project, hold your mouse cursor over the indicator. A box describing its meaning appears. To get a list of Project icons and their meanings, go to Help, click the Index tab, and type **icon** in the Search box. Click Search and then click Indicator Fields.

Lines of progress

Progress lines offer an additional visual indicator of how you're doing. As you can see in Figure 14-2, a progress line zigzags between tasks and forms, showing left-or-right-pointing peaks. These peaks indicate late or early tasks (calculated according to the status date you use when tracking). A progress line that points to the left of a task indicates that the task is running late. Progress lines that point to the right show that, wonder of wonders, you're running ahead of schedule. (Treasure these: They don't seem to appear often in projects!)

Displaying progress lines

By default, Project doesn't display progress lines. You have to turn them on. And while you're at it, you might as well specify when and how they appear. Here's how to make settings for and display progress lines:

1. **Display Gantt Chart view.**

2. **Choose Tools⇨Tracking⇨Progress Lines.**

   The Progress Lines dialog box appears, as shown in Figure 14-3.

3. **If you want Project to always show a progress line for the current or status date, select Always Display Current Progress Line and then select At Project Status Date or At Current Date.**

4. **If you want progress lines to be displayed at set intervals, do the following:**

   a. *Select Display Progress Lines at Recurring Intervals, and then select Daily, Weekly, or Monthly.*

   b. *Specify the interval settings.*

   For example, if you select Weekly, you can choose every week, every other week, and so on, as well as which day of the week the line should be displayed for on the timescale. Figure 14-4 shows a project with progress lines at regular intervals.

5. **Choose whether you want to display progress lines beginning at the Project Start or on another date.**

   To use the Project Start date, simply select the Project Start option in the Begin At section of the dialog box. To select an alternate start date, select the second option and then select a date from the calendar drop-down list.

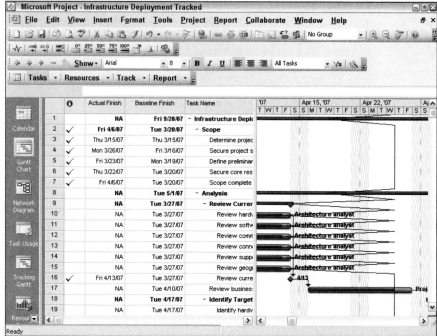

Figure 14-2:
The progress line shows where a task should be relative to your plan.

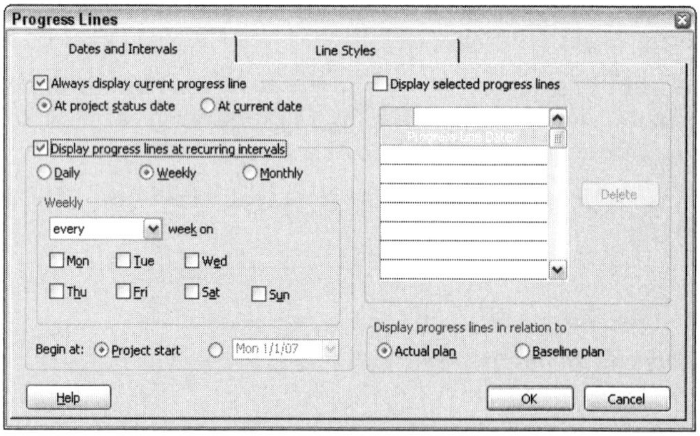

Figure 14-3:
These two tabs allow you to control just about everything about progress lines.

6. **If you want to display a progress line on a specific date, click Display Selected Progress Lines and then choose a date from the Progress Line Dates drop-down calendar.**

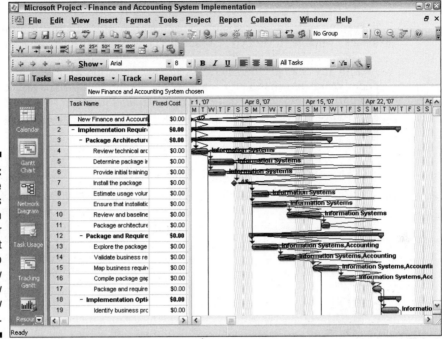

Figure 14-4:
Multiple
progress
lines can
get rather
busy, but
they do
show
clearly how
delays grew
over time.

You can make this setting for multiple dates by clicking subsequent lines in this list and selecting additional dates.

7. Finally, you can choose to display progress lines in relation to actual or baseline information.

If a task has been tracked to show 50 percent complete and you choose to have Project display progress lines based on actual information, the peak appears relative to the 50 percent *actual* line, not the complete baseline taskbar.

8. Click OK to save your settings.

You can use your mouse to add a single progress line quickly. On the Tracking toolbar, click the Add Progress Line tool. Then click the Gantt chart at the location on the timescale where you want the line to appear in the chart. To delete the line, right-click it and choose Progress Lines. In the Progress Lines dialog box, click the item you want to delete in the Progress Line Dates list, click Delete, and then click OK.

Formatting progress lines

In keeping with the almost mind-boggling array of formatting options Project makes available to you, you can modify how progress lines are formatted.

As with any changes to formatting, you're tampering with the way Project codes visual information for readers. You should be cautious about making formatting changes that cause your plan to be difficult to read for those who are used to Project's default formatting.

To modify progress line formatting, follow these steps:

1. **Choose Tools⇨Tracking⇨Progress Lines.**

2. **Click the Line Styles tab, if necessary, to display the options shown in Figure 14-5.**

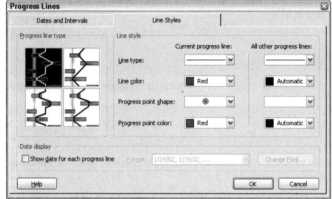

Figure 14-5: Select line styles and colors with these settings.

3. **In the Progress Line Type display, click a line style sample.**

4. **In the Line Type fields, click a style from the samples shown.**

   You can make two settings here: one for the Current Progress Line and one for All Other Progress Lines.

5. **You can change the line color, progress point shape, and progress point color by making different choices in those boxes.**

6. **If you want a date to appear alongside each progress line, select the Show Date for Each Progress Line option and then select a date from the Format field.**

7. **If you want to change the font used for the displayed date, click the Change Font button and make your changes.**

8. **Click OK to save your settings.**

When worlds collide: Baseline versus actual

One of the most obvious ways to view the difference between your baseline estimates and what you've tracked in your project is through taskbars. After you track some progress on tasks, the Gantt chart shows a black bar superimposed on the blue taskbar that represents your baseline. For example, in Figure 14-6, Task 6 is complete; you can tell this by the solid black bar that extends the full length of the baseline taskbar. Task 8 is only partially complete; the black, actual task line only partially fills the baseline duration for the task. Task 9 has no recorded activity on it; there is no black *actual* line at all, only the blue baseline taskbar.

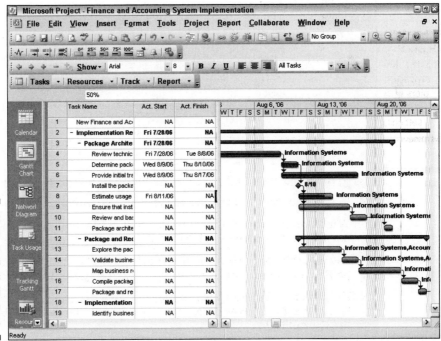

Figure 14-6:
The solid line on taskbars represents actual activity in your project.

Learn by the Numbers

Visual indicators such as taskbars and indicator icons are useful to alert you to delays or variances between estimated and actual performance, but they don't provide any detailed information. To get the real lowdown on how far ahead (or behind) you are, down to the day or penny, you need to give the numbers a scan. The numbers that Project provides reveal much about whether you're on schedule and within your budget.

Two tables you can display in Gantt Chart view bring your situation into bold relief. The Cost table and Variance table provide information about dollars spent and variations in timing between baseline and actual activity.

The Cost table is shown in Figure 14-7. Here you can review data that compares baseline estimates of fixed costs and actual costs. These two sets of data are presented side-by-side in columns. In the project shown in Figure 14-7, you've spent $190,350 so far, and your baseline estimate was $182,750, giving you a variance of $7,600 over your budget.

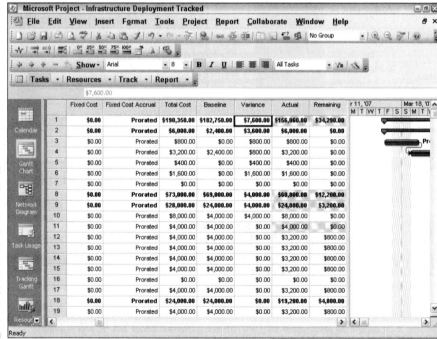

Figure 14-7:
The Variance column shows the difference between the total cost and the baseline.

To display a table, choose View⇨Table and click the table name.

Figure 14-8 shows the Variance table. This table is to your scheduling what the Cost table is to your budget. It shows the variance between baseline start and finish dates and task durations, as well as the timing that actually occurred on tasks after your project got going.

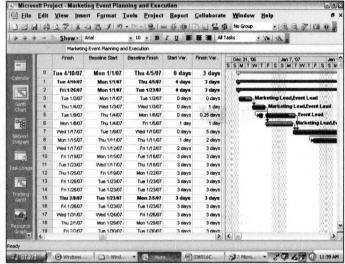

Figure 14-8:
Use this table to see what delays are doing to your schedule.

If you created a slack task to help you deal with delays that might come up, the total variance shown here will tell you how many days you may have to deduct from the duration of the slack task to get back on track. Read more about making adjustments in your plan to deal with delays and cost overruns in Chapter 15 and about slack in Chapter 10.

Acronym Soup: BCWP, ACWP, EAC, and CV

In any view, you can insert several columns of data to give you some calculated analyses of what's going on in your project budget. Much of this data will mean more to an accountant than to most in-the-trenches project managers. If only to make your accountant feel more comfortable, you should become familiar with some of the most common calculations. Also, many organizations require information on these specific numbers in project reports:

✔ **BCWP (budgeted cost of work performed):** Referred to in some circles as *earned value,* BCWP is essentially a calculation of the value of the work that you've completed expressed in dollars. For example, if a task has $2,000 of costs associated with it and you record that the task is 50 percent complete, the earned value for that task is $1,000 (50 percent of the baseline estimated costs).

✔ **ACWP (actual cost of work performed):** This calculation looks at actual costs, including tracked resource hours or units expended on the task plus fixed costs. Whereas BCWP looks at the baseline *value* of work, ACWP looks at actual tracked *costs.*

✔ **EAC (estimate at completion):** This is a total of all costs on a task. For a task in progress, EAC calculates the actual costs recorded to date plus the remaining baseline estimated costs.

✔ **CV (cost variance):** This represents the difference between *planned costs* (that is, costs included in the baseline for a task) and the combination of actual costs recorded to date plus any remaining estimated costs. This number is expressed as a negative number if you're under budget and as a positive number if you're like the rest of us (over budget).

Studying these numbers can help you see what it has cost to get where you are today on your project.

Calculations behind the Scenes

While you're happily entering resource hours and fixed costs into your project, Project is busy making calculations that can shift around task timing and resource workload in your plan. These calculations relate to how tasks are updated, how the critical path is determined, and how earned value is calculated. If you're a control freak, you'll be happy to know that you can, to some extent, control how Project goes about making these calculations.

Remember that the new Change Highlighting feature helps you see what effect an individual change has on your project. See Chapter 10 for more about this feature.

Going automatic or manual

By default, Project is on automatic as far as calculations go. When you make a change to your plan, Project recalculates totals, the critical path, and so on without you having to lift a finger. However, you can change that default setting and have Project wait for you to initiate calculations manually. You do so in the Calculation tab of the Options dialog box (Tools➪Options). Figure 14-9 shows the settings available there.

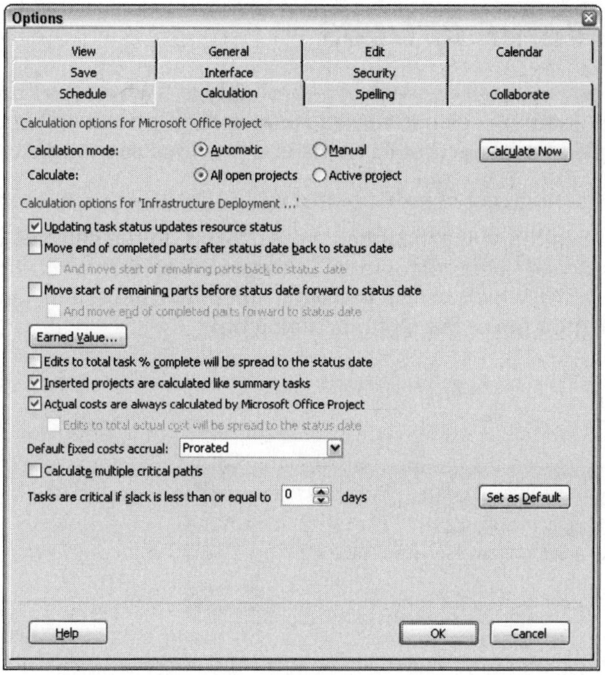

Figure 14-9:
Click the
Calculate
Now button
to make
Project
perform
calculations
on your
command.

If you change the Calculation mode to Manual, you must click the Calculate Now button in this dialog box any time you want Project to perform all its calculations. You also have the choice here of setting different modes for only the current project or for all open projects.

So why would you choose to use manual calculation? You might want to make a lot of changes and not have Project take the milliseconds required to recalculate between each change, slowing down your entry work. You can put things on manual, make all your changes, and then use the Calculate Now button to make all the changes at once.

In addition, because even with Change Highlighting on it's not always easy to spot all the items that have been recalculated when you make a series of changes, it might be easier to make all the changes in manual mode, print your Gantt Chart view, and *then* recalculate and compare the two. This approach shows you the cumulative calculations that occurred when all your changes were made so you can see whether you're happy with the revised plan. (This feature is especially useful for trying out what-if scenarios.)

In Project 2007, you can also take advantage of the Multiple Undo feature. This means you can leave your calculations on automatic, make changes, and then undo them, thereby undoing the calculations in sequence. For more on Multiple Undo, see Chapter 10.

Earned-value options

Your first question about earned value probably is, "Why does Project use *BCWP* in its column names but *earned value* in the Options dialog box?" Don't ask. Just be glad I explained both terms in a previous section ("Acronym Soup: BCWP, ACWP, EAC, and CV").

The second question you probably have is, "What do the settings you can make to the earned-value calculation do to your project?" Well, start by looking at Figure 14-10, which shows you what's behind the Earned Value button on the Calculation tab of the Options dialog box.

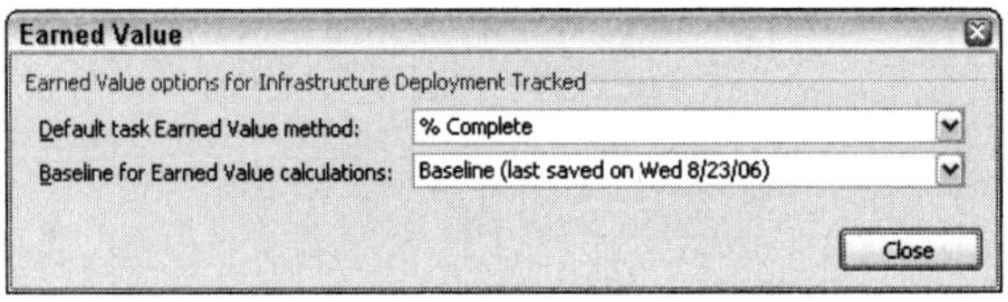

Figure 14-10:
Here are
two simple
settings to
use for
calculating
earned
value.

The Default Task Earned Value Method setting provides two choices:

- ✔ **% Complete:** This setting calculates earned value using the percent complete that you record on each task. This assumes that for a task that's halfway complete, half the work hours have been used.

- ✔ **Physical % Complete:** Use this setting if you want to enter a percent of completion that is not based on a straight percent-complete calculation. For example, if you have a four-week task to complete a mail survey, 50 percent of the effort might happen in the first 25 percent of the duration of the project: designing, printing, and mailing the survey. Nothing happens for two weeks while you wait for responses, and then there's a flurry of activity when the responses come back. So a straight calculation that 50 percent of the task is completed 50 percent of the way through wouldn't be accurate. If your projects have a lot of tasks like this, you might consider changing your settings to use this method. Then, you can display the Physical % Complete column in your Gantt chart sheet, and enter what you consider more accurate percent-complete information for each task.

The second setting in the Earned Value dialog box is the Baseline for Earned Value Calculations drop-down list. As I mention earlier, *earned value* is the value of work completed, expressed in dollars, according to the baseline: A $2,000 task at 50 percent complete (for example) has a $1,000 earned value of work performed. Therefore, the baseline against which you calculate this value is hugely important. Choose any of the 11 possible baselines you may have saved in your project here. After you make these two choices, click Close to close the Earned Value dialog box.

You should explore one more option in the Options dialog box that concerns earned value calculation. The Edits to Total Task % Complete Will Be Spread to the Status Date option, which is not selected by default, affects how Project distributes changes in your schedule. If this option is left deselected, calculations go to the end of the duration of tasks in progress, rather than up to the status date or the current date. If you do select this option, calculations spread changes across your plan up to the status date or the current date, and no farther. Selecting this choice helps you see changes to your project in increments of time, rather than across the life of tasks in progress.

If I were you, I'd leave the Edits to Total Task % option not selected for the most accurate reflection of progress on your project.

How many critical paths are enough?

The last group of settings on the Calculation tab of the Options dialog box concerns critical path calculations.

The Inserted Projects Are Calculated Like Summary Tasks option is straightforward. If you insert another project as a task in your project, having this setting selected allows Project to calculate one critical path for your entire project. If you don't select it, any projects you insert are treated like outsiders — that is, they're not taken into account in the master project's critical-path calculations. If an inserted project won't have an effect on your project's timing, you may want to clear this option.

If following one project's critical path is too tame for you, try getting critical with multiple paths. By selecting the Calculate Multiple Critical Paths option, you set up Project to calculate a different critical path for each set of tasks in your project. Doing so can be helpful if you want to identify tasks that, if delayed, will cause you to miss your final project deadline or the goals of a single phase in your project.

Finally, you can establish what puts a task on the critical path by specifying the number of days of slack critical tasks might have. By default, tasks with no slack are on the critical path. However, you can change this situation if you want to be alerted that tasks with only one day of slack are critical — figuring that one day isn't much padding and that these tasks are still in jeopardy.

If you want all the settings on the Calculation tab to pertain to all projects, click the Set as Default button before clicking OK to save the new settings in the Options dialog box.

Chapter 15

You're Behind: Now What?

In This Chapter

▶ Reviewing your plan versions and notes to understand what went wrong

▶ Trying out what-if scenarios

▶ Working with the Analysis toolbar

▶ Understanding how getting more time or more people will help

▶ Adjusting your timing going forward

*I*n almost every project comes a time when you feel like the floor dropped out from under you. Suddenly — and this one just snuck up on you — you're $20,000 over budget. Or you're going to miss that drop-dead deadline by two weeks. All the aspirin in the world isn't going to solve this one.

Of course, you have a general idea of what happened because you're smart, you kept in touch with your team, and you have Project and all its columns of data. Still, somehow things are off track, and you need to take action at this point. First, you have to justify what occurred (abbreviated *CYA*), and then you have to fix things so that you can go forward and just maybe save your project, your job, or both.

How do you save the day when things go off track? What you have to do at this point involves analyzing your options and making some tough choices. This is stuff you did before you ever heard of Microsoft Project. However, Project can help you try out some possible solutions and anticipate the likely results. After you decide what to do, you have to implement your solutions in Project.

Justifying Yourself: Notes, Baselines, and Interim Plans

If you've kept interim plans, multiple baselines, and task notes in Project, it's much easier to explain how you got into this mess to the powers-that-be.

Interim plans and multiple baselines demonstrate how you made adjustments when major changes or problems occurred. Using these two items indicates to your boss that you were on top of things all the way and probably kept him or her in the loop by generating printouts or reports reflecting major changes as they came up. (If you didn't, print them now from the interim plans or baselines you saved along the way — and let them paint a picture of what happened.)

A *baseline* saves all project data; an *interim plan* saves only the start and finish dates of tasks in the project. Chapter 12 deals with interim plans and baselines.

To view or print information from various baselines or interim plans, follow these steps:

1. **Display Gantt Chart view.**

2. **Right-click the column heading area of the sheet pane and then click Insert Column.**

   The Column Definition dialog box appears, as shown in Figure 15-1.

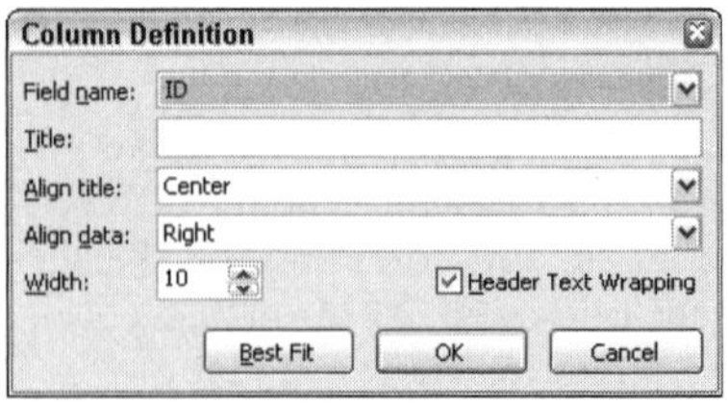

Figure 15-1:
Insert as
many
columns as
you like in
any view
with a sheet
pane.

Column Definition	
Field name:	ID
Title:	
Align title:	Center
Align data:	Right
Width:	10	☑ Header Text Wrapping
	Best Fit OK Cancel

3. **In the Field Name box, choose a column name.**

   For example, you might choose Start 1-10 and Finish 1-10 for any one of your interim plans (or choose Baseline through Baseline 10 for baseline data).

4. **If you need to, repeat Steps 2 and 3 to display additional columns. Click OK to display the column(s).**

In addition to interim plans and baselines, task notes should include information about resource performance on a task, vendor problems, or late deliveries. Notes that are especially important to add are those you make when someone in authority over you has asked for a change and okayed more money or time to make that change. (Don't worry, this hardly ever happens.)

To add a note to a task, either display the task note column in a sheet pane or double-click a task and add the note on the Notes tab of the Task Information dialog box.

What If?

Just as you can get too close to a problem to see a solution, you can get too close to your project to recognize what you need to do. With Project's filtering and sorting features, though, you can slice and dice various aspects of your project a little differently to get a fresh perspective.

You can also use tools such as resource leveling to solve resource conflicts. Resource leveling might not always solve problems to your taste, but it's a good way to let Project show you one what-if scenario that will solve most resource problems instantly.

See Chapter 10 for more information about how to use resource leveling.

Sorting things out

Sometimes when things won't sort themselves out, it's time to sort your tasks. Project allows you to sort tasks by several criteria, including start date, finish date, priority, and cost.

How can sorting help you? Well, here are a few examples:

- ✔ **To cut costs:** Consider sorting tasks by cost. Then you can focus on the most expensive tasks first to see whether there's room to trim nice-to-have-but-pricey items.

- ✔ **To delete tasks to save time:** Display tasks by priority and then look at the low-priority tasks as the first candidates for the waste bin.

- ✔ **To review task timing:** Sort by duration in descending order to see the longest tasks first.

If you want to apply a preset sorting order, simply choose Project➪Sort and then choose an option from the submenu, such as by Start Date or by Cost.

If you want to see additional sort criteria — or sort by more than one criterion — follow these steps:

1. **Choose Project➪Sort➪Sort By.**

   The Sort dialog box appears, as shown in Figure 15-2.

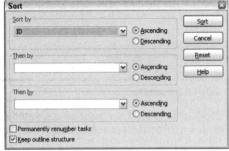

Figure 15-2:
Sort by up to
three
criteria in
ascending
or
descending
order.

2. **In the Sort By list, select a criterion.**

3. **Select either Ascending (to sort from lowest to highest) or Descending (to sort from highest to lowest).**

   With a date field, the sorting order would be soonest to latest and latest to soonest, respectively; with a text field, alphabetical would be the order.

4. **(Optional) If you want a second criterion, click the first Then By box and make a selection.**

   For example, if you choose to sort first by Cost and then by Type, tasks are sorted from least expensive to most expensive, and then (within each cost level) by type (Fixed Duration, Fixed Units, and Fixed Work).

5. **(Optional) If you want to add a third criterion, click the second Then By box and make a selection.**

6. **Click Sort.**

To return to your original task order, choose Project⇨Sort⇨By ID. Tasks are now back in *task ID number* order, which is Project's standard sorting criterion.

Filtering

Chapter 10 deals with how you create and apply filters in Project. Now is a good time to call on your knowledge of those features. Especially in larger projects, where it's not always easy to scan hundreds of tasks and notice which are running late or over budget, filters can home in on exactly where your trouble lies.

You can choose to have tasks that don't meet filter criteria removed from your display or simply highlight tasks that meet the criteria on-screen.

Table 15-1 lists some filters that are useful when you're trying to identify and solve problems with your schedule.

Table 15-1	Filters to Isolate Problems
Filter Name	*What It Displays*
Critical	Tasks in the project that must be completed according to schedule to make your final deadline (critical path)
Cost Overbudget	Tasks that exceed budgeted expenditures
Incomplete Tasks	Tasks that haven't been marked as complete
Late/Overbudget Tasks	Tasks that are running later than their baseline estimate and are over budget
Should Start By	Tasks that should have started as of a specified date
Slipped/Late Progress	Tasks that are running late and have no progress recorded
Update Needed	A task that should have had progress tracked by now
Overallocated Resources	Tasks with resources assigned that are overbooked at some point during the life of the task
Slipping Assignments	Tasks that involve resource work that should have begun by now
Work Incomplete	Tasks that should have had all their work recorded by now
Work Overbudget	More work hours have been put in on the task than you had estimated

Don't see all these choices in the More Filters dialog box? Remember, when you use this dialog box (Project⇨Filtered For⇨More Filters), you have to enable the Task option to see task-related filters and the Resource option to see resource-related filters.

You might also consider exporting your Project information to a program such as Excel so you can use analysis tools, such as pivot tables, to figure out what's going on. If that idea excites you, you might want to check out *Excel Data Analysis For Dummies* by Steven Nelson.

Examining the critical path

One of the most useful filters is the one called Critical. This displays or highlights all tasks that are on the critical path. If you're running late, knowing which tasks can't slip helps you identify where there is no room for delay — and, conversely, where you can delay noncritical tasks and still meet your deadline. You might use the Critical filter to help you determine how to free up overallocated resources or get a task that's running late back on track.

You can look at the critical path in any Gantt Chart or Network Diagram view. Figure 15-3 shows Gantt Chart view of a project with the critical path highlighted. Figure 15-4 shows Network Diagram view with the same filter applied.

If you need a closer look at task timing, consider modifying the timescale display to use smaller increments of time, such as days or hours. To do so, right-click the timescale itself and then choose Timescale.

Use resource leveling one more time

If you performed manual resource leveling earlier in your project to solve resource conflicts, consider trying it again. With changes to tasks and tracked activity, resource leveling may give you some new options to solve conflicts.

If resource leveling is set to Automatic, Project automatically performs this calculation every time you modify your schedule. To see whether this is set to automatic or manual, choose Tools⇨Level Resources to bring up the Resource Leveling dialog box, as shown in Figure 15-5. If the Manual radio button is selected, click the Level Now button to run resource leveling.

What's driving the timing of this task?

The Task Drivers feature, new to Project 2007, allows you to review what is causing tasks to fall in a certain timeframe, such as dependencies or task constraints. You simply select a task and then click the Task Drivers button, which displays a pane listing all factors that affect the timing of that task.

By using this feature, which you can read more about in Chapter 10, you can determine whether a task that you'd like to happen earlier could do so if you remove some dependency or constraint affecting it. For example, early in your planning, you may have thought that the training task couldn't start until all the equipment was delivered, but now that half the equipment is here, you realize you could start the training now and complete it later. By understanding what is driving the timing of the task, you can better search for a solution if that timing is causing problems.

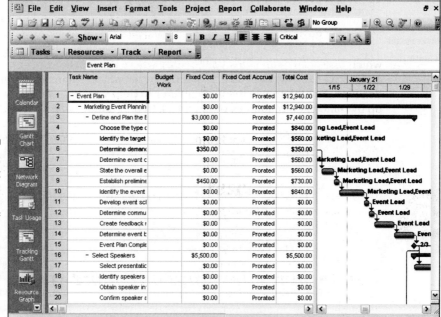

Figure 15-3:
Gantt Chart view shows you columns of data and a more precise timescale for each task.

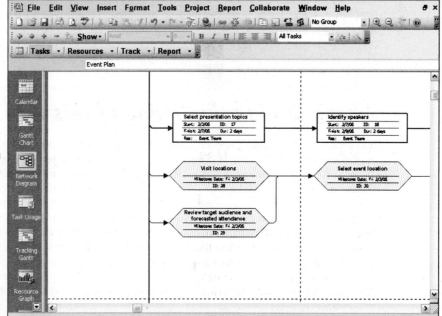

Figure 15-4:
Network Diagram view gives you a feel for workflow and dependencies among tasks.

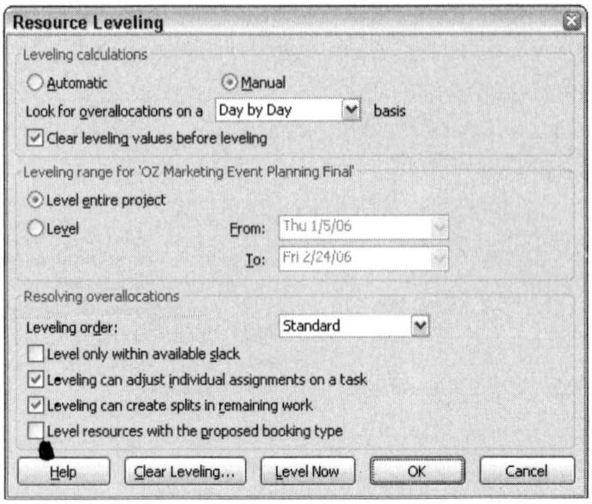

Figure 15-5:
Here's
where you
determine
whether you
or Project
will control
resource
leveling.

Using the Analysis Toolbar

Although your project woes might make you feel like entering analysis with an expensive shrink, save some money and just use the Analysis toolbar instead.

The Analysis toolbar allows you to use the Program Evaluation and Review Technique (PERT) to figure out a task's duration based on information you enter about optimistic, pessimistic, and expected scenarios. Getting information about these three possible futures can help you analyze where your project is headed if you don't make some changes.

The default settings for pessimistic, optimistic, and expected durations of a task suggest that the expected outcome is most likely and also that both the optimistic and pessimistic outcomes are equally likely. You can change that by modifying the weight you give to each task scenario. For example, the default probability for *expected* is 4 of 6; *pessimistic* and *optimistic* are each 1 of 6. If you adjust the pessimistic setting to 3 of 6, you're saying it's more likely than the optimistic outcome. Project then performs a calculation to create a weighted average of the three. This weighted average provides a likely task duration, a pessimistic task duration, and an optimistic task duration.

To display the Pert Analysis toolbar, right-click the toolbar area and choose PERT Analysis from the toolbar list to display the PERT Analysis toolbar, as shown in Figure 15-6 with the PERT Entry Sheet displayed.

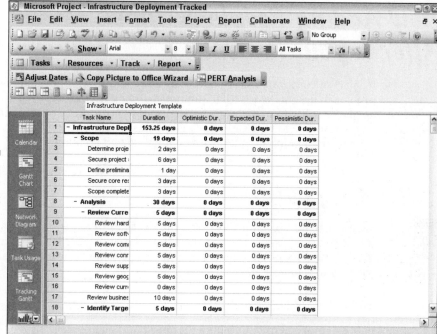

Figure 15-6:
View your
Gantt chart
from an
expected,
optimistic,
or
pessimistic
viewpoint
using these
tools.

To perform an analysis, you first have to enter the three categories of durations. Then you can perform the calculation and display three possible futures in your Gantt chart. Follow these steps to use the PERT analysis:

1. **Select the task you want to analyze.**

2. **Display the PERT Analysis toolbar and click the PERT Entry Sheet button.**

   The PERT Entry Sheet is displayed.

3. **Enter the optimistic, expected, and pessimistic durations for the task in the appropriate fields.**

4. **Click Calculate PERT.**

   Project estimates a task duration based on the average of the three durations you entered. You can click the Optimistic Gantt, Expected Gantt, and Pessimistic Gantt buttons on the PERT Analysis toolbar to see what each scenario does to your project timing.

If you want to change the default weights for each scenario, click the Set PERT Weights button on the PERT Analysis toolbar and enter new values. Remember that the sum of all three numbers has to be equal to 6, so you have to change at least two fields to make things jibe.

How Adding People or Time Affects Your Project

It's part of corporate human nature to want to throw money and people at problems; in some cases, that instinct is on target. However, you don't always have the ability to draw on endless supplies of resources or an endless amount of time to play with. Because of this, you may have to play around with a combination of options involving time and resources.

Hurry up!

Saving time in Project means doing things faster or adjusting the timing of things to use up slack. You are likely to find that making this adjustment is like an intricate puzzle: Correct one thing, and something else pops up to cause you aggravation.

To accomplish work faster, you have two options:

- ✔ **Get more people to help with tasks.** Adding people adds money, so you might get back on track time-wise — but it will cost you.

- ✔ **Modify the scope of tasks.** Modifying the scope of the task may have an effect on its quality. If you do two inspections instead of three or you shorten your QA cycle by a week, you may run the risk of other types of problems down the road.

Changing the timing of tasks and shifting dependencies uses up slack to make up for delays but may leave you with no wiggle room. The next time a problem comes up, you'll be up against the wall with no slack to save you.

In reality, combining small modifications for both time and money is often what helps you save the day.

Throwing people at the problem

With effort-driven tasks, things get accomplished when the specified amount of effort is expended. So, a task with a duration of 3 days based on a standard calendar requires 3 days × 8 hours per day to be completed (a total of 24 hours of effort). One resource performing this task working full time takes three days to complete it; three resources working full time take one day to complete 24 hours of work. When you add resources to such a task, Project automatically recalculates its duration.

Changing how resources are assigned

Beyond simply adding resources to a task, you can also make modifications to existing assignments. On any given project, you might have dozens (or even hundreds) of resources working on tasks. All those people are working according to their working calendars, the percentage of resource time you assigned to particular tasks, and their ability to do the job. Take a look at how you assigned folks to begin with to see whether you could save some time or money by modifying those assignments.

You can modify assignments in several ways:

- ✔ If someone is working at, say, only 50 percent capacity on a task, consider upping the person's assignment units.

- ✔ If you have someone available who could perform a given task more quickly, switch resources on a task and then shorten its duration.

- ✔ Consider having some people work overtime or be overbooked at various points during the project. You may have modified an overbooked resource's assignments earlier to get rid of a conflict, but now you find that there's no choice but to have the resource work that occasional 12- or 14-hour day!

Remembering the consequences

Before you get carried away making changes to resources, think a minute. Adding resources to effort-driven tasks can shrink them, helping your project get back on track. However, depending on the resources' hourly rates, this approach may cost you more.

Remember that three people working on a task won't necessarily geometrically shrink the duration of the task. That's because three people have to coordinate their efforts, hold meetings, and generally do the things people do when they interact that make their work a tad less efficient than when they work alone. If you add resources, Project shrinks the task geometrically: Consider going in and adding a little time to the task to accommodate the inefficiencies of multiple resources.

The other concern about adding resources to tasks is that it could cause more resource conflicts, with already busy people getting overbooked on too many tasks that happen in the same timeframe. If you have the resources and they have the skills and the time, though, beefing up the workforce is definitely one way to perform some tasks more quickly.

To add resources to a task, you can use the Resources tab in the Task Information dialog box or choose the task and click the Assign Resources tool button on the Standard toolbar.

Shifting dependencies and task timing

Time is a project manager's greatest enemy. There's never enough time, and what there is gets eaten up like a bag of chips in a room full of hungry Little Leaguers.

Here are some ways you can modify task timing to save time:

- ✔ **Delete a task.** You heard me. If a task represents a step that could be skipped, just get rid of it. This doesn't happen often, but sometimes — on rethinking your project — you realize that a few things aren't necessary or have already been handled by someone else.

- ✔ **Adjust dependencies.** Couldn't the revision of the manual start a few days before *all* the feedback comes back? Could the electrical and plumbing go on at the same time instead of one after the other (assuming that the electrician and the plumber can stay out of each other's way)? Use the Predecessors tab of the Task Information dialog box shown in Figure 15-7 to modify dependencies. In the Lag column, you can enter a negative number to allow tasks to overlap.

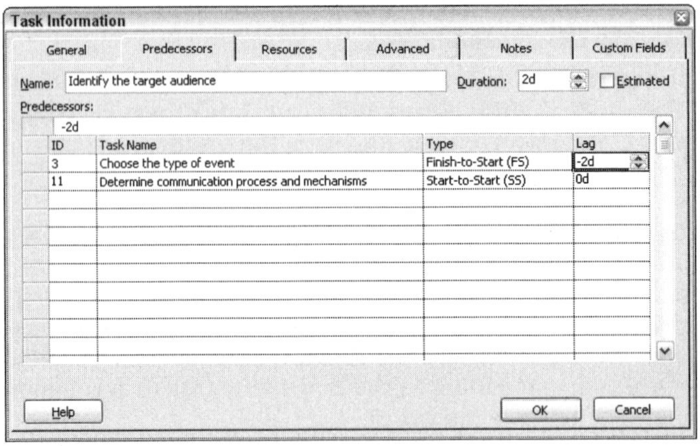

Figure 15-7: Review a task's dependencies here and modify lag to allow tasks to overlap.

- ✔ **Modify constraints.** Perhaps you set a task to start no earlier than the first of the year because you don't want to spend money on it until the new fiscal year budget kicks in. To save time, consider whether you could allow it to start a week before the end of the year but bill the costs in January. Examine any constraints such as this — specifically, those created to verify the timing logic.

✔ **Check external dependencies.** If you've inserted a hyperlinked task to represent another project and set dependencies with tasks in your project, check with the other project manager to see whether he or she can hurry up some tasks. Or if the timing relationship isn't absolutely critical, delete the hyperlink to the other project. It could be slowing you down more than you realize.

If you've set resource leveling to automatic, Project may have delayed some tasks until overbooked resources are freed up. Choose Tools⇨Level Resources and change the setting to Manual.

When All Else Fails

Okay. You've monkeyed with resource assignments and shifted task dependencies around to save time, and deleted tasks and assigned cheaper workers to save money. Still, it's not enough. This is the scenario where you have to say to your boss, "You can have it on time, you can have it on budget, or you can have quality work: Choose two."

If your boss throws money at you, go ahead and add resources to tasks, as discussed in the earlier section, "Throwing people at the problem." If she opts for time or quality, read on.

All the time in the world

If your boss is willing to give you more time, grab it. When you do, you have to update your project in a few ways:

✔ **Add to slack.** If you have a Slack task, you can simply add to its duration, giving more waffle room to all other tasks. (See Chapter 10 for more about slack.)

✔ **Modify task durations.** Take tasks that are running late and give them more time to be accomplished. In Project, this means increasing their durations or pushing out their start dates to a later time.

✔ **Review your task constraints.** If you specified that some tasks couldn't finish any later than a certain date but now you're moving your deadline out three months, you may be able to remove or adjust those original constraints accordingly.

After you work in the extra time provided to you, make sure that the new timing of tasks doesn't cause new resource conflicts, review the Resource Graph view, and then reset your baseline to reflect the new schedule. You reset a baseline by choosing Tools⇨Tracking⇨Save Baseline. When asked whether you're sure that you want to overwrite the existing baseline, reply Yes. Or choose Baseline 1-10 in the Save Baseline dialog box to save to a different baseline and preserve the original.

Don't forget to inform your team members of the new timing and provide them with an updated version of your plan. You can do that easily using Project Web Access, which I discuss in Chapters 18 and 19.

And now for something completely different

If your manager tells you to cut some corners and sacrifice quality, you have license to modify the scope of the project. You can cut out some tasks that might ensure higher quality, such as a final proofreading of the employee manual. You can hire cheaper workers. You can use cheaper paper or computer equipment.

In Project, this means you have to do the following:

- ✓ **Take less steps:** Delete tasks. (Click the ID of the task in Gantt Chart view and click Delete.)

- ✓ **Use less expensive resources:** Delete one set of resource assignments and assign other resources to tasks in the Assign Resources dialog box.

- ✓ **Use less expensive materials:** Change the unit price for materials you've created in Resource Sheet view, as shown in Figure 15-8, or lower the price of a Cost resource.

You can also take a more sweeping approach: Just redefine the goal of the project. If your goal was to launch a new product line, perhaps you can modify your goal to simply manage the design of the new product and then leave the launch to a later date or another project manager. If you were supposed to produce 10,000 widgets, could your company get along with 7,500? To make such changes, you may have to slice and dice entire phases of your project — or even start from scratch and build a new plan.

Consider saving your current project plan with a new name to give you a head start. Clear the baseline (Tools⇨Tracking⇨Clear Baseline), make your modifications, and then save a new baseline.

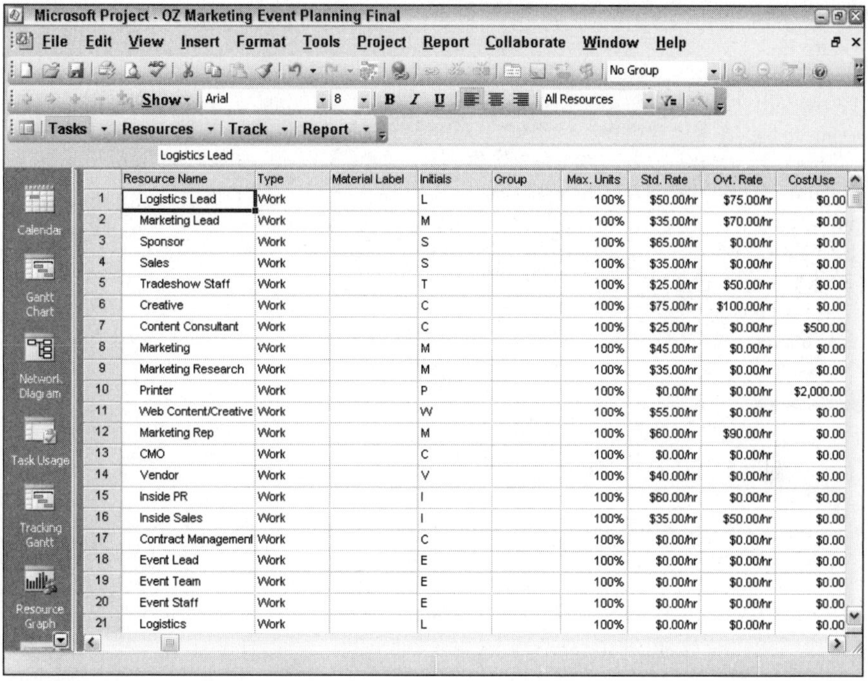

Figure 15-8:
Use the
Resource
sheet to
quickly
modify unit
prices.

What Does Project Have to Say About This?

One final word of caution: When you take certain steps, such as deleting tasks or modifying dependency relationships, your action may just cause Project to alert you to a potential problem you hadn't thought of. If that happens, Project shows you a Planning Wizard dialog box like the one in Figure 15-9. If you make changes on your own instead of using the Planning Wizard, you may be more apt to back yourself into a problem situation.

These dialog boxes offer you options — typically to go ahead and proceed, to cancel, or to proceed but with some modification. Read these alerts carefully and consider the pros and cons of what will happen if you proceed.

Figure 15-9:
Here the
wizard
wants to be
sure that
you know
that deleting
a summary
task takes
all its
subtasks
with it.

Chapter 16

Spreading the News: Reporting

- -

In This Chapter

▶ Generating standard reports

▶ Creating custom reports

▶ Dazzling people with Visual Reports

▶ Using graphics and formatting in reports

▶ Making printer settings

- -

*H*ere it is. The big payoff. The reward you get for inputting all those task names, entering all those resource hourly rates, and tracking activity on dozens of tasks during those late-hour sessions in the first hectic weeks of your project. You finally get to print a report, getting something tangible out of Project that you can hand out at meetings and use to impress your boss.

Reports help you communicate about your project, conveying information about resource assignments, how costs are accumulating, and what activities are in progress or coming up soon. You can take advantage of built-in reports or customize those reports to include the data that's most relevant to you. New to Project 2007 are Visual Reports that offer graphic possibilities to help paint a picture of your progress.

Knowing that you'll want to impress people, Project also makes it possible to apply certain formatting settings to reports and add drawings to help get your point across.

Off the Rack: Standard Reports

Standard reports are already designed for you, offering a lot of choices regarding the information you can include. You don't have to do much more than click a few buttons to generate them. Essentially, you select a category of report, choose a specific report, and print it. If the plain-vanilla version of a report isn't quite right, you can modify standard reports in a variety of ways.

You can also print any view in Project; just display the view and click the Print tool button. The entire project is printed in whatever view you have on-screen at the time. Or you can choose File➪Print; in the Print dialog box that appears, you can choose to print only certain pages of your project or only a specific date range from the timescale. Any filters or grouping that you've applied will show in the printed document.

What's available

Project has five categories of standard reports: Overview, Current Activities, Costs, Assignments, and Workload. Each category contains several pre-designed reports (as you can see in the dialog box for Overview Reports, as shown in Figure 16-1), for a total of 22 standard reports.

Figure 16-1:
From the
Overview
category,
you can
choose one
of five
reports.

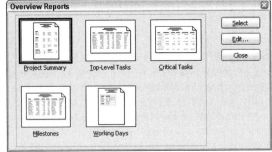

Standard reports vary in content, format (for example, a table versus a columnar report), and sometimes in page orientation (landscape or portrait). You can edit each report to change its name, the time period it covers, the table of information that it's based on, and filters applied to it. You can also sort information as you generate the report and add formatting, such as borders or gridlines.

Going with the standard

The standard report is simplicity itself. You could practically do this one in your sleep.

Or better yet, you could create a macro to generate your reports with a single-keystroke shortcut (more about macros in Chapter 17).

Follow these steps to generate any standard report:

1. **Choose Report⇨Reports.**

    The Reports dialog box appears, as shown in Figure 16-2. All five categories of reports, plus a custom report category, are accessible through the Reports dialog box.

Figure 16-2:
Choose a
report style
here.

2. **Click the category of standard report you want and then click Select.**

    A dialog box named after the category of report you selected appears (refer to Figure 16-1).

3. **Click one of the standard reports shown here and then click Select.**

    A preview of the report appears, like the one of Unstarted Tasks shown in Figure 16-3.

4. **To print, click the Print button.**

    You can also click Page Setup to change those settings, or use the Zoom, One Page, and Multiple Pages tool buttons to change how your report previews.

Clicking Close returns you to the Reports dialog box, which lists the category of reports. You have to start all over again if you do this.

When you click Print, an additional dialog box appears for some reports, asking for a date range or other data specific to that report.

A standard report, with a twist

Some people are happy with the cookie-cutter standard reports that Project provides; others like to add their own spin to their reports. That's okay because even though standard reports are prebuilt, you can still get under the hood and tinker a little.

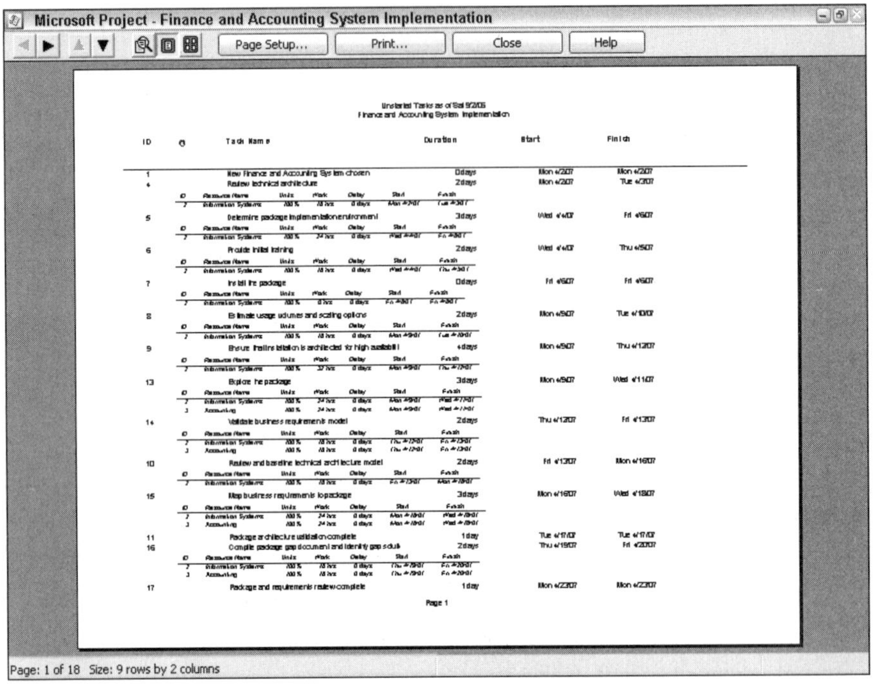

Figure 16-3:
You may have to click a report preview to zoom in so you can read its details.

You can edit three categories of modifications for a standard report:

- ✔ **Definition:** This includes the report name, the time period, the table of information, any filters applied, and whether summary tasks should appear.

- ✔ **Details:** Details can be included for tasks (such as notes or predecessors) and for resource assignments (such as notes or cost). You can also choose to show totals, and add a border around the report or gridlines between details.

- ✔ **Sort:** You can sort by up to three criteria in ascending or descending order.

When modifying standard reports, you'll encounter some variations. For example, when you try to edit a Project Summary report, all you get is a text formatting dialog box. However, the majority of reports are edited through one dialog box, as shown in the procedure that follows.

To edit a standard report, follow these steps:

1. **Choose Report⇨Reports.**

   The Reports dialog box appears.

2. **Click Custom and then click Select.**

3. **Click a specific report and then click Edit.**

   Depending on the type of report you chose, the Resource Report, Task Report, or Crosstab Report dialog box appears. The settings in these dialog boxes are the same except for some default choices (for example, which filter is applied). Figure 16-4 shows a Task Report dialog box.

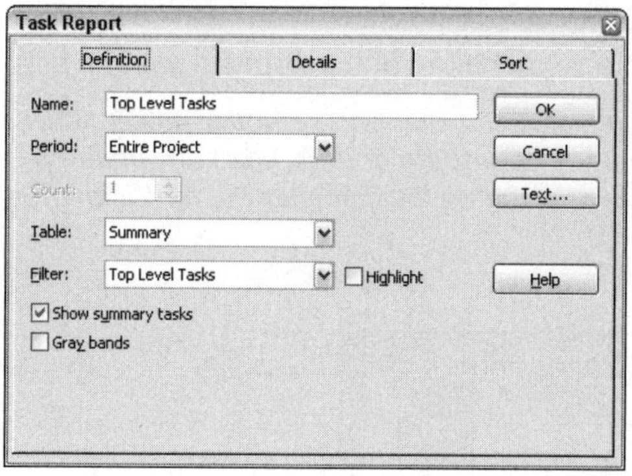

Figure 16-4:
You can
make three
tabs' worth
of settings.

4. **Click the Definition tab, if it's not already displayed, and make your selections:**

   a. *If you want a new name for the report, type the name in the Name field.*

   b. *In the Period box, choose the period of time you want the report to reflect.*

   If you choose an increment of time from the Period field, such as week (rather than choosing Entire Project), you can set the Count counter to reflect the number of increments. For example, you might set Count to **3** for three weeks, which provides a report on the project covering data in three-week increments.

   c. *If you'd like a different table of information to be included, make a choice from the Table field.*

   If you don't change this setting, the table currently displayed in the project is used.

   d. *If you want to apply a filter to tasks, choose one from the Filter field.*

   To highlight tasks that match the filter's criteria, rather than simply exclude those tasks that don't meet the criteria from the report, select the Highlight checkbox.

5. **Click the Details tab (as shown in Figure 16-5) and make your selections:**

    a. Select various check boxes to include different types of information, such as task notes or resource assignment costs.

    b. If you want a border around these elements, select the Border around Details checkbox.

    c. If you want gridlines in the report, select the Gridlines between Details checkbox.

    This gives your report more of the appearance of a table.

    d. To include totals of dollar amounts or hours, select Show Totals. If you use a currency other than dollars, you can set that by choosing Tools⇨Options and setting the currency on the View tab.

Figure 16-5:
Some of these options may be selected already, depending on the standard report you're editing.

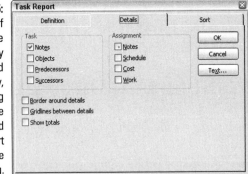

6. **Click the Sort tab and make your selections:**

    a. In the Sort By field, click a sort criterion, and then select either Ascending or Descending to choose a sort order.

    b. If you want to sort by additional criteria, repeat Step 6a with the Then By boxes.

7. **Click OK to save your settings.**

8. **In the Reports dialog box, click Select to generate the report preview.**

You can find more details about sorting in Chapter 15.

Crosstabs: A different animal

Crosstab reports present slightly different settings when you edit them. Figure 16-6 shows the Definition tab of the Crosstab Report dialog box. A *crosstab report* tabulates a unique piece of data relative to column and row definitions. Essentially, the cell formed by the column and row intersection represents the unique data.

Figure 16-6: Here you have to choose which three elements define the crosstab.

For example, you may have columns that list days and rows that list resources. The piece of information where the column and row intersects is resource work on a particular day. The report shows the hours of work by each resource day by day.

When you edit a crosstab, you define the column, the row, and the piece of data being compared. On the Details tab for the Crosstab Report dialog box, you can make settings such as whether to include row or column totals, to insert gridlines, and to display values of 0.

A Custom Job

Not impressed with the standard reports? Or perhaps none of those reports quite fits your information needs? That's okay. You can create as many custom reports as your heart desires.

A custom report starts out with a report type, which can be task, resource, monthly calendar, or crosstab. After you choose that basic category, you simply work with the same Reports dialog box that you use to edit a standard report.

Follow these steps to create a custom report:

1. **Choose Report⇨Reports.**

   The Reports dialog box appears.

2. **Click the Custom category and then click Select.**

   The Custom Reports dialog box appears, as shown in Figure 16-7. You have two options: edit an existing report or create an entirely new custom report.

Figure 16-7:
The Custom Reports dialog box lets you start with an existing set of data.

3. **Decide whether you want to base your custom report on an existing report or create a new report, and proceed accordingly.**

   a. *If you want to base your custom report on an existing report:* Choose a report in the Reports list and then click Edit.

   b. If you want to create a report, not based on any other report: *Click New. Click one of the categories in the dialog box that appears and then click OK.*

4. **In the Report dialog box, make choices to define your new report and then click OK.**

   The choices in this dialog box are discussed in detail earlier in the section, "A standard report, with a twist."

If you create a custom report based on an existing report, be sure to give it a unique name.

Get a New Perspective on Data with Visual Reports

If you just love the capabilities that PivotTable reports in Excel and Visio offer, you'll be glad to know that the same capability has come to Project 2007 in the form of Visual Reports. Pivot tables allow you to view data from a variety of perspectives beyond the Project standard report capabilities. Pivot tables offer perspectives that are especially useful for data analysis.

The Visual Reports feature allows you to select the fields you want to view and to modify your reports on the fly.

Getting an overview of what's available

Project offers six categories of Visual Reports as well as custom reports that you can build yourself. Some are based on *timephased data* (data distributed over time, such as allocations of resource time or costs), and some aren't. The report categories include

- ✔ **Task Usage:** Based on timephased data for tasks, this category of report gives you a peek at information such as cash flow and earned value over time.

- ✔ **Resource Usage:** Based on timephased resource data, these reports include cash flow, resource availability, resource costs, and resource work data.

- ✔ **Assignment Usage:** Also based on timephased data, this category of reports provides information in areas such as baseline versus actual costs and baseline versus actual work.

- ✔ **Task Summary, Resource Summary, and Assignment Summary:** These three categories of reports provide diagram views of a variety of work and cost data. These three categories are not based on timephased data.

Creating a Visual Report

Generating a Visual Report is simplicity itself; you simply choose a report, decide whether you want to generate it in Excel or Visio, and view or print the report.

You need to know a couple of things before you create a Visual Report. First, to access Visual Reports, you have to have installed .NET Framework 2.0 from Microsoft (a free download) before you installed Project. Second, if you have a version of Excel or Visio that's earlier than 2007, you have to add .NET Programmability support. Visit the Microsoft Project page at www.office. microsoft.com/project to get information about both products.

If you want to customize a Visual Report, you need some knowledge of pivot tables in Excel or Visio. Because covering pivot tables in those products is beyond the scope of this book, I heartily recommend *Excel 2007 For Dummies* (Greg Harvey) and *Visio 2007 For Dummies* (John Paul Mueller; both from Wiley).

Follow these steps to generate a standard Visual Report:

1. **Choose Report➪Visual Reports.**

   The Visual Reports dialog box appears (see Figure 16-8).

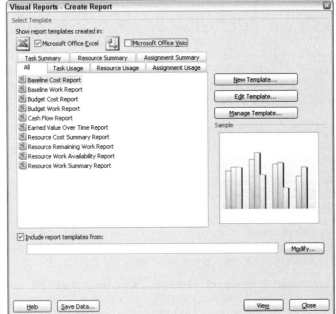

Figure 16-8:
The Visual Reports dialog box offers several categories of reports.

2. **Use the check boxes in the Show Report Templates Created In area to specify whether the report should be shown in Excel or Visio.**

3. **Click a report to select it.**

4. **Click the View button.**

   The report is generated in the selected application (see Figure 16-9).

You can modify the Visual Reports templates or create your own templates by using the New Template and Edit Template buttons in the Visual Reports dialog box. Editing a template allows you to add or remove fields from it; creating a new template involves specifying the format (Excel or Visio), choosing the data you want to report on, and selecting fields to include.

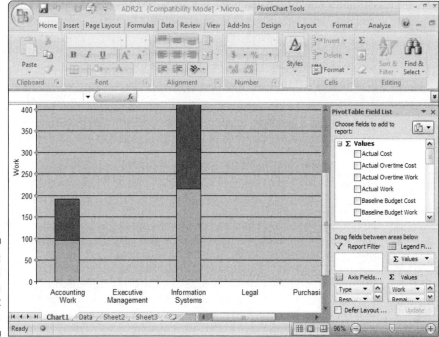

Figure 16-9:
A Visual
Report on
project
costs.

Spiffing Things Up

These days, image is everything. You and your project may be judged to some extent by how professional your printed information looks. Even if your project is a million dollars over budget and four months behind, making your reports or other printouts look good can make delivering bad news easier.

To create impressive documents, make sure you cross the *t*'s of formatting text and dot the *i*'s of visual design.

Using graphics in Project

Wouldn't your company logo look spiffy in the header of your report? Or what about including a picture of the new product box in Gantt Chart view of your New Product Launch project?

Graphics can add visual information or just plain make your plan look nicer. You can insert graphics in your project file by using three methods. You can

- ✔ **Cut and paste a graphic from another file.** A graphic you cut and paste essentially can't be edited by you in Project.

- ✔ **Insert a link to an existing graphics file.** Linking keeps your Project file smaller.

- ✔ **Embed a graphic.** Embedding lets you edit the graphic's contents in Project, using the tools of an image program such as Paint.

You can't add graphics willy-nilly, however. You can add graphics in only a few places: the chart pane of any Gantt Chart view; a task note; a resource note; or a header, footer, or legend used in reports or printouts of views.

For example, you may put pictures of resources in the resource note field so that you can remember who's who. Or you may include a photo of your corporate headquarters in the header of your report.

Remember, graphics swell the size of your Project file like a sponge in a pail of water. If you're thinking of using a lot of graphics, be sure they don't detract from the main information in your printouts. Or, try linking to them instead of inserting them in the file.

Follow these steps to insert a graphic in your Gantt chart, using object linking and embedding:

1. **Display Gantt Chart view.**

2. **Choose Insert➪Object.**

   The Insert Object dialog box appears, as shown in Figure 16-10.

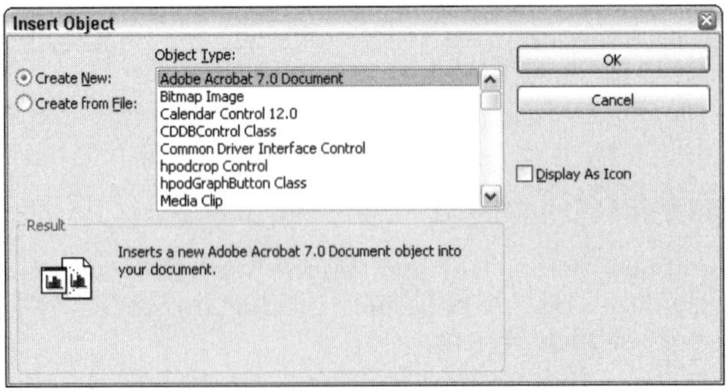

Figure 16-10: You can insert a wide variety of objects using this dialog box.

Insert Object	⊠
Object **Type:**	OK
⊙ Create **New:** Adobe Acrobat 7.0 Document	Cancel
○ Create from **File:** Bitmap Image	
Calendar Control 12.0	
CDDBControl Class	
Common Driver Interface Control	
hpodcrop Control	☐ **Display As Icon**
hpodGraphButton Class	
Media Clip	
Result	
Inserts a new Adobe Acrobat 7.0 Document object into your document.	

If you want to insert an existing graphics file, do the following:

1. **In the Insert Object dialog box, select Create from File.**

   The choices in the dialog box change to those shown in Figure 16-11.

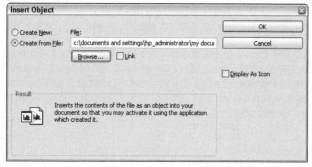

2. **Type the filename in the File field or click Browse to locate the file.**

3. **To link to the file, select the Link checkbox and then click OK.**

   If you don't select this option, the object is embedded in your file.

4. **To insert the object as an icon, select Display As Icon.**

   When you display the object as an icon, those viewing your project on a computer can click the icon to view the picture.

5. **Click OK.**

   The image appears in the Gantt Chart pane.

6. **Use the resizing nodes on the corners of the image to expand or shrink it, or click the image to move it around the pane.**

If you want to insert a blank graphics placeholder instead of inserting an existing graphics file, follow these steps:

1. **In the Insert Object dialog box, select Create New.**

2. **From the Object Type list, choose the type of object you want to insert.**

   For example, you might select Bitmap Image, Microsoft Word Picture, or Paintbrush Picture.

3. **If you want to insert the object as an icon, select Display as Icon.**

   When you display the object as an icon, those viewing your project on a computer can click the icon to view the picture.

4. Click OK.

You see a blank object box, along with tools, similar to the one in Paint shown in Figure 16-12.

5. Use the tools of the program from which you inserted an object to make, draw, insert, or format the new graphic object.

When you close this window, you go back to your Project file; double-click the object to open its editing environment any time you like.

To insert an object into a notes field, open the Task or Resource Information dialog box and then click the Insert Object tool. The Insert Object dialog box appears. Then just proceed as in the preceding steps. A similar tool is available in the Page Setup dialog box, where you can use the Header, Footer, or Legend tabs to insert objects.

Formatting reports

You probably cut your computing teeth by formatting text in word processors, so formatting reports will be a breeze. You have all the usual formatting options available to you whenever you generate a report in Project.

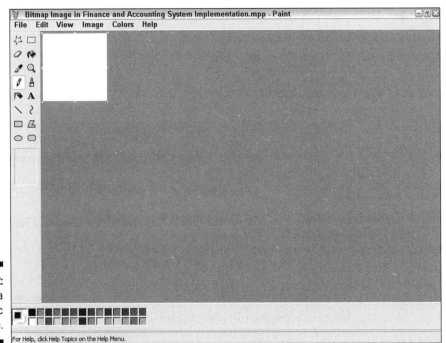

Figure 16-12:
Add a
graphic
here.

As with any other business document, your goal in formatting text should be readability. Remember, in addition to dealing with neat columns of data, you also may be dealing with labels of dates or resource names wedged alongside taskbars in the chart pane. Keep the following points in mind when formatting Project text:

- ✔ **Font:** Choose simple sans serif fonts, such as Arial.

  If you're publishing your project on the Web, consider using *Verdana,* which is a font created for readability online.

- ✔ **Color:** Will the printout be in color or black and white? Will the use of too many colors become confusing for the reader? Will certain colors, such as yellow, be difficult to read?

- ✔ **Font size:** Use a font size that is readable, without making it so big that the taskbar labels become too crowded.

- ✔ **Effects:** Avoid text effects that can make some text difficult to read (such as bold, italic, or underlining). Use such effects only to call attention to a few elements of your project.

To edit report text, just follow these steps:

1. **Choose Report⇨Reports.**

   The Reports dialog box appears.

2. **Click a report category and then click Select.**

3. **In the Reports category dialog box that appears, click the specific report that you want to generate.**

4. **Click Edit.**

   The specific report dialog box opens. With some reports, the Text Styles dialog box opens at this point because there are no other settings you can change in those reports. If this happens, skip Step 5 and proceed with Step 6.

5. **Click the Text button.**

   The Text Styles dialog box appears, as shown in Figure 16-13.

6. **In the Item to Change box, click the item that you want to format.**

7. **Make your selections in the Font, Font Style, Size, or Color fields.**

8. **If you want to format another item, select it in the Item to Change box and repeat Step 7.**

9. **When you're finished, click OK.**

10. **To view the report in preview, click Select.**

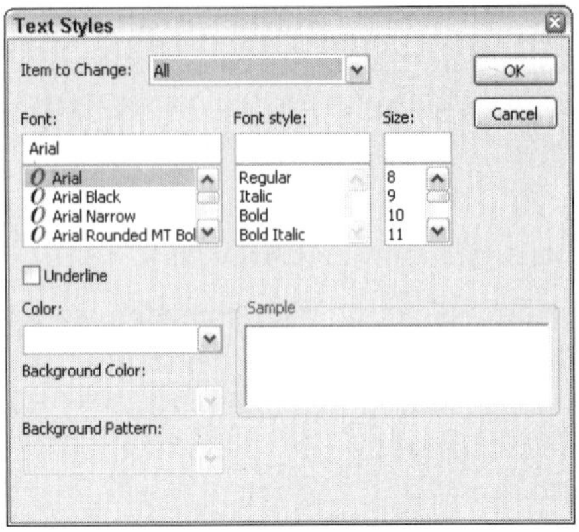

Figure 16-13:
This dialog
box
contains
many
familiar text
settings.

Call the Printer!

The proof of the report is in the printing, but you should see to several adjustments before you click that button to print. With Project, it's not just margins or page orientation that you need to set (although you do have to set those, too). You can also put useful information in headers and footers as well as set legends that help your reader understand the many bars, diamonds, and other graphic elements many Project views and reports display.

Working with Page Setup

The Page Setup dialog box can be used to control printouts of both reports and any currently displayed Project view. You can get to this dialog box in a few different ways:

✓ **To make settings for printing the current view:** Choose File⇨ Page Setup.

✓ **To modify the page setup for a report:** Select Page Setup from the preview of the report. Choose Report⇨Reports, click a report category, and then click a specific report. When you click Select to generate a specific report, the print preview appears. Click the Page Setup button that appears there.

The Page Setup dialog box, as shown in Figure 16-14, contains six tabs. In the case of reports, all tabs may not be available to you. For example, reports don't contain graphic elements such as taskbars, so you can't set a legend to appear on them. Also, you have access to the View tab only when you're printing the currently displayed view.

Figure 16-14:
You can control how your document is laid out and printed.

When size is important

The Page tab contains some basic page settings that determine the orientation, the paper size, and the way the contents are scaled to fit the page. By making these settings, you influence how much can fit on each page and how many pages long your document will be.

Here are the choices you have on this tab (shown in Figure 16-14):

- ✔ **Portrait or Landscape orientation:** No doubt you've dealt with these before. Portrait is set up like the Mona Lisa with the short edge of the paper running across the top of the page; Landscape is when the long edge of the paper runs across the top instead.

- ✔ **Scaling:** You can use the Adjust To or Fit To settings. The Adjust To setting is based on a percentage of the original size. The Fit To setting gives you some control over scaling to fit to the width of a single page or the height of a single page.

- ✔ **Other:** This area is a catchall for two options: Paper Size and First Page Number. All the standard choices for paper size are available in the Paper Size list, including index cards and envelopes. First Page Number can be left as Auto (in which case the first page is numbered 1, the second page, 2, and so on), or you can enter another number there yourself.

Keeping things within the margins

I won't bore you by defining what a margin is. However, I will remind you that margins serve the dual purpose of controlling how much information can fit on each page and also creating a border of white space that frames your document (making it cleaner looking and easier to read).

To set margins using the Page Setup dialog box, follow these steps:

1. **Click the Margins tab, which is shown in Figure 16-15.**

   As you modify margin settings, the preview shows you where they will appear on your page.

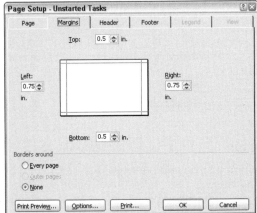

Figure 16-15: Set margin settings here.

2. **Use the arrows to set the Top, Bottom, Left, and Right margins.**

   Click the up arrow for a wider margin and the down arrow for a narrower margin.

3. **If you want a border representing the margin, use the Borders Around options.**

   Here you can choose to print a border on Every Page, on only Outer Pages (prints a border on the first and last pages only; available only when printing a Network Diagram view), or None.

Setting margins to be less than ½ inch (.5") could cause your printed output to be cut off because printers can only print so close to the edge of a page.

Putting all the right stuff in headers and footers

Throughout the life of a project, you'll print many versions of your project, many reports, and many types of information using various tables. Headers and footers are a great feature to help you and your readers keep track of all this information.

You can use the Header (as shown in Figure 16-16) and Footer tabs of the Page Setup dialog box to set and preview header (top) and footer (bottom) contents.

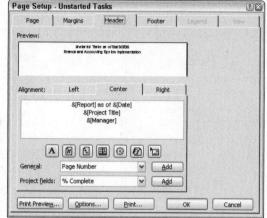

Figure 16-16:
The Header
and Footer
tabs are
identical.

You can also get to this area of the Page Setup dialog box by choosing View➪ Header and Footer.

Here are the settings you can make on these tabs:

✔ **Text location:** Specify that the text you enter is to appear on the Left, at Center, or to the Right of the header or footer by clicking the corresponding tab and then typing the text.

✔ **Format text:** Use the tool buttons; or, quickly insert such things as the page number, the date, or a picture file.

✔ **Select standard text:** Insert additional text by using the General and Project Fields lists. The General list includes such things as Total Page Count, Project Title, and Company Name. The Project Fields list includes all the fields available in Project. You might use these to alert the reader to key fields to review or the nature of the printout. To add General or Project Field items, select them from their respective lists and then click Add to add them to the Left, Center, or Right tab.

Working with a legend

A *legend* acts as a guide to the meanings of various graphic elements, as shown in Figure 16-17. The Legend tab bears a striking resemblance to the Header and Footer tabs except that the legend is generated automatically, so all you can specify here is the text that fits in the box to the left of the legend.

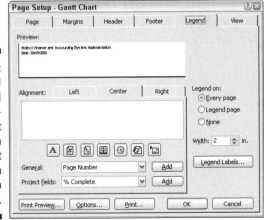

Figure 16-17:
The legend
is printed
automat-
ically, but
you can
insert
information
in the box to
the left of it.

The Legend tab of the Page Setup dialog box has only two settings that differ from the Header and Footer tabs:

✔ You can print the legend on every page or on a separate legend page; or, you can decide to not print a legend.

✔ You can establish the width of the text area of the legend (the area where you can insert elements such as the page number or the date).

Unlike a header or footer, where you have to enter something to have any-thing appear, a legend prints by default. If you don't want a legend to print, choose this tab and then set the Legend On setting to None.

What to print?

If you're printing a currently displayed view, the View tab of the Page Setup dialog box is available to you, as shown in Figure 16-18.

You can make the following settings here:

✔ **Print All Sheet Columns:** Prints every sheet column in the view, regard-less of whether it's currently visible on-screen. With this option not selected, only the columns that show in your view will print.

✔ **Print First # Columns on All Pages:** Allows you to control a specific number of columns to print.

✔ **Print Notes:** Prints every task, resource, and assignment note. These items are printed on a separate notes page.

✔ **Print Blank Pages:** Choose this setting if you want to print blank pages: for example, use this setting to print a page that represents a time in your project when no tasks are occurring. If you want a smaller number of pages in your printout, don't choose this setting.

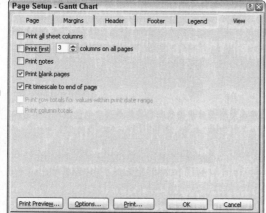

Figure 16-18:
This tab
is not
available if
you're
printing a
report.

✔ **Fit Timescale to End of Page:** Scales the timescale to allow you to fit more of your project on the page.

✔ **Print Row Totals for Values within Print Date Range:** Adds a column containing row totals. Pertains to printouts of Usage views.

✔ **Print Column Totals:** Adds a column containing column totals. Pertains to printouts of Usage views.

Get a preview

Granted, although software print previews aren't quite as exciting as movie previews, they help you get everything right before you print your project. The Print Preview feature is accessible from many places in Project:

✔ Choose File➪Print Preview (to preview the current view).

✔ Click the Print Preview button on the Standard toolbar.

✔ Click Print Preview on any tab of the Page Setup dialog box.

✔ Generate a print preview when you select a specific report to print.

You can use the tool buttons in this view to do the following:

✔ Move around the pages of the report by using the Page Left, Right, Up, and Down arrows on the toolbar, as well as the horizontal and vertical scroll bars.

✔ View more detail by clicking the Zoom tool button and then clicking the report.

✔ Focus on a single page or all the pages of your report by using the One Page and Multiple Pages tool buttons.

✔ Modify margins and the orientation of the printout by displaying the Page Setup dialog box.

✔ Display the Print dialog box by clicking Print.

✔ Close the preview by clicking Close.

So Let's Print!

Last but not least, here's how to actually print that document for which you've made all the wonderful settings discussed in this chapter. For this, you need to deal with the Print dialog box, which you've seen a million times in almost any other Windows program on the planet. (See Figure 16-19 for a quick refresher.)

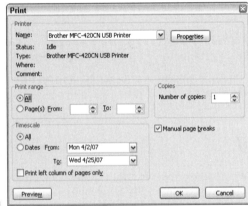

Figure 16-19: Control the printer, the number of copies, and what prints.

Here are the settings you encounter in this dialog box:

✔ The first area of this dialog box concerns the printer you will use. You can choose a printer in the Name list, and click the Properties button to control printer settings such as color quality and paper source.

✔ The Print Range area allows you to print All pages or to select a page range From one page number To another.

✔ The Copies area contains one simple setting: Click the up arrow here to print more copies or the down arrow to print fewer (but no less than 1).

✔ The Timescale settings are unique to Project's Print dialog box: Here you can choose to print the entire timescale (the entire length of your project) or only a range of dates within your project. Along with Print Range, this setting helps control how much of your Project will print.

✔ If you want the leftmost column of the page to print on every page, select Print Left Column of Pages Only. For example, you may want the task ID number column to print on both pages when a printout width stretches over two pages.

✔ Finally, if you've inserted manual page breaks in your project, you can select the Manual Page Breaks check box to include these breaks in your printed report. Leave this deselected if you want the Print feature to control where pages break.

After you make all your settings and you're ready to print, just click OK.

Chapter 17

Getting Better All the Time

*H*ave you ever finished a project and then wondered how the heck everything ended up the way it did? The total budget numbers mystically appear to be several thousand dollars over estimate; you missed your final deadline by three weeks; and somewhere along the line, you lost track of three people who were supposed to be working on tasks. But you delivered your deliverables (somehow), and you can finally stuff your project file in the bottom of your drawer. Or can you?

Don't think of Microsoft Project as just a giant electronic to-do list; rather, it's a sophisticated tool to manage your projects. And the logical by-product of that management is a fantastic treasure trove of information that you can use to become a better Project user — and thus a better project manager.

After you send out the last memo on your project and accept your last kudos or criticism from your boss, take a moment to look over your Project plan one more time.

Learning from Your Mistakes

When I teach classes in using project management software, people are often a bit overwhelmed at all that a product such as Project can do. They're reeling from all the data that they have to input as well as all the information that Project throws back at them. They can't see straight for all the views, reports, tables, and filters that they can use to access information on their projects.

Here's the secret that I tell them: You won't understand every nuance of your Project plan on your first project. You won't even uncover all that Project can do on your second project. But gradually, as you master the ins and outs of Project and understand what you can get out of it, you'll become better at absorbing all that information — and at understanding how it can help you avoid mistakes on your future projects.

The best way to gain that benefit is to review every project when it's finished to see what you did right and what you did wrong. Then you can use what you discover to do better on your next project.

It was only an estimate

You know what they say: If you don't study history, you're doomed to repeat it. And repeating mistakes is the last thing you want to do where project management is concerned.

Consider these strategies to debrief yourself on what happened in your last project:

- **Compare your original baseline plan against the final actual activity (as shown in Figure 17-1).** Even if you created interim or baseline plans to adjust for drastic changes, look at the widest gap between what you expected to happen in your initial plan and what did happen. This can be the best way to see the areas where you tend to underestimate most.

- **Review the notes you made on your tasks to remind yourself of changes or problems that came up along the way.** Insert the column named Notes on your Gantt Chart sheet and read through all the notes at one sitting.

- **Note which resources delivered on their promises and which didn't; if you manage some of them, provide them with constructive feedback.** For those you don't manage, keep some notes on hand about how well or how fast they worked and make future assignments with those notes in mind. Also note which outside vendors performed and which didn't (and consider crossing the latter off your vendor list).

- **Assess your own communications to others in saved e-mails or memos.** Did you give your team enough information to perform effectively? Did you keep management informed about changes or problems in a timely way?

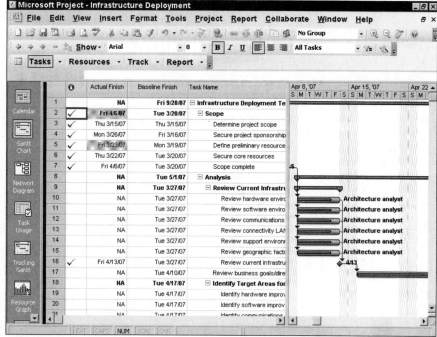

Figure 17-1:
Baseline
and actual
figures,
displayed
side by side,
paint an
interesting
picture of
your
planning
strengths
and weak-
nesses.

Debrief your team

No project is the province of a single person. Even if no one else ever touched your Project plan, your team still provided input for that plan through the hours of activity they reported and the information they provided to you during the course of your project.

Consider these suggestions for refining your communications process:

✔ **Ask people how the process of reporting actual activity worked.** Did you use e-mail, schedule notes, route files, or use the Project Web Access tools such as Timesheet to gather resource information? Should you consider taking advantage of all the benefits of online collaboration for your next project?

✔ **Would your team rate your communications as frequent and thorough enough?** Did you share enough of your project with resources, or did you inundate them with too much information? Did you send an entire Project file to people regularly when a simple report on a specific aspect of the project would have served you and them better? Did your management team feel that your reporting on the project was sufficient for their needs? Should you learn to take more advantage of other software, such as Excel and Visio, accessed through Visual Reports?

Debrief yourself?

Don't forget to sit down and have a good talk with yourself about what went on during your project. Did your team give you the kind of information you needed to operate efficiently, or should you lay down more stringent ground rules for reporting in the next project? Were you swamped with work throughout the project, and would it be wise to find someone to make updating entries for you the next time around? Did management give you information about company changes in a timely way so that you could make adjustments to keep your project on schedule?

It's often the case that in the heat of the project battle, many of us don't have time to stop and change processes or get the help we need. Review the notes you kept in the Project notes areas to see what types of snafus made you pull your hair out. Then institute changes before you begin the next project.

✔ **Did you integrate activity on various projects successfully so that resources weren't overbooked or underutilized?** If people on your team reported conflicts with other projects, consider using some special Project tools, such as hyperlinking to tasks in other project plans, creating a deliverable-based plan, or developing a master project (which involves inserting several projects into a master plan so you can view resource conflicts across them).

Building on Your Success

Although it's human nature to focus on all the things that went wrong with a project, the fact is that you probably did many, many things right. So before you start planning your next project, take the good stuff and put it in a place where you can find it easily later.

Create a template

One option is to create a template. *Templates* are simply files you save that contain certain settings. When you open a template, you can save it as a Project document with a new name and have all those settings already built in.

Project contains its own templates for common projects (see Chapter 1 for more about starting projects based on a template), but you can save any of your projects as templates. If you often use the same set of tasks in your projects — as people in many industries do — you'll save yourself the time of creating all those tasks again.

If you work with Project Server and Project Web Access on an enterprise level, consider adding templates on a global level for use across your company. See Chapters 18 and 19 for more about enterprise-level project management.

In addition to any tasks in the project, templates can contain any or all of the following information for those tasks:

- ✔ All the information for each baseline
- ✔ Actual values
- ✔ Rates for all resources
- ✔ Fixed costs
- ✔ Notations of tasks that you publish to Microsoft Project Web Access

You can save all this information or only selected items. For example, if you created a lot of fixed costs (such as equipment) and resources with associated rates — and you'll use those in most of your projects — you could save a template with only fixed costs and resource rates.

To save a file as a template, follow these steps:

1. **Open the file you want to save and then choose File➪Save As.**

   The Save As dialog box appears, as shown in Figure 17-2.

   Microsoft saves templates in a central folder called *Templates*.

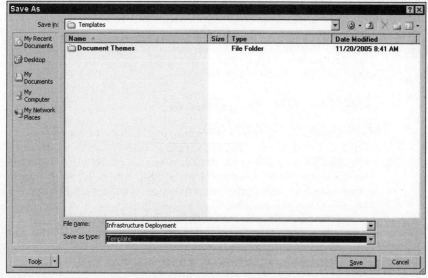

Figure 17-2:
Save a file
as a
template.

2. **In the Save As Type list, click Template.**

   Project selects the Templates folder as the Save In location.

3. **Click Save.**

   The Save As Template dialog box appears, as shown in Figure 17-3.

   Choose which information about values and resource rates will be saved with all the tasks in the project in the template.

Figure 17-3:
Save values and resource rates with the tasks in the project in a template.

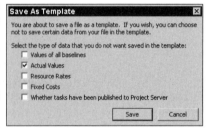

4. **Select the check boxes for the information that you want saved in the template.**

5. **Click Save.**

   The file is saved in the template format with the MPT extension.

When you open a new project and want to use a saved template, click On Computer in the New Project task pane. The Templates dialog box appears, and any templates you've saved will appear in the list on the General tab. Just open the template, and then save it as a Project file with a new name.

Master the Organizer

Project has this marvelously flexible nature that allows you to customize a lot of things. For example, you can create your own tables of data to display in views that contain sheet panes. You also can create your own filters, reports, and calendars. If you have any kind of a life, you don't want to spend your evenings re-creating all that stuff for your next project. Instead, use the Organizer to copy them to other Project files.

The Organizer allows you to take information in one file and copy it to another file. You can also rename the items. Some of the most commonly used types of items you can copy with Organizer include

✔ Calendars

✔ Forms

✔ Tables

✔ Reports

✔ Views

✔ Fields

✔ Groups

✔ Toolbars

✔ Filters

Follow these steps to use the Organizer:

1. **Open the project that you want to copy things from and the project that you want to copy things to.**

2. **In the file you want to copy to, choose Tools➪Organizer.**

   The Organizer dialog box appears, as shown in Figure 17-4.

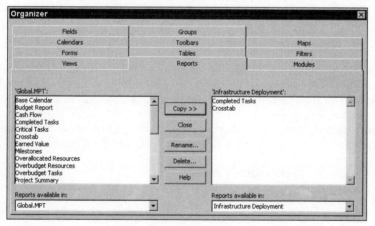

Figure 17-4:
You have eleven sheets' worth of stuff you can copy here!

3. **Click the tab for the type of information you want to copy.**

4. **If necessary, choose other files to copy to or from.**

   By default, Project uses the Global template as the file to copy from; the file from which you open the Organizer becomes the file to copy to. To use other files, select another file from the [Item] Available In box on the left (copy from) or right (copy to) of the dialog box. (Depending on the tab you display, this item might be Views Groups, Reports, and so on.) These boxes contain the Global.mpt file and any other files you have open.

5. **Click an item in the list on the left that you want to include in the file on the right and then click the Copy button.**

   The item appears in the list on the right.

6. **(Optional) To rename an item**

   a. Click it and then click the Rename button.

   b. In the Rename dialog box that appears, enter a new name and then click OK.

7. **To copy additional items on the same tab, repeat Step 5.**

8. **To copy an item on a different tab, repeat Steps 3–7.**

9. **When you finish copying items from one file to another, click the X in the upper-right corner.**

   All the items are copied, and the Organizer dialog box closes.

Handy little timesavers: Macros

If you were paying attention, you noticed a lot of activities in your project that you did again, and again, and again. No, I'm not talking about all those cups of coffee you downed in the wee hours. I'm talking about things such as generating a weekly report, or inserting your five department projects into a single master schedule, once every quarter, to review resource allocations.

You don't have to reinvent the wheel to perform actions such as these. Instead, you can create a *macro* — a combination of keystrokes, text entries, and so on that you can record and play back any time you like.

For example, suppose you generate and print a report on current activities every week. Doing so requires the following keystrokes and entries:

1. **Choose Report⇨Basic Reports.**

2. **Click Current Activities.**

3. **Click Select.**

4. **Click Tasks Starting Soon.**

5. **Click Select.**

6. **Type a unique date for tasks that start or finish after a point in time.**

7. **Click OK.**

8. **Type a unique date for tasks that start or finish before a point in time to complete the specified range.**

9. **Click OK.**

10. **Click Print to print the report.**

If you record all those keystrokes, you have to go through a ten-step process. But, after they're recorded, that process is reduced to three steps when you play back the macro.

1. **Start your macro.**

2. **Enter the first part of the date range.**

3. **Enter the last part of the date range.**

 One great use I've seen for macros is to copy a range of tasks that is repeated again and again in your project — for example, a Q&A procedure that's repeated ten times throughout a project. In recording the macro, just select the absolute range and copy it, go to the first blank task and paste it, ten times. While the macro's running, you can go get yourself another cup of coffee.

Recording a macro

Recording a macro is a simple process: You just start recording, do whatever you usually do to perform the action, and then stop recording. You run macros by selecting them from a list of macros or by using a keystroke short-cut. You also can edit them if you need a slightly different series of keystrokes for a slightly altered sequence of steps.

Here's how you record a macro:

1. **Choose Tools⇨Macro⇨Record New Macro.**

   The Record Macro dialog box appears, as shown in Figure 17-5. Macros that you record can be played back by using a shortcut key that you designate here.

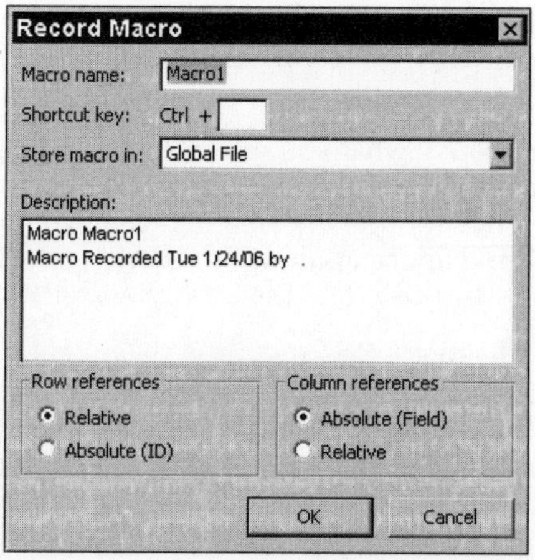

Figure 17-5:
Designate a
shortcut
key here.

Record Macro dialog box:

Macro name: Macro1
Shortcut key: Ctrl +
Store macro in: Global File

Description:
Macro Macro1
Macro Recorded Tue 1/24/06 by .

Row references
- Relative
- Absolute (ID)

Column references
- Absolute (Field)
- Relative

OK   Cancel

2. **In the Macro Name box, type a name.**

   Make the name descriptive of what the macro does.

3. **In the Shortcut Key box, type a letter (numbers or symbols won't work).**

   When you press Ctrl plus that key, the macro plays back.

4. **If you like, edit or add to the description of the macro.**

   This is especially useful if you think others will use it.

5. **Select whether row and column references will be relative or absolute.**

   - *Relative references:* If you select (say) the task in the third row displayed in a sheet and perform an action on it, Project selects the task in the third row whenever you run the macro.

   - *Absolute references:* Project selects a specific, named task, no matter what row it occupies.

6. **Click OK to begin recording.**

   Every keystroke you make during this time becomes part of the macro.

7. **After you complete your keystrokes, choose Tools⇨Macro⇨ Stop Recorder.**

Here are some points to keep in mind about recording macros:

- ✔ **Naming:** Macro names have to start with a letter and can't contain spaces. Use the underscore to separate words in a macro name (Weekly_Report, for example).

- ✔ **Keystroke presets:** Several keystroke shortcuts are already reserved by Project for use with built-in functions. For example, pressing Ctrl+K inserts a hyperlink. Project displays a message telling you this if you choose such a shortcut and then gives you an opportunity to choose another letter or number.

- ✔ **Entering unique information:** If what you record includes entering specific information (such as a name or a date range), you're presented with a blank box into which you enter new information when you run the macro — even if you entered information while recording the macro.

Running and editing macros

To run a macro, your best bet is to use the shortcut key that you entered when you created it. (See the preceding section.) This two-keystroke combination runs the macro, pausing for you to fill in any requested information.

Alternatively, you can do the following:

1. **Choose Tools⇨Macro⇨Macros.**

2. **Choose a macro in the list of macros shown in the Macros dialog box, as shown in Figure 17-6.**

3. **Click Run.**

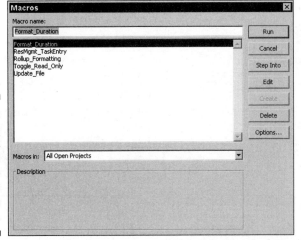

Figure 17-6:
The Macros
dialog box
lists all
available
macros in
any open
projects.

To edit a macro, you might want to simply re-record it, which is sometimes the quickest way to do it. If you prefer to edit it instead, do the following:

1. **Choose Tools⇨Macro⇨Macros.**

2. **In the Macros dialog box that appears, choose the macro that you want to modify and then click Edit.**

    The Microsoft Visual Basic editor opens; your macro is displayed in Visual Basic code, as shown in Figure 17-7. Visual Basic code uses certain syntax to code keystrokes and text entry.

    • *To edit the code:*

       You can edit this code much as you edit text in a word processor-generated document. Although you have to be familiar with the Visual Basic programming language to make most changes, you can make some edits without being a programmer. For example, any items in quotes are text entries or names of things, such as reports. For example, it's pretty easy to change a macro that generates the report named `"Tasks Starting Soon"` so that it generates the report `"Tasks in Progress"`. Just replace the existing report name (within the quotation marks) with the new report name.

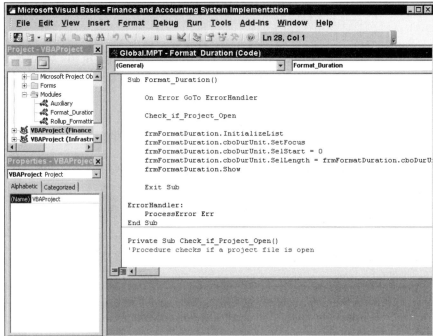

Figure 17-7:
Edit your
macro here.

• *To delete something within the code:*

> If you want to delete a piece of the process, you can usually figure that out from the code. For example, if you see the line `If project is empty, alert the user and end the macro` and you don't want the macro to include that step, just select it and then press Delete.

Monkeying around with Visual Basic for anything much more complex could mess up your macro. Because I don't want to write another book on Visual Basic at this point, I suggest that you keep your life and mine simple: Delete the first macro and walk through the procedure again, re-recording it as a new macro.

Customizing Project Guide

Project Guide provides a great way to walk yourself or other users through the logical steps of setting up a Project file. However, your organization might require additional or different steps for your specific projects. For example, you might want to set up some internal accounting codes in all your projects. You can customize Project Guide to give yourself and others in your organization a great tool for building enterprise projects in a consistent way.

By creating an XML format file, you can customize Project Guide content for your organization. Essentially, you build a series of XML pages that you direct Project to use for Guide content. I won't give you a primer in creating XML files, but I will tell you the procedure for directing Project to use your custom content.

To specify custom Project Guide content, do the following:

1. **Choose Tools⇨Options.**

   The Options dialog box appears.

2. **Click the Interface tab to display it, as shown in Figure 17-8.**

3. **In the Project Guide Content section of the dialog box, select the Use Custom Content radio button.**

4. **Enter the location of your XML file in the XML File for Custom Content field.**

   You can also click the Browse button there to locate the file, find it in the Browse dialog box that opens, and then click OK.

5. **Click OK.**

   The new Project Guide content is displayed in the Project Guide area and toolbar.

Part V
Working with Enterprise Projects

The 5th Wave   By Rich Tennant

"It's a solid ID management and tracking system, Ted. Over 15 years on the Kalahari and we never lost a single lion."

In this part . . .

Here's where Project Professional comes into its own: Serving the enterprise via Project Server and Project Web Access, you can get some serious online collaboration going. You can share documents online with your team, get perspective on your organization's resource pool to make efficient assignments, and get your human resources to report their work time. This part gives you a glimpse of what Project Server and Project Web Access can do if your organization decides to go the enterprise route with Project.

Chapter 18

Project Web Access for the Project Manager

*I*f you think that Project Server is like an add-on *applet* (a tiny application) that works with Project, you're wrong. It's actually a full-fledged software product that enables you to take your project — and all its accompanying resources, tracking, and reporting — into the world of the Internet.

Project Server comprises two main components: the Project Server database where project data is stored; and Project Web Access, the browser-like interface that connects you and others to that database.

Note: To make life simple, I mostly simply refer to Project Web Access going forward because that's the interface and set of tools you'll be working with. However, Project Web Access is useless without Project Server: Before you can actually perform the steps in this chapter and use Project Web Access, somebody must install Project Server on your company network and configure it for your company's standards and requirements. This usually requires that IT-type people stay up nights installing and configuring software and that another team of people design the implementation. After all that is accomplished, you can actually perform the steps listed here and not just read about them.

With Project Web Access (which works only with the Professional edition of Microsoft Project), you can enhance communications, interactions, and documentation for each and every project you undertake. This chapter looks at who should use Project Web Access as well as how it can help any project manager.

Figuring Out Whether Project Web Access Is for You

Just as you don't need a Hummer to run to the corner grocery store for milk once a week, Project Web Access can be too high-powered a solution for some organizations. Implementing Project Server and Project Web Access involves not only money for product licenses but also requires some other specific commitments:

- ✔ Time to install and configure it
- ✔ Effort to standardize how Project is used across your organization
- ✔ Time and money to train people to use the tools
- ✔ Ongoing maintenance of the Project Server database

Therefore, before you jump in with both feet to the Project Web Access world, you should be sure that the benefits of using it outweigh the effort required.

Project Web Access is useful to organizations that have an *enterprise orientation,* which means they make the effort to centralize information online in some fashion so it's standardized and available throughout the company.

Typically, this scenario is worthwhile for mid- to large-sized companies that manage several projects at once across departments or disciplines. The features accessed through Project Web Access provide the managers of these companies with a way to orchestrate resources more efficiently and also get a broad perspective on the efficiency and success of their project management efforts across the organization.

Another plus to using Project Web Access is that it can make all project information for the company available online through a company intranet that can be accessed from anywhere in the world.

The benefits of using a Project Web Access solution include

- ✔ Standard formats, reports, and resource information that can be accessed and shared by all project managers for consistency among multiple projects

✔ The ability to see, on an enterprise-wide level, how resources are being allocated (as in Figure 18-1, where you can assign resources with an eye to the big picture)

✔ A perspective on all the projects in the company, which can help management prioritize and strategize overall enterprise efforts

✔ A greater capability to collaborate among projects

✔ More efficient methods for resources to track their time on project tasks without anybody having to reenter the information in Project

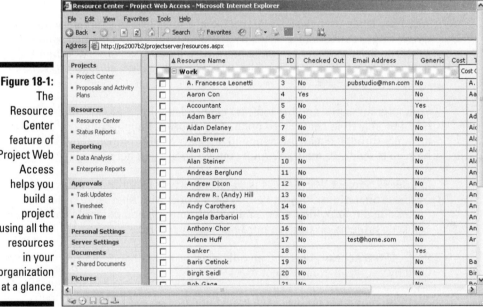

Figure 18-1: The Resource Center feature of Project Web Access helps you build a project using all the resources in your organization at a glance.

If you have a company LAN or intranet, you can set up Project Server and Project Web Access to deliver all these benefits and more.

Not every member of your team has to have Project installed to interact with it as long as he has access to your LAN or intranet, access to Project Web Access, and appropriate network permissions.

The downsides to Project Server with Project Web Access include

✔ The cost for licenses

✔ The time to install and maintain the server as well as to train users

✔ The need to ensure that projects are handled in a uniform way across your enterprise (If you don't do this, the information you receive through Project Server may be inaccurate and out of date.)

If your most tech-savvy person whom you will call on to install and configure Project Server needs some help, I recommend you take a look at *Microsoft Project 2007 Bible* (Wiley). Author Elaine Marmel does a stellar job of walking you through Project Server issues (which I say not because she's a friend, or a fellow Wiley author, but because she's just plain good!).

Getting a Handle on What You Can Do with Project Web Access

Way back when there was no Internet, companies had to share information by passing around memos. The guy in Manufacturing had no idea what the people in Sales were up to until a handwritten purchase order was hand-delivered to his desk and he realized that he didn't have enough products on hand to fill the order.

Computer networks and the Internet changed all that. Suddenly information could be shared in centralized online repositories. People could communicate instantly through e-mail. An action in one part of the company could instantly be seen in another, and that group could respond and act accordingly.

In a sense, Project Web Access is to Project what the Internet is to standard business operations. Project Web Access works with Microsoft Project Professional to provide the centralized information and communications that can keep projects on track in our I-need-it-now world.

Project Web Access gives you an online project Command Central that can be used by people in your project to

- ✔ **Communicate online,** exchanging updates on progress and sending suggested new tasks to project managers.
- ✔ **Make, view, and accept or decline task assignments** from a standardized resource pool.
- ✔ **Update activity on tasks** by using a timesheet interface (as shown in Figure 18-2).
- ✔ **Send and request status reports and review project information.**
- ✔ **Manage project documents,** creating and comparing multiple versions of projects and setting up document libraries.
- ✔ **Attach important documents to a project.** For example, you might include a goal statement or Excel budget file with your project for others to view online.
- ✔ **Use analysis tools** to model what-if scenarios and determine risks and progress on projects.

✔ **Create and refine proposals**. This is a new feature in Project 2007 that allows you to begin to build your project ideas before you're ready to commit the time to building a full-blown project plan.

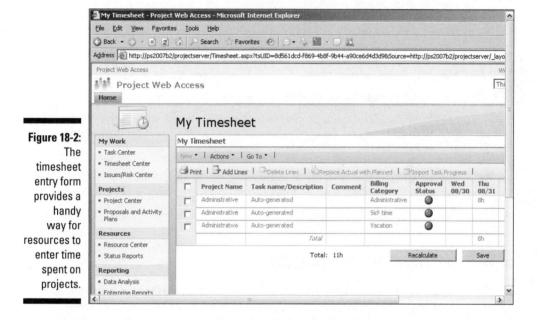

Figure 18-2:
The
timesheet
entry form
provides a
handy
way for
resources to
enter time
spent on
projects.

Planning to Use Project Server and Project Web Access

Before your administrator begins installing Project Server, you have to sit down and do some thinking about how you'll use it in your organization. During the installation process, you have to make some design choices based on how you want to use the product.

Tools built into the Project Collaborate menu become available to you when Project Server is installed, so you can perform much of your work with Project Web Access right from your copy of Microsoft Project.

Get a team together

First figure out who at your organization should be part of this process. For example, you'll probably need senior management input, *end user* (the people on your project teams) input, the experience and expertise of all the project managers in your company who use the enterprise features, and somebody (or three or four somebodies) from your IT department who actually have to set the thing up.

As with most network-oriented computing, everybody has a role to play and has to be set up to use features on the network based on that role. Project Server provides a user model with three types of participants, providing various information and access requirements accordingly:

- ✔ **Managers,** who oversee the day-to-day operations of a project
- ✔ **Team members,** who perform the work on the project
- ✔ **Shareholders,** such as clients and senior management, who require regular updating on project progress, often across several projects in an organization

You should analyze how these roles relate to the functions in your project teams and work with your IT folks to set up Project Server permissions accordingly.

Gather information

Next, set up a process to research and come to an agreement on all the enterprise-wide information you need to enter into Project Server, such as resources, their rates, their calendars of availability; WBS (work breakdown structure) code structure; standard report formats; custom fields you'd like to include in the Project Server Enterprise Global Template (kind of like the Global Template in Project 2007, but available online); and filters, views, tables, and so on.

The key word in this planning process is *standardization*. By standardizing the information in your projects and making that information available online, you increase efficiency in building projects and provide mechanisms for comparing projects in an apples-to-apples way.

Standardize processes

Pay special attention to the reporting process that different people use on their projects. Standardizing reporting processes and formats ensures that those who read reports about multiple projects can easily and quickly understand what they're looking at. Also, determine how project performance will be assessed. For example, the way in which earned value is used in creating tasks produces different measures of progress on projects.

Don't forget the training!

Project Web Access requires that different people in your organization learn new tricks. Your IT people need time to get up to speed on setting up and maintaining the Project Server database. Project managers have to learn to use the timesheet reports to track projects.

Team members require some training on the status report and timesheet features in Project Web Access. Build in time and money to your implementation process to make effective training happen.

You can bone up on reporting by going to Chapter 16.

Coordinate with IT

Finally, work with your IT people to identify the Project Server features that you want to use in your organization. For example, if maintaining an online discussion is important to your company, you may want to create discussion boards on your Project Web Access site.

Planning for problems

One final word about implementing Project Server and Project Web Access at your organization: Because you will now be sharing resources and information with others on a daily basis, put a little thought into how you'll deal with problems when they come up. For example, what happens if you want to use a resource but another project manager already has that resource assigned to a project? Or how do various project managers make use of tools, such as resource leveling, to resolve resource conflicts?

Make sure that everybody understands the rules of etiquette involved in working in an enterprise-wide fashion, sharing people, equipment, and information.

Looking Over the Project Web Access Tools

So what goodies become available to you after your organization has been through the somewhat daunting task of getting everything set up? It's time for a closer look at how you'll use specific Project Web Access features in your projects.

Chapter 19 goes into more detail about how end users use various Project Web Access features.

Make assignments and delegate tasks

Because the main focus of Project Web Access is to help you interact with your team members, one of its most useful features is the capability to post resource assignments and delegate work on tasks.

When you make assignments to projects, you can do so by using this resource pool. This central repository of resources ensures consistency of resource calendars, rates, and so on across your company's projects. Assigning resources from this pool (as shown in Figure 18-3) to your project tasks also lets you see where resources are overbooked on multiple projects.

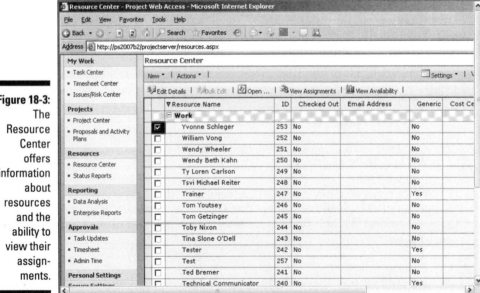

Figure 18-3: The Resource Center offers information about resources and the ability to view their assignments.

From the Resource Center, you can also view resource assignments and availability to help you plan your resource strategy. Figure 18-4 shows the current assignments for one resource — a very busy guy!

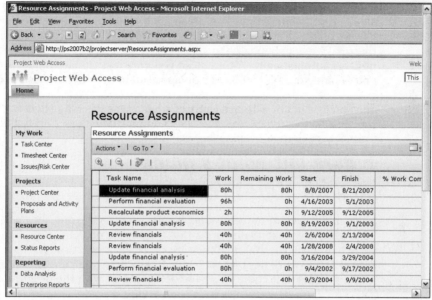

Resource Assignments - Project Web Access - Microsoft Internet Explorer

File   Edit   View   Favorites   Tools   Help

Back ▾   ▾ ▾ Search Favorites

Address http://ps2007b2/projectserver/ResourceAssignments.aspx

Project Web Access   Welc

Project Web Access   This

Home

Figure 18-4:
Viewing
resource
data in a
central
location
helps any
busy project
manager.

Resource Assignments

My Work	Resource Assignments

Actions ▾ | Go To ▾ |

Task Name	Work	Remaining Work	Start	Finish	% Work Com
Update financial analysis	80h	80h	8/8/2007	8/21/2007	
Perform financial evaluation	96h	0h	4/16/2003	5/1/2003	
Recalculate product economics	2h	2h	9/12/2005	9/12/2005	
Update financial analysis	80h	80h	8/19/2003	9/1/2003	
Review financials	40h	40h	2/6/2004	2/13/2004	
Review financials	40h	40h	1/28/2008	2/4/2008	
Update financial analysis	80h	80h	3/16/2004	3/29/2004	
Perform financial evaluation	80h	0h	9/4/2002	9/17/2002	
Review financials	40h	40h	9/3/2004	9/9/2004	

My Work
- Task Center
- Timesheet Center
- Issues/Risk Center

Projects
- Project Center
- Proposals and Activity Plans

Resources
- Resource Center
- Status Reports

Reporting
- Data Analysis
- Enterprise Reports

After you make assignments, the folks on your team can access timesheets for their specific assignments and can get e-mail notification of those assignments. Team members can delegate assignments to others on the team. Then, the team member can review and approve status reports on work performed on the task before sending those reports on to the project manager.

Of course, you don't want everyone on a project to be able to pass the buck when it comes to assignments: The project manager has control over who can — and can't — delegate tasks in a project.

Track your progress

In Chapter 13 of this book, I tell you all about gathering resource-activity information and entering it in your Project file to track progress. This can be a somewhat tedious process. Wouldn't it be nice if your resources could just enter their work in timesheets that could be automatically imported into Project to do your tracking for you? Well, I've got a surprise for you. . . .

One huge perk to using Project Web Access is the functionality that it gives your team members to track their activity on tasks and also report their progress to you online. Project managers can request updates or send reminders shortly before updates are due.

Team members can use the Microsoft Project Web Access interface to enter actual activity into a timesheet. Web Access communicates directly with Project on the project manager's computer. As the project manager, you can then make manual updates to your project plan or let Project make its own updates automatically. You can also generate task update requests to help you remind your team to keep you apprised of their activity and progress.

You can find out how to use features such as the tracking sheet in Chapter 19.

Figure out what's going on with status reports

You can design and request *status reports,* such as the one shown in Figure 18-5, which are essentially forms that the people on your project can complete to explain the status of their tasks. These aren't used to track and record actual work performed. Instead, they help team members describe various issues that come up and what's going on with the progress of tasks.

Status Report Request

| Report Title | Title: |
| Name the status report request. | Progress Weekly Status Report |

Frequency
Indicate how often the report is due.

Recurrence:
⦿ weekly ○ monthly ○ yearly

Due [every ▼] week on:

☐ Sunday ☑ Monday ☐ Tuesday ☐ Wednesday
☐ Thursday ☐ Friday ☐ Saturday

Start Date
When does the first reporting period begin?

Start:
9/4/2006

Resources
Select the resources who should respond to this status report request.

These resources' responses will be sent to you.

Available Resources:
Adam Barr
Administrator
Aidan Delaney
Alan Brewer
Alan Shen
Alan Steiner
Andreas Berglund

Resources who should respond:
A. Francesca Leonetti
Aaron Con

Add >
< Remove

Figure 18-5:
You specify exactly what you want to see in a status report.

You can request status reports and then work with your team's responses. One of the nice things about status reports for you, as a project manager, is that you can assemble all the individual reports into a complete status report for the project. Then you can make that report available to shareholders to update them on the latest news.

Getting set up

Before you can begin, you have to create a Project Server account and then publish a project to the Web. You use the Enterprise Options on the Tools menu to create a Project Server account, which involves entering the Project Server URL and some access settings. Then you can use the Publish command on the File menu to publish a project to the server. Ask your IT guy for some help on this, such as providing you with the proper server URL and advising you on how you should access that server. Or, again, I recommend the *Microsoft Project 2007 Bible* by Elaine Marmel (Wiley) if you feel like tackling this on your own.

Working with the Gang Online

This section gets you hands-on with Project Web Access, where you can try out some of its tools for team interaction. This isn't an exhaustive rundown of all Project Web Access has to offer, but it does get you working with the interface and exploring the tools it offers. Depending on your projects and your organization, you may take advantage of many other options.

Check resource availability and assignments

One of the really cool things about Project Server is how it empowers project managers to make resource assignments in a way that takes into account one set of shared resources across a whole organization. The Enterprise Resource Pool, which the Project Server administrator from your IT group can set up, is available through the Resource Center. By using the Enterprise Resource Pool, you can make assignments without having to re-create entries for all your resources every time you create a project.

Here are the steps involved in checking the availability and assignments of resources through Project Web Access:

1. **Open your Project Server site and click Resource Center in the Action pane.**

   Project displays the Resource Center. The resources for your enterprise are listed here.

2. **Select a check box to enable a resource.**

3. **Click the View Assignments button.**

   The amount of work hours that the selected resource is assigned to on specific tasks, along with the remaining hours of work on those tasks, are listed, as shown in Figure 18-6. This list also shows the scheduled start and finish dates of tasks.

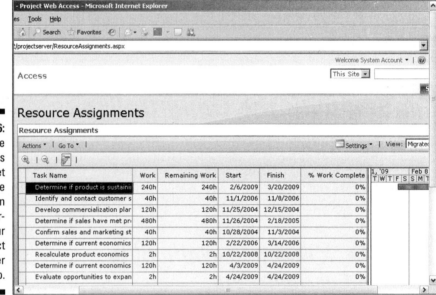

Figure 18-6: The resources here are set up by the person administering your Project Server setup.

4. **Choose Go To➪View Availability.**

   The resource's available work hours are listed day by day, starting with the current date (see Figure 18-7).

TIP

While viewing assignments, you can quickly view the taskbar for any task by clicking it and then clicking the Scroll to Task button.

Build a project team

With an entire resource pool at your disposal, after you know who is available for your project, you can build a project team.

Follow these steps to build your project team:

1. **Click the Project Center link on the Action pane to display it.**

   The Project Center is displayed.

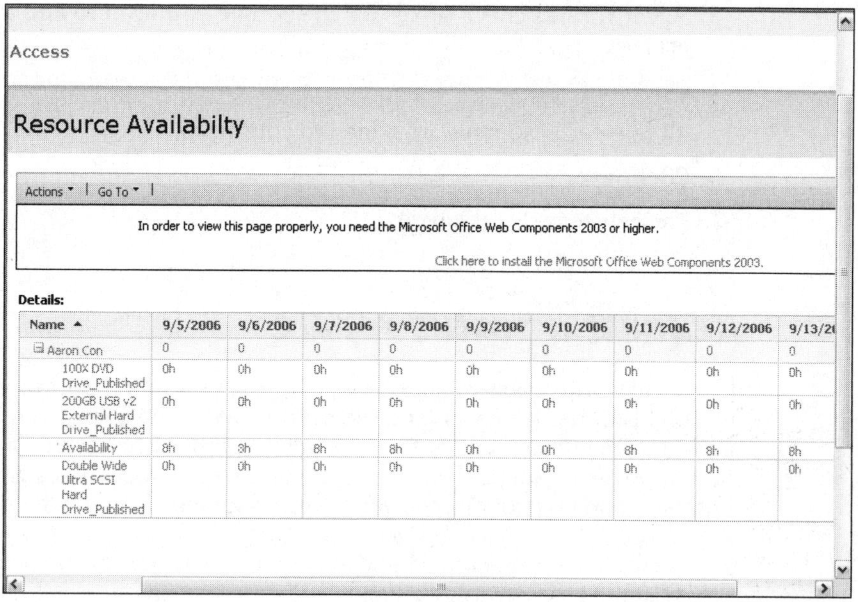

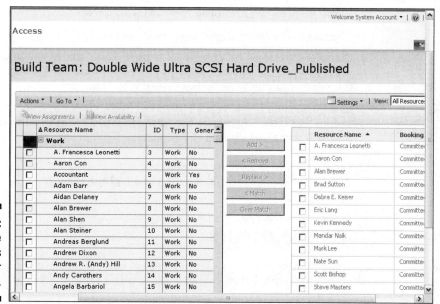

Figure 18-7:
Viewing
availability
of resources
helps you
create the
best
resource
plan.

2. **Choose your project from the list and then choose Actions⇨ Build Team.**

   The Build Team window, as shown in Figure 18-8, appears.

Figure 18-8:
Choose the
resources
for your
project.

3. **Select various check boxes for the people you want to add to your project.**

4. **Click Add.**

   All selected resources are added to your team.

5. **Click Save.**

   The new team list is saved.

Request a status report

In an ideal world, every resource on your project would report to you faithfully on his or her progress (and the news would all be good). In reality, the news is often not so good, but there's nothing Project or I can do about that. However, Project Server does provide a way for you to design status reports — and regularly nudge your team to submit them to you.

You can design a status report and also request that your team submit these reports at intervals by using a handy wizard.

To request a status report, follow these steps:

1. **From the Project Web Access home page, click the Status Reports link on the Action pane.**

   The Status Reports page appears.

2. **In the Request area, choose New⇨New Request.**

   The Status Report Request page, as shown in Figure 18-9, appears.

3. **Complete the form by entering a report name, the frequency that the report should be submitted to you, the start date for the report, and the resources you want to have send it to you.**

4. **In the last area of the report titled Sections, click the Insert Section button and type a name for the new section. Repeat this for every section you want included in the report.**

5. **Click Send.**

   The request for the report is sent to each of the resources you indicated.

Share documents

One other great use of Project Web Access is as a place to share documents with your team. Follow these steps to work with shared documents:

1. **From the Project Web Access home page, click the Shared Documents link on the Action pane.**

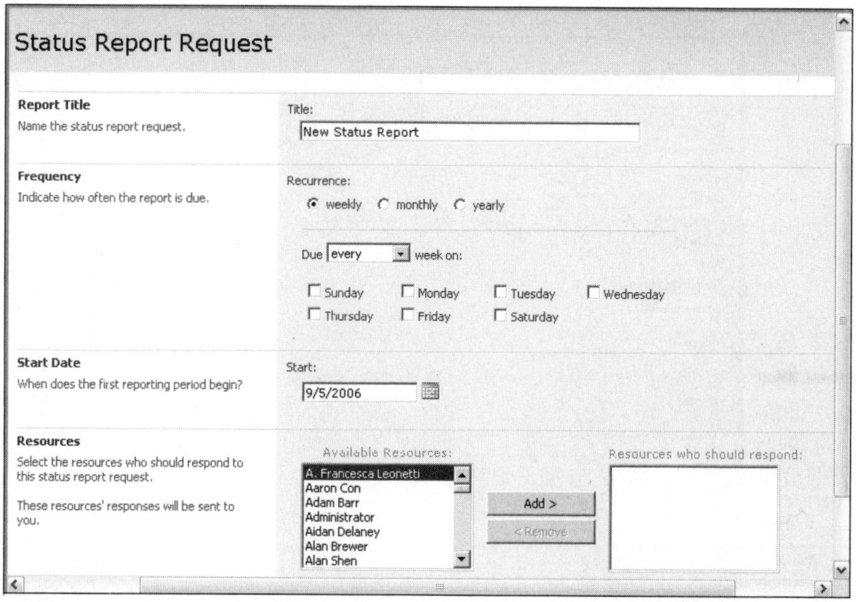

Figure 18-9:
Enter
information
for the
report
you're
designing.

> **Status Report Request**
>
> **Report Title**
> Name the status report request.
>
> Title:
> New Status Report
>
> **Frequency**
> Indicate how often the report is due.
>
> Recurrence:
> ⦿ weekly ○ monthly ○ yearly
>
> Due every ▾ week on:
>
> ☐ Sunday ☐ Monday ☐ Tuesday ☐ Wednesday
> ☐ Thursday ☐ Friday ☐ Saturday
>
> **Start Date**
> When does the first reporting period begin?
>
> Start:
> 9/5/2006
>
> **Resources**
> Select the resources who should respond to this status report request.
>
> These resources' responses will be sent to you.
>
> Available Resources:
> A. Francesca Leonetti
> Aaron Con
> Adam Barr
> Administrator
> Aidan Delaney
> Alan Brewer
> Alan Shen
>
> Add >
> < Remove
>
> Resources who should respond:

The Shared Documents window, as shown in Figure 18-10, appears.

2. **You have several options at this point:**

   • *Choose New⇨New Document.* This opens Word so you can create a document.

   • *Choose New⇨New Folder and enter a new folder name.* The folder appears in your Shared Documents list.

   • *Choose Upload⇨Upload Document or Upload Multiple Documents to upload an existing document.* If you upload a document, use the Browse button that appears (see Figure 18-11) to locate and upload the file.

   • *Choose Actions⇨Open with Windows Explorer and then drag and drop documents from Windows Explorer into the Shared Documents list.*

3. **To create a new document library, click the Documents link on the Project Web Access home page. On the page that appears, click Create.**

A few more Project Web Access features that are useful to your project team are covered in Chapter 19. Project Web Access is so feature rich that I don't have the room to fully do it justice in this book. Fortunately, the interface and tools are easy to use, and the Help information is actually quite helpful. Explore the topics of interest to you, and you'll be a Project Web Access pro in no time.

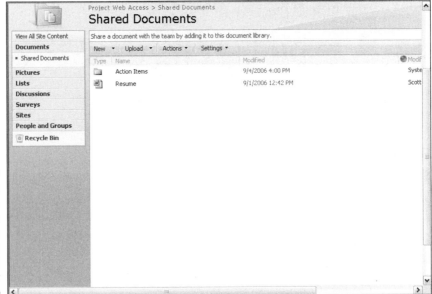

Figure 18-10:
All documents you share with your team are placed here.

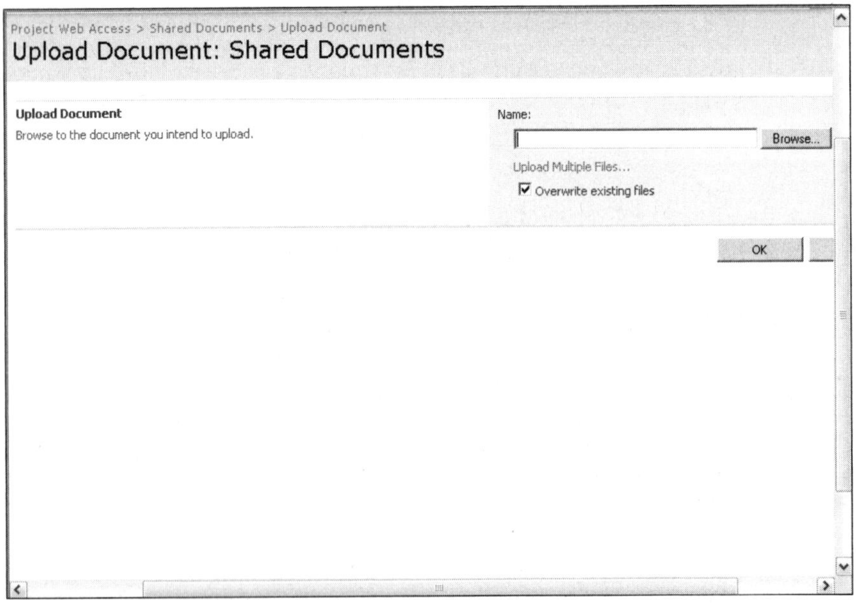

Figure 18-11:
Browse for a document to upload to your document library.

Chapter 19

Project Web Access for the End User

. . . .

In This Chapter

▶ Using Timesheet to enter actual work

▶ Looking at project information

▶ Setting up alerts and reminders

▶ Viewing information about a Project Web Access user

. . . .

Project Web Access is a marvelous tool for project managers to make assignments, track progress, and communicate, but it also offers great advantages to project team members.

Essentially, you can think of Project Web Access as a metaphorical two-way street. That is, project managers can post projects, notify resources of assignments, and request status reports, but the members of your project team can also initiate actions. For example, they can record the time they've spent on tasks, take a look at project information, send status reports to managers, and set up alerts and reminders to keep them on top of their commitments.

Seeing Project Web Access from the User's Perspective

The main Project Web Access home page is shown in Figure 19-1. In the various categories shown on the left here (My Work, Projects, Resources, Reporting, and so on), you can view a wealth of project information. You can also use the links in the Actions pane along the left side of the screen to move around the site.

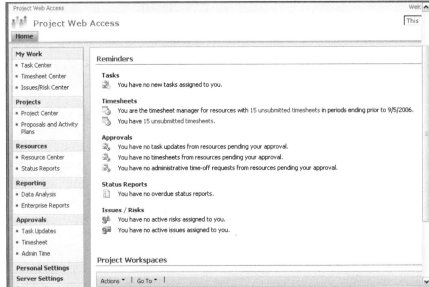

Figure 19-1:
The Project
Web
Access
home page
is filled with
various links
you use to
get around.

By using the various categories in the Actions pane, you can accomplish many things, including entering the hours you have spent on tasks, viewing project information, getting reminders of what is coming due (or is overdue), and communicating with other resources on your project.

For information about the features of Project Web Access that are useful to a project manager, see Chapter 18.

Reporting Work Completed

Okay, put aside your project manager hat (if you have one) and imagine for a moment that you're working on a project team. Your project manager — I'll call him Milt — has assigned you to tasks, and you have deadlines (way too many in your humble opinion) to meet.

The Timesheet feature (which you access through Project Web Access) enables you to view your tasks and enter information about the actual time you spent on them. Milt can check your timesheet (as shown in Figure 19-2) and track progress automatically.

Here's how to get to Timesheet view:

1. **Display the main Project Web Access page for your project.**

2. **Click the Timesheet Center link in the Actions pane.**

A list of timesheets for various time periods in the project appear, as shown in Figure 19-3.

3. **Click the Click to Create link for the appropriate time period.**

A timesheet like the one shown in Figure 19-4 labeled My Timesheet appears.

As you can see in Figure 19-4, Timesheet view looks something like a spreadsheet. To enter work on tasks, follow these steps:

1. **Click the cell for a task and task category you want to update.**

2. **Enter the actual time you spent on a task on that particular day.**

Use a number (such as 3, for three hours) in the appropriate date field.

3. **After you enter all updates, click the Save or the Save and Submit button at the bottom of the timesheet.**

If you click Save and Submit, a dialog box appears asking you to choose the person you want to submit the timesheet to. Use this Browse feature to choose the person and then click OK to send the timesheet.

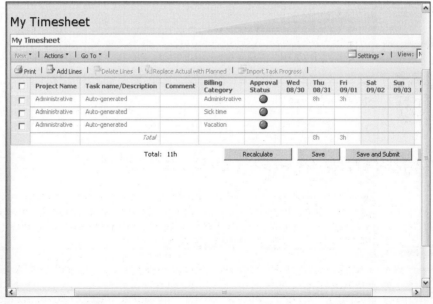

Figure 19-2:
Timesheet view can be opened using Project Web Access.

After you click Save, the changes that you make in the timesheet get stored in the Project Server database, but they haven't been used to update the project yet. That's up to Milt, your faithful project manager. Clicking Save and Submit causes Project Web Access to send an e-mail to your manager, who can accept or reject the updates in the project. Milt, the project manager, can log on to Project Web Access and then click the Approvals link. All timesheets are displayed. You can accept or reject these by clicking the Approve or Reject button.

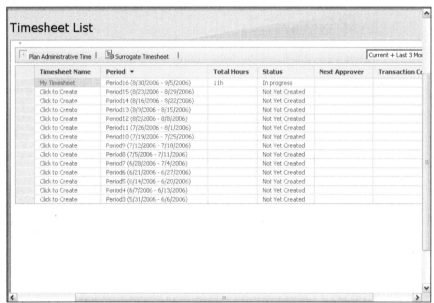

Figure 19-3:
The
Timesheet
List.

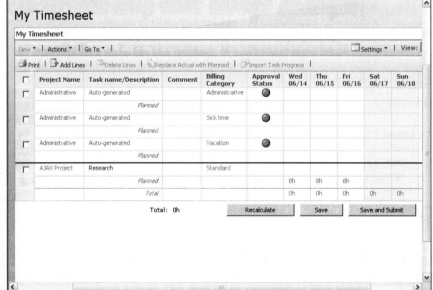

Figure 19-4:
Timesheet
view allows
resources to
track time
spent on
tasks.

Viewing Project Information

Project team members often don't have Project itself loaded on their comput-ers, so they need a way to view the project plan. They can do that by using Project Web Access. (Viewing project information works pretty much the same whether you're wearing a project manager or team member hat.)

To view a project, follow these steps:

1. **Display the Project Web Access page.**

2. **Click the Project Center link in the Actions pane.**

   All the projects you have access to (as shown in Figure 19-5) are displayed.

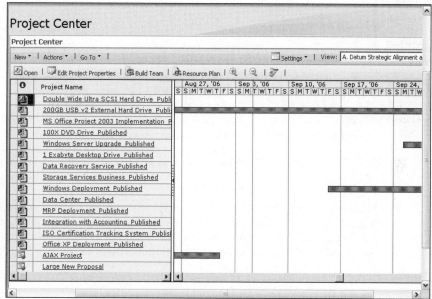

Figure 19-5: See an overview of several projects going on at once.

3. **Click the link for the project that you want to view and then click Open.**

   The project is displayed (see Figure 19-6).

Your team members cannot edit this project plan, which is just as well: I recommend that one person be responsible for making all the edits to the plan to avoid confusion.

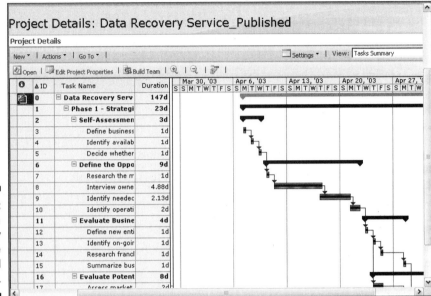

Setting Up Alerts and Reminders

I don't know about you, but when I discovered a feature in my e-mail program that allowed me to be reminded of my various obligations, I became a happy camper. No more missed meetings, and no more forgotten deadlines. (Well, almost none.)

Because project team members quickly begin to use the Project Web Access site as their own command central regarding their project commitments, it's useful for them to be able to set similar reminders and alerts for project tasks you assign them to or status reports that are due.

To set up your alerts and reminders, follow these steps:

1. **Click the Personal Settings link in the Actions pane.**

   The Personal Settings window appears.

2. **Click the Manage My Alerts and Reminders link.**

   The Manage My Alerts and Reminders window, as shown in Figure 19-7, appears.

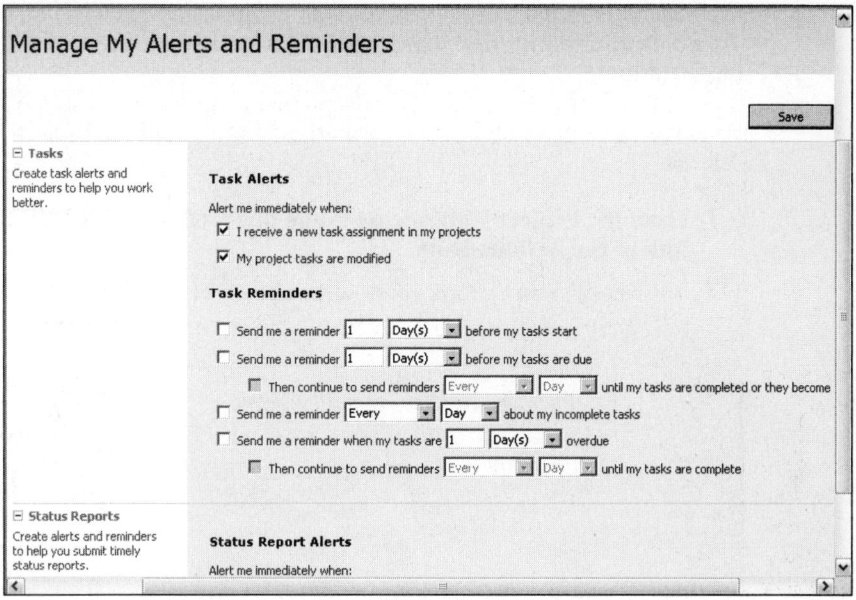

Figure 19-7:
Create and
manage
helpful
reminders to
keep you on
track.

3. **In the Task Alerts area, you can request to be notified about various events.**

   Make settings here to be notified when you are assigned to a task or when the task is modified.

4. **In the Task Reminders area, you can set up all kinds of reminders to let you know a task will start or be due soon.**

   You can even make a setting to be reminded periodically about any incomplete or overdue task.

5. **In the Status Report Alerts area, adjust settings to alert you to respond to status report requests.**

   You can choose to be notified when a new status report request appears or when a status report is due or overdue.

6. **Click Save to save all your settings.**

Viewing Information about Other Users

When you work on projects, you work with other people for the most part. How many times have you been working on a deadline and found you had to contact somebody only to forget that person's name, e-mail address, or even what department he works for?

By using the People and Groups tools in Project Web Access, you can update your own information and look up information about others in your organization.

Follow these steps to look up information about people in Project Web Access:

1. **From the Project Web Access home page, click the People and Groups link in the Actions pane.**

   The People and Groups window, as shown in Figure 19-8, appears.

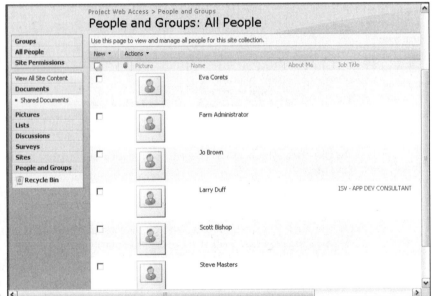

Figure 19-8:
Access
information
about your
co-workers
here.

2. **Double-click any person's name in the list to display a detailed information form, as shown in Figure 19-9.**

3. **If an e-mail address is listed and you want to e-mail this person, simply click the e-mail address.**

   A blank message opens.

4. **When you finish viewing the person's information, click Close.**

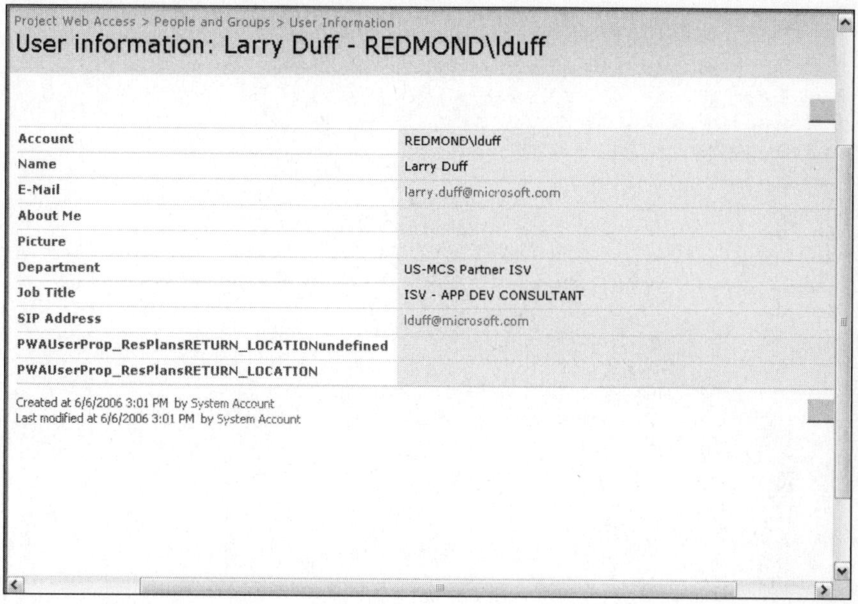

Project Web Access > People and Groups > User Information
User information: Larry Duff - REDMOND\lduff

Account	REDMOND\lduff
Name	Larry Duff
E-Mail	larry.duff@microsoft.com
About Me	
Picture	
Department	US-MCS Partner ISV
Job Title	ISV - APP DEV CONSULTANT
SIP Address	lduff@microsoft.com
PWAUserProp_ResPlansRETURN_LOCATIONundefined	
PWAUserProp_ResPlansRETURN_LOCATION	

Created at 6/6/2006 3:01 PM by System Account
Last modified at 6/6/2006 3:01 PM by System Account

Figure 19-9:
View details
for a co-
worker.

If you prefer talking with somebody over the phone rather than sending an e-mail, use NetMeeting, an online meeting software program from Microsoft. From the People and Groups window, select a check box to select a person, and then choose Actions➪Call/Message Selected Users. This opens NetMeeting, which allows you to connect with this person in a variety of ways such as with text, video, or by phone.

If you want to discover more about Project Web Access, see Chapter 18, which covers several tasks a project manager might find useful.

Part VI
The Part of Tens

The 5th Wave   By Rich Tennant

"Hold on people. It seems the Japanese have a 40 teraflop fruitcake in development, and plan to release it –get this –one week before Christmas! Okay, we've got our work cut out for us."

In this part . . .

*T*en fingers, ten toes — things that come in tens are just a natural! This part gives you two handy lists of ten: Ten Golden Rules of Project Management, and Ten Project-Management Software Products to Explore. The first of these chapters offers new users of Project (as well as seasoned veterans) some pointers on getting your project to perform. The second chapter looks at add-on products and supplemental software to enhance Microsoft Project

Chapter 20

Ten Golden Rules of Project Management

*Y*ou've heard this one: You can have your deliverable on time, on budget, or done right: Choose two. That's an example of some traditional project management wisdom. But how does that wisdom translate to the use of project management software?

Well, it's simple: If you assign additional resources to a Project schedule, you add costs and time to your schedule because resources have costs attached and can work only according to their work calendars. So, clearly, making changes that might improve quality — such as adding more or higher-priced resources — affects the time and money needed for your project. That adage about time being money is still true, but now you can clearly see the effect that one action has on other aspects of your project (especially if something you do tinkers with time or money) — and it's all visible in Project's many views and reports.

So what project management adages should you be aware of as you begin to use Project? Here are ten to tack up on your office wall.

Don't Bite Off More Than You Can Manage

As I mention elsewhere in this book (see Chapter 1), you must have an understanding of the goal of your project as well as the scope of its activities before you start to build a Project schedule. Don't plan a full marketing campaign if all you can anticipate at this point is what the market-research phase will look like. Because the additional elements of an actual marketing campaign hinge on that market research, do first things first: Build your project in phases. That way, you'll have less reworking of later tasks that simply couldn't be anticipated when you began. You'll also have less need to manipulate the baseline for those later tasks: If they're too far in the future, by the time you get there, their time demands won't look anything like what you originally set aside for them.

Don't set tasks that are far in the future in stone too early in the game.

Here are some Project features that help you with this process:

- ✔ The capability to combine subprojects into a master project with linking
- ✔ Network Diagram view, which helps you visualize phases of your project graphically
- ✔ The flexible nature of Project outlines, allowing you to hide or display different phases of a project

See Chapter 5 for more about the best ways to manipulate outlines.

Get Your Ducks in a Row

Before you start creating your project, do your homework. If you don't have all the information that you need when you sit down at your computer to work with Project, you'll find yourself constantly stopping, mid-plan, and running off to find that information. This isn't a very efficient way to work.

Here are some things to research before you sit down to build a project schedule:

- ✔ **Resource information:** For people, this includes the full name, contact information, manager and manager's contact information, skills, cost, schedule, and timing conflicts. For equipment or facilities, find out their availability and cost.

- ✔ **Team structure:** Does everyone do his or her own tracking, or does someone else on the team input everyone's progress? Who updates the schedule for changes? Who gets copies of which reports? Should your team have access to the master schedule online? Does everyone on the team have the technology to communicate using collaborative features such as Project Web Access?

✔ **Management expectations:** Does management expect to see Basic reports on a regular basis? Would they prefer that you use Visual reports, instead? Do you need to get budget approval at various phases in your project planning; if so, from whom? Are cross-enterprise interests involved that require you to report to or get approval from multiple sources? (See Chapter 16 for the lowdown on reports.)

✔ **Company policies:** These include company work policies regarding resource hours and overtime, the holiday calendar, how your company charges overhead costs or markups to projects, and what information can — and can't — be shared with clients or vendors.

The Enterprise resource features in Project 2007 help you call on company information stored on your server, such as obtaining a list of enterprise resources, for consistency across projects.

Now you're ready to sit down and start inputting a Project project! (Is there an echo in here?)

Plan for Murphy

You know he's out there: Murphy and his darn law! Most projects don't happen on time or on budget. This is especially true of lengthier and more complex projects. Your job is to do the most accurate planning that you can — and make prudent adjustments whenever a wrench is thrown into the works. Project gives you lots of tools to do that. But beyond all the automated features of Project, you can anticipate change by planning for it.

As I describe in Chapter 6, the *critical path* in a project is indeed critical. Every wise project manager builds extra time, and even extra money, into schedules. When the project comes in but a week late and $5,000 over budget, only the project manager knows that it was really four weeks later and $25,000 costlier than what the first schedule — the one with no allowance for Murphy — reflected.

Add time to the duration of every task if possible to account for shifts in schedule. Also add a resource to every phase of your project to pad your budget just a bit to help you deal with overages.

Instead of a work or material resource, use the new Project 2007 cost resource type to add a set amount to a task or phase. You can even name the extra cost resource *Murphy,* if you like!

Don't Put Off Until Tomorrow

Project management software can make many aspects of your life easier, but the thing that overwhelms most people when they begin to use Project is the amount of time spent inputting data and keeping it up to date. True, those tasks can be cumbersome, but what you can get back from those automated updating and reporting capabilities more than makes up for the upfront work.

Don't forget about the capability to import tasks from Outlook into Project. This helps speed up some of that data entry in the planning phase.

However, if you don't tend to the task of tracking progress on a project, you can wind up behind the proverbial eight-ball. Track just as often as you can — at least once a week. This not only saves you from facing a mountain of tracking data to be entered, but this also means that you and your team can see the true picture of your project at any point in time. That way, you can promptly spot disaster coming and make adjustments accordingly.

Delegate, Delegate, Delegate!

Don't try to do everything on a project yourself. Although creating and maintaining your Project file on your own might seem to give you more control, doing so is just about impossible in larger projects. Of course, you don't want dozens of people going in and making changes to your plan because you run the risk of losing track of who did what and when. However, a few simple practices make a few fingers in the project pie helpful, not harmful:

- Designate one person whose mission is to enter all tracking data into the master file for you. Or, you can automate tracking by using the Request Progress Information feature.
- Break your project into a few subprojects and assign people whom you trust to act as managers of those phases. Let them deal with their own tracking and adjustments, and then assemble the phase projects into a master project so you can monitor their changes.
- Enlist the help of your IS/IT person(s) to set up Project Server with Project Web Access to provide enhanced collaborative features and share documents with your team.
- Set uniform procedures for your team up front. Don't have one person report time on an inter-office memo sheet, somebody else e-mail you his progress, and let others stick the work they did on tasks into the Timesheet willy-nilly. Work up a strategy that uses Project features to communicate consistently.

If you work in a large enterprise, begin practicing enterprise project management techniques right away. By setting up portfolios of projects and designating resource pools, you can collaborate with other project managers for the most efficient processes. See Chapter 19 for more about how to do this.

CYA (Document!)

Everyone knows the project management adage to CYA, but Project makes it a lot easier. Try using these features to document the details of your project:

- Use the Notes area for both tasks and resources to make a record of background information, changes, or special issues (as shown in Figure 20-1). (See Chapter 4.)

- Use the routing feature of Project to route schedules to people for review. This builds an electronic paper trail of where information went and who responded. (See Chapter 9.)

- Customize reports to incorporate all pertinent information and help you document trends and changes. (See Chapter 16.)

- Try using the new Visual Reports to paint the picture of project status for visually inclined stakeholders. (See Chapter 16.)

- Save multiple versions of your project, especially if you make changes to your baseline in later versions. This provides a record of every step in your project planning, which you can refer to when questions arise down the road. (See Chapter 12.)

Figure 20-1:
Keep
track of
changes to
personnel,
budget, and
timing in
task notes.

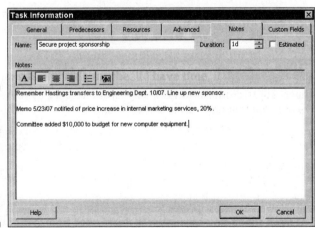

✔ Share updates to your plan through Project Web Access so that nobody can say he or she was out of the loop when some important change came down. (See Chapter 18.)

Keep Your Team in the Loop

I've worked in offices where I spent more time wrestling with whom to keep informed about what than I did working. If I didn't include marketing and finance in every e-mail on a new product launch, I'd be called on the carpet the next day, or (worse) some vital action step would fall through the cracks because someone didn't know he or she was supposed to take action. Try these methods of keeping communication channels open:

✔ Use Project features that allow you to integrate with Outlook or other e-mail programs to route Project files or other communications.

✔ Build address lists in your e-mail program specific to your project team so that every message goes to everyone, every time.

✔ Review progress with your team by meeting regularly, whether in person, over the phone, online in a chat area, or by using meeting software. Make sure that each team member has the latest version of the Project schedule to refer to during these meetings.

✔ Use the Send to: Exchange Folder command to post the latest version of a project in a folder on your network so others know what's going on.

✔ If you run SharePoint Services, you can use the integrated task pane in Project to work with the Shared Workspace feature. Shared Workspace is a great, centralized place to post and exchange project-related documents created in any Office 2007 application.

✔ Display the work-breakdown structure code on reports so you can easily refer to specific tasks in large projects without confusion.

Take advantage of the Printing wizard in the Project Guide. This feature helps you find the best way to print various views of your project to share hard copy updates with your team.

Measure Success

When you begin your project, you should have an idea of what constitutes success and a way to measure that success. Success can involve attaining many goals, such as

   ✔ Customer satisfaction

   ✔ Management satisfaction

   ✔ Being on budget

   ✔ Being on time

When you start your project planning, know how you'll measure your success. Will success in budgeting mean that you don't exceed your original estimates by more than ten percent? Will your project be considered on time if you worked the estimated amount of weeks on it minus a two-month period when you went on hold for a union strike, or is the total working time less important than meeting a specific deadline? How will you measure customer satisfaction? Will management satisfaction be a done deal if you get a promotion or if your division receives more funding? Does a successful product launch include high sales figures after the launch, or was your project successful merely because you got it out the door?

Place milestones in your project (as shown in Figure 20-2) that reflect the achievement of each type of success. When you reach each milestone, you can pat your team on the back. Knowing what success looks like helps you motivate your team to get there.

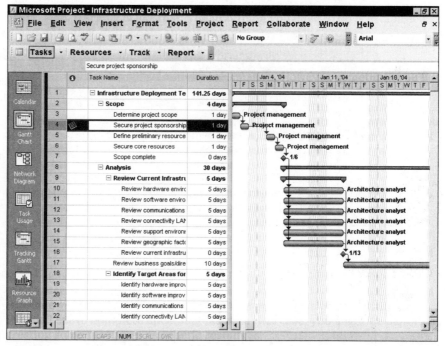

Figure 20-2:
Milestones provide markers along the way that give your team a feeling of achievement.

Have a Flexible Strategy

Stuff happens. There's never been a project that didn't require accommodations for surprises along the way. The mark of a good project manager is that he or she is alert to these changes and makes adjustments to deal with them quickly.

This isn't always easy: It's really, really hard to be the messenger bearing bad news. However, avoiding a problem in your project, hoping it will go away, has a nasty habit of snowballing. The following tools can help you stay alert to changes and make adjustments:

- ✔ The Resource Substitution Wizard helps you make changes when the one resource you counted on suddenly wins the lottery and disappears.

- ✔ The new Change Highlighting feature can help you see where changes to your schedule pay off in a trimmer budget or faster schedule.

- ✔ Use the Portfolio Modeling feature to try what-if analyses on your project to anticipate how possible changes might affect you.

- ✔ Use various views (such as Network Diagram view shown in Figure 20-3) to see the critical path of your project and track how much slack you have left. Adjusting tasks to efficiently use up their slack can keep you on schedule in a crisis.

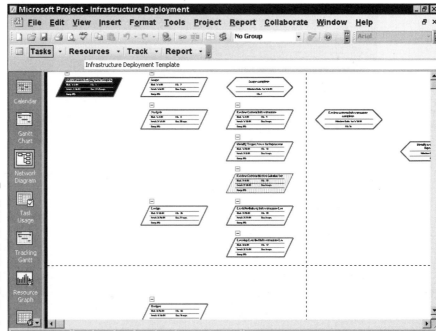

Figure 20-3:
A critical path can be seen several ways using Project's views and filters.

Remember that Project 2007 offers new features to help you try out what-if scenarios and determine what's driving the timing of tasks (see Chapter 15). Use these to figure out the best way to proceed.

Learn from Your Mistakes

One of the greatest gifts that Project offers you is the capability to look back after you complete a project so that you can learn from your mistakes. You can review your original schedule and every version after that to see how well you estimated time and money and figure out how to do it better.

By using records of your project, you can spot trends. Where do you always seem to miss on timing? Do you always allow way too little time on market research and way too much time for Q&A? Do you always forget to budget for temporary help during rush times, or do you overstaff early on when you could get by with fewer people?

Use the wealth of information in Project schedules to educate yourself on your own strengths and weaknesses as a project planner and manager and to get better with each project you take on.

 Use the Portfolio Analyzer tool to get the bigger picture across all the projects and programs for which you're responsible.

Chapter 21

Ten Project Management Software Products to Explore

. . . .

In This Chapter

▶ Looking at add-on software

▶ Discovering software that integrates with Project-generated plans

▶ Reviewing separate software products that help project managers with project-related tasks

. . . .

*I*f you've followed this book to this point, you've probably figured out by now that project management software — just like a project manager — wears a lot of hats. Microsoft Office Project does everything from allowing you to create tasks and assign resources to tracking progress, analyzing cost overruns, and analyzing scheduling conflicts. It handles graphics, complex calculations, and interactions with the Web.

Software designers always have to make trade-offs among features, deciding which ones to include and how much functionality to give each feature. Most Project features do everything you need, but others are less complete. Some features might not quite get the job done as well as a more specialized tool that you can use in conjunction with Project. Third-party software partners work with Microsoft to create add-on software to provide Project with greater functionality: for example, generating a greater variety of graphic reports. In other cases, software handles specialized functions that Project doesn't incorporate, such as managing the hundreds of drawings involved in construction projects.

Consider this the when-two-heads-are-better-than-one chapter. This chapter describes ten interesting software tools that you can use with Project. Most of the makers of these tools offer some kind of free demo of their product on company Web sites. Plenty of products are out there, so use this chapter as a starting point as you consider ways to extend Project's functionality.

DecisionEdge Chart and Report Products Enhance Project's Own Tools

Makers of business intelligence software such as DecisionCharts and DecisionReports for Microsoft Project, DecisionEdge (www.decisionedge.com) offers reporting and graphics software products that add functionality to Project. You can use these tools to help you visualize resource challenges, get a handle on your project schedule status, and gauge how well you're performing.

Go to the DecisionEdge Web site to see a sample gallery of charts and reports that use a variety of graphic effects and colors to get your message across. Check out the *Dashboard charts,* which show a combination of several different charts in one report; these help your executives get a one-glance overview of your progress.

Even with the more graphical options in Project's new Visual Reports feature, you can benefit from the more advanced graphics capabilities of DecisionEdge's products.

Cobra Squeezes the Most from Cost/Earned Value

WST Corporation (www.welcom.com), which makes its own complete project management package called Open Plan, also produces *Cobra,* a cost/earned value management software package that you can use with Project plans. Cobra tools offer functionality in estimating, what-if modeling of costs, and budget forecasting based on information in your Project schedule. I especially like the multiple rate files feature that makes it easy to juggle several resource rates within a single project.

Cobra not only allows you to define certain budget calculations yourself, but it also offers more flexibility than some of Project's costing features. In addition, the Chart Template Designer lets you play around with a variety of 3-D charts, which you can manipulate and rotate in several ways, expanding your options for presenting Project data in three dimensions.

MindManuals Helps You Visualize Project Information

MindManuals (www.mindjet.com/us) offers *MindManager Pro,* which is a software product that helps you get your team thinking together in creative ways. This visual mapping software is touted as a visual thinking tool. MindManager is offered in Basic and Pro versions, and you can also get MindManager Viewer 6, which allows you to view and navigate MindManager maps.

MindManager maps allow you to attach files, connect to RSS feeds, and more. After you organize your ideas and information, you can use these details as the basis for your Project file. As of this writing, you can download a free 21-day trial to see all the power MindManager offers.

Innate Integrates Projects Large and Small

Innate Timesheets and Innate Resource Manager from Innate Management Systems (www.innateus.com) are especially helpful if you're juggling multiple projects that range from small to large. You can use Innate to manage the human resources who work on smaller projects in your organization and are also busy on larger projects that you plan in Microsoft Project. Innate Timesheets can group resources in various useful ways.

The Innate Resource Manager helps you scope out resource availability and prioritize resource assignments. Innate Timesheets is tracking software, but it offers more than Project does in this area. You can do productivity comparisons across several tasks or projects. You can also tap into sophisticated billing systems and integrate project information with accounting and payroll systems in ways that enhance Project 12 budget-tracking features.

PlanView Models Your Workforce Capacity

PlanView, Inc. (www.planview.com) produces the software product *PlanView Enterprise,* which helps you sort through the various layers in your organization. The role-modeling features in PlanView allow you to analyze and manage risk, give priorities to strategies, and set up scenarios to prepare for inevitable emergencies in your project.

The PlanView Project Portfolio Management product focuses on specific project work, featuring easy-to-use dashboards for managing your project portfolios.

PlanView is closely integrated with Microsoft Project, so you can share information about processes and people on a project between the two products. PlanView templates can also be used to give you a head start on your Project plan.

Tenrox Streamlines Business Processes

The buzzword today is *enterprise,* and Tenrox (www.tenrox.com) puts the focus on business processes, such as performance analysis, resource planning, purchasing, and revenue and cost accounting. One of the best uses of this software for the Microsoft Project user is as a bridge to various enterprise and accounting packages such as SAP and ADP Payroll.

Project Portfolio Management and Professional Services Automation for service delivery and invoicing are Web-based solutions that can be very useful in a geographically diverse project team setting. You should take a look at these packages also if you have a need for RFI, quotation, and evaluation functions in your projects. Tenrox also offers a set of proposal management tools to help you get the project off the ground in the first place.

Project KickStart Gives Your Project a Head Start

Project KickStart from Experience In Software (www.experienceware.com) is a simple-to-use program with a wizard-like approach that helps you lay the groundwork for small to midsize projects. If you need a little help getting started with a project, you can create your plan here in 30 minutes or less, and then use the hot link to port information to Microsoft Project.

Project KickStart is designed to help you figure out your project strategy as you come up with a list of tasks. Planning icons remind you to map out the goals of your project and plan for obstacles. Libraries of typical goals and challenges make building them into your plan simple, and you can add your own specific company or industry phrases to the libraries. Links to Outlook, Word, and Excel also offer you some flexibility in sharing information among the Office family of products, which includes Project. Check out the free trial download and online demo to get an idea of what Project KickStart can do for your projects.

Project Manager's Assistant Organizes Drawings for Construction Projects

Originally created for the construction industry, Project Manager's Assistant, CS Project Lite, and CS Project Professional from Crest Software (www.crestsoft.com) are useful for any industry that uses a lot of drawings.

Essentially, these are database products that help you track drawings, issue copies, develop production plans, and manage changes over the life of the project. Although the product doesn't integrate directly to Project, it's an additional software product that might prove useful to many project managers — and it does integrate to any ODBC (open database connectivity) database.

Graphic designers and new product designers who generate drawings can catalog them here. If you manage scientific or engineering projects, you might also find this software useful for managing schematics or diagrams. By placing links to this database in your Project plan, you can make this information available to your project team.

TeamTrack Solves Mission-Critical Issues

TeamTrack from Serena Software, Inc. (www.serena.com) offers "Web-architected workflow management solutions." In English, that means that the software helps you identify problems and defects that may crop up in your processes — and find solutions. The software allows you to create visual maps for your processes and share that data among your team members. The Web focus here means that people can get to the process data online without having Project running. Serena offers ProjectBridge to help integrate their system with Microsoft Project.

One nice feature of this software is that it notifies you when a problem occurs or deadlines have passed without activity. TeamTrack even helps you identify issues that might arise when "non-talking" systems communicate. In other words, if you integrate two pieces of software to share data and data comes into Project that causes a problem, you won't even know it because you're not inputting it. TeamTrack flags such problems to help you avoid missing a critical situation before it's too late.

Serena's Web site offers a free evaluation download and online case studies to help you decide whether TeamTrack is right for you.

EPK-Suite Eases Portfolio Mangement Chores

EPK-Suite from EPK Group (www.epkgroup.com) is built on Project Server 2003 and Windows SharePoint Services platforms and integrates through Project Web Access, so this technology works seamlessly with Project.

EPK-Suite offers portfolio management, resource and capacity planning, timesheets, and collaboration features with an easy-to-use interface. Check out the new features in version 4, including Web-based planning and resource request/planning tools.

Part VII
Appendixes

The 5th Wave

By Rich Tennant

@RICHTENNANT

"Well, here's your problem. You only have half the ram you need."

In this part . . .

This part of the book dives into the incredibly useful companion CD (chock full of project-management goodies). You get the lowdown on what's on the CD and how to make use of it.

Then — by way of the last word(s) — you get a handy glossary that will have you talking like a project manager in no time.

Appendix A

On the CD

· ·

In This Appendix

▶ System requirements

▶ Using the CD with Windows

▶ What you'll find on the CD

▶ Troubleshooting

· ·

System Requirements

*M*ake sure that your computer meets the minimum system requirements shown in the following list. If your computer doesn't match up to most of these requirements, you may have problems using the software and files on the CD. For the latest and greatest information, please refer to the ReadMe file located at the root of the CD-ROM.

✔ A PC with a Pentium or faster processor

✔ Microsoft Windows XP or later

✔ A CD-ROM drive

If you need more information on the basics, check out these books published by Wiley Publishing, Inc.: *PCs For Dummies,* by Dan Gookin; *Windows XP For Dummies* and *Windows 2007 Professional For Dummies,* both by Andy Rathbone.

Using the CD

To install the items from the CD to your hard drive, follow these steps:

1. **Insert the CD into your computer's CD-ROM drive. The license agreement appears.**

Note to Windows users: The interface won't launch if you have autorun disabled. In that case, choose Start⇨Run. In the dialog box that appears, type D:\start.exe. (Replace D with the proper letter if your CD-ROM drive uses a different letter. If you don't know the letter, see how your CD-ROM drive is listed under My Computer.) Click OK.

2. **Read through the license agreement, and then click the Accept button if you want to use the CD.**

3. **The CD interface appears. The interface allows you to install the programs and run the demos with just a click of a button (or two).**

What You'll Find on the CD

The following sections are arranged by category and provide a summary of the software and other goodies you'll find on the CD. If you need help with installing the items provided on the CD, refer back to the installation instructions in the preceding section.

Shareware programs are fully functional, free, trial versions of copyrighted programs. If you like particular programs, register with their authors for a nominal fee and receive licenses, enhanced versions, and technical support.

Freeware programs are free, copyrighted games, applications, and utilities. You can copy them to as many PCs as you like — for free — but they offer no technical support.

GNU software is governed by its own license, which is included inside the folder of the GNU software. There are no restrictions on distribution of GNU software. See the GNU license at the root of the CD for more details.

Trial, demo, or *evaluation* versions of software are usually limited either by time or functionality (such as not letting you save a project after you create it).

Empire Suite, from WSG System Corp.

Demo version, Windows

This suite of solutions includes Empire Time for both Project Financial Management and Resource Skills Management. Customized user interfaces make managing these aspects of projects simple for all users, and advanced reporting and analytics help you get the most from your Project data.

Learn more at www.wsg.com.

EPK Suite 4.1, from EPK GROUP, LLC

This software, based on Project Server, offers an integrated approach to planning for your projects. You can inventory resources, prioritize projects, control processes, and more with EPK Suite. Before running the EPK-Suite SETUP, you must obtain a product installation key. To get one simply go to www.epkgroup.com/productkey.htm.

EPK GROUP Web site: Http://epkgroup.com/

Milestones Professional, from Kidasa Software

Trial version

Milestones Professional offers you advanced formatting, calculation, Web publishing, and reporting features that take you beyond what you can do with Project alone.

Go to Kidasa's Web site at www.kidasa.com to learn more about all their products.

Milestones Project Companion 2006, from Kidasa Software

Trial version

Milestones provides advanced formatting, calculation, Web publishing, and reporting tools compatible with Microsoft Project 2007.

Kidasa Software Web site: www.kidasa.com

MindManager Pro 6, from Mindjet Corporation

Trial version

If you've always wanted to see what your ideas look like, try MindManager to map brainstorming and plans into graphical strategy blueprints. At the time of publication, the new trial version wasn't available. You can now download it at www.mindjet.com/us/download/.

Mindjet Web site: www.mindjet.com/us

PERT Chart Expert, from Critical Tools, Inc.

Demo version

With this software you can create stunning PERT chart project plans with way more bells and whistles than Microsoft Project provides. If you want to impress people with graphical views of your workflow, this is one to check out.

Critical Tools Web site: www.criticaltools.com

PertMaster Project Risk, from PertMaster

Evaluation copy

You can use this as stand-alone software or as an add-on for Microsoft Project. Use the tools provided here to run schedule and cost risk analyses.

Go to www.pertmaster.com to explore the full feature set.

PlanView Project Portfolio, from PlanView

Demo version

PlanView is touted as a comprehensive decision-making platform for enterprises, meaning it can help you prioritize and strategize the goals for your project.

PlanView Web site: http://planview.com

Project KickStart, from Experience in Software

Trial version

Project KickStart offers a wizard-like brainstorming tool to help you with project planning and scheduling.

Visit www.projectkickstart.com for more information.

WBS Chart Pro, from Critical Tools, Inc.

Trial version

You can use the underlying structure of your project's WBS code to create tree-style diagrams of your task hierarchies using WBS Chart Pro.

Critical Tools Web site: www.criticaltools.com

Troubleshooting

I tried my best to compile programs that work on most computers with the minimum system requirements. Alas, your computer may differ, and some programs may not work properly for some reason.

The two likeliest problems are that you don't have enough memory (RAM) for the programs you want to use, or you have other programs running that are affecting installation or running of a program. If you get an error message such as Not enough memory or Setup cannot continue, try one or more of the following suggestions and then try using the software again:

- ✔ **Turn off any antivirus software running on your computer.** Installation programs sometimes mimic virus activity and may make your computer incorrectly believe that it's being infected by a virus.

- ✔ **Close all running programs.** The more programs you have running, the less memory is available to other programs. Installation programs typically update files and programs; so if you keep other programs running, installation may not work properly.

- ✔ **Have your local computer store add more RAM to your computer.** This is, admittedly, a drastic and somewhat expensive step. However, adding more memory can really help the speed of your computer and allow more programs to run at the same time.

Customer Care

If you have trouble with the CD-ROM, please call the Wiley Product Technical Support phone number at 800-762-2974. Outside the United States, call 1-317-572-3994. You can also contact Wiley Product Technical Support at http://support.wiley.com. Wiley Publishing, Inc., will provide technical support only for installation and other general quality control items. For technical support on the applications themselves, consult the program's vendor or author.

To place additional orders or to request information about other Wiley products, please call 877-762-2974.

Appendix B

Glossary

• •

Atual: The cost of the percentage of work that has been completed on a task.

ACWP (actual cost of work performed): Cost of the actual, real work done on a project to date, plus any fixed costs.

ALAP (as late as possible): A constraint put on a task's timing to make the task occur as late as possible in the project schedule, taking into account any dependency relationships. *See also* dependency.

ASAP (as soon as possible): A constraint put on a task's timing to make the task occur as early as possible in the project schedule, taking into account any dependency relationships. *See also* dependency.

BAC (budget at completion): The sum total of all costs involved in completing a task. *See also* baseline cost.

baseline: The detailed project plan against which actual work is tracked.

baseline cost: The total planned costs for a project's tasks, before any actual costs are incurred.

BCWP (budgeted cost of work performed): Also called *earned value,* this term refers to the value of work that has been completed. For example, a task with $1,000 of costs accrues a BCWP of $750 when it's 75 percent complete.

BCWS (budgeted cost of work scheduled): The percentage of the plan that's completed multiplied by the planned costs. This calculated value totals a task's completed work and its remaining planned costs.

booking type: A category for resources that specifies whether they are committed to the project or simply proposed to be involved.

calendar: The various settings for hours in a workday, days in a workweek, holidays, and nonworking days on which a project schedule is based. You can set Project, Task, and Resource calendars.

change highlighting: A feature that highlights any changes you make in your project since you last saved it.

circular dependency: A timing relationship among tasks that creates an endless loop that can't be resolved.

collapse: To close a project outline to hide subtasks from view.

combination view: A Project view with task details appearing at the bottom of the screen.

constraint: A parameter that forces a task to fit a specific timing. For example, a task can be constrained to start as late as possible in a project. Constraints interact with dependency links to determine a task's timing.

cost: The amount of money associated with a project task when you assign *resources,* which are equipment, materials, or people with associated fees or hourly rates.

critical path: The series of tasks that must occur on time for the overall project to meet its deadline.

critical task: A task on the critical path. *See also* critical path.

crosstab: A report format that compares two intersecting sets of data. For example, you can generate a crosstab report showing the costs of critical tasks that are running late.

cumulative cost: The planned total cost to date for a resource's effort on a particular task. This calculation adds the costs already incurred on a task to any planned costs remaining for the uncompleted portion of the task.

cumulative work: The planned total work of a resource on a particular task. This calculation adds the work completed on a task to any planned work remaining for the uncompleted portion of the task.

current date line: The vertical line in a Gantt Chart indicating today's date and time. *See also* Gantt Chart.

CV (cost variance): The difference between the baseline costs and the combination of actual costs to date and estimated costs remaining *(scheduled costs).* The cost variance is either *positive* (over budget) or *negative* (under budget).

deadline date: A date you assign to a task that doesn't constrain the task's timing. However, if a deadline date is assigned, Project displays an indicator symbol if the task runs past the deadline.

dependency: A timing relationship between two tasks in a project. A *dependency link* causes a task either to occur before or after another task, or to begin or end at some point during the life of the other task.

detail task: *See* subtask.

duration: The amount of calendar time it takes to complete a task.

duration variance: The difference between the planned (baseline) task duration and the current estimated task duration, based on activity to date and any remaining activity still to be performed.

EAC (estimate at completion): The total planned cost for resource effort on a specific task. This calculation combines the costs incurred to date with costs estimated for a task's remaining work.

earned value: A reference to the value of work completed. A task with $1,000 of associated costs has an earned value of $750 when it's 75 percent complete. *See also* BCWP.

effort-driven: A type of task that requires an assigned amount of effort to be completed. When you add resources to an effort-driven task, the assigned effort is distributed among the task resources equally.

enterprise custom fields: Custom fields stored in a global file; these fields can be used to standardize Project plan content across an organization.

enterprise resources: A feature that allows you to save all resource information for resources used across an organization in one location.

estimated duration: A setting that indicates that you are using a best guess of a task's duration. When you enter an estimated duration for a task, you can then apply a filter to display only tasks with estimated duration, which reflects the fact that they have questionable timing.

exception: A specified date or date range that is not governed by the default working time calendar.

expand: To open a project outline to reveal both summary tasks and subtasks.

expected duration: An estimate of the actual duration of a task, based on work performance to date.

external task: A task in another project. You can set links between tasks in your project and external tasks.

finish date: The date on which a project or task is estimated to be — or actually is — completed.

finish-to-finish relationship: A dependency relationship in which the finish of one task determines the finish of another task.

finish-to-start relationship: A dependency relationship in which the finish of one task determines the start of another task.

fixed duration: The length of time required to complete a task remains constant no matter how many resources are assigned to the task. A half-day seminar is an example of a fixed-duration task.

fixed-unit: A type of cost for which the resource units are constant; if you change the duration of the task, resource units don't change. This is the default task type.

fixed-work: A type of task for which the number of resource hours assigned to the task determine its length.

float: *See* slack.

Gantt Chart: A standard Project view that displays columns of task information alongside a chart that shows task timing in bar chart format.

gap: *See* lag.

generic resources: A type of resource that allows you to make skill-based assignments based on a skill/code profile.

grouping: The organization of tasks by a customized field to summarize costs or other factors.

ID number: The number automatically assigned to a task by Project based on its vertical sequence in the project list.

indent: To move a task to a lower level of detail in the project's outline hierarchy.

lag: The amount of downtime that can occur between the end of one task and the beginning of another. Lag is built into a dependency relationship between tasks when you indicate that a certain amount of time must pass before the second task can begin.

leveling: A calculation used by Project that modifies resource work assignments for the purpose of resolving resource conflicts.

linking: (1) To establish a connection between tasks in separate schedules so that task changes in the first schedule are reflected in the second. (2) To establish dependencies among project tasks.

material resources: The supplies or other items used to complete a task (one of two resource categories; the other is work resources).

milestone: A task of zero duration, which marks a moment in time or an event in a schedule.

network diagram: An illustration that graphically represents workflow among a project's tasks; one of the Microsoft Project standard views.

node: In Network Diagram view, a box containing information about individual project tasks.

nonworking time: The time when a resource is not available to be assigned to work on any task in a project.

outdent: To move a task to a higher level in a project's outline hierarchy.

outline: The structure of the summary and subtasks in a project.

overallocation: When a resource is assigned to spend more time on a single task or a combination of tasks occurring at the same than that resource's work calendar permits.

overtime: Any work scheduled beyond a resource's standard work hours. You can assign a different rate than a resource's regular rate to overtime work.

percent complete: The amount of work on a task that has already been accomplished, expressed as a percentage.

PERT chart: A standard project management tracking form indicating workflow among project tasks. This is a *network diagram* in Project. *See also* network diagram.

predecessor: In a dependency link, the task designated to occur before another task. *See also* dependency *and* successor.

priorities: A ranking of importance assigned to tasks. When you use resource leveling to resolve project conflicts, priority is a factor in the leveling calculation. A higher-priority task is less likely than a lower-priority task to incur a delay during the leveling process. *See also* resource leveling.

progress lines: Gantt Chart view bars that overlap the baseline taskbar and allow you to compare the baseline plan with a task's tracked progress.

project: A series of tasks that achieves a specific goal. A project seeks to meet the triple requirements of timeliness, quality, and budget.

project calendar: The calendar on which all new tasks are based; the project calendar can be standard, 24 Hour, or use a Night Shift.

Project Guide: A wizard-like help feature that takes Project users through various steps to build a Project schedule.

project management: The discipline that studies various methods, procedures, and concepts used to control the progress and outcome of projects.

Project Server: A Web-based companion product of Microsoft Project that enables team members to enter information about their tasks into an overall project schedule without having Project installed on their own computers.

recurring task: A task that will occur several times during the life of a project. Regular project team meetings or quarterly inspections are examples of recurring tasks.

resource: A cost associated with a task. A resource can be a person, a piece of equipment, materials, or a fee.

resource driven: A task whose timing is determined by the number of resources assigned to it.

resource leveling: A process used to modify resource assignments to resolve resource conflicts.

resource pool: (1) Resources that are assigned as a group to an individual task, such as a pool of administrative workers assigned to generate a report. (2) A group of resources created in a centralized location that multiple project managers can access and assign to their projects.

resource sharing: A feature that allows you to copy resources you created in another project to your current plan.

Resource Substitution Wizard: A wizard that replaces an unavailable resource with another of similar skill and cost.

roll up: The calculation by which all subtask values are *rolled up* — summarized — in a single summary task.

Shared Workspace: A feature of Windows SharePoint Services in which you can share documents online that were created with various Microsoft Office 2007 applications.

slack: The amount of time that you can delay a task before the task becomes critical. Slack is used up when any delay in a task will delay the overall project deadline. Also called *float.*

split tasks: Tasks that have one or more breaks in their timing. When you split a task, you stop it part way and then start it again at a later time.

start date: The date on which a project or task begins.

start-to-finish relationship: A dependency relationship in which the start of one task determines the finish of another task.

start-to-start relationship: A dependency relationship in which the start of one task determines the start of another task.

subproject: A copy of a second project inserted in a project. The inserted project becomes a phase of the project in which it is inserted.

subtask: A task detailing a specific step in a project phase. This detail is rolled up into a higher-level summary task. Also called a *subordinate task. See also* roll up.

successor: In a dependency relationship, the later of two tasks. *See also* dependency.

summary task: In a project outline, a task that has subordinate tasks. A summary task rolls up the details of its subtasks and has no timing of its own. *See also* roll up.

task: An individual step performed to reach a project's goal.

template: A format in which a file can be saved. The template saves elements such as calendar settings, formatting, and tasks. New project files can be based on a template to save the time involved in reentering settings.

timescale: The area of a Gantt Chart view that displays units of time; when placed against those units of time, taskbars graphically represent the timing of tasks.

tracking: Recording the actual progress of work completed and the costs accrued for a project's tasks.

Value List: An alternative to entering data manually: a customizable feature of Project that allows you to create a list of values in a field from which a user can choose.

variable rate: A shift in resource cost that can be set to occur at specific times during a project. For example, if a resource is expected to receive a raise or if equipment lease rates are scheduled to increase, you can assign variable rates for those resources.

WBS (work breakdown structure): Automatically assigned numbers that designate an outline structure for each project task. Government projects often require WBS codes.

work breakdown structure: *See* WBS.

work resources: The people or equipment that perform work necessary to accomplish a task. *See also* material resources.

workload: The amount of work that any resource is performing at any given time, taking into account all tasks to which the resource is assigned.

workspace: A set of files and project settings that you can save and reopen together so that you pick up where you left off on a set of projects.

Index

• S •

Wiley Publishing, Inc.
End-User License Agreement

5.   Limited Warranty.   G

(a)   WPI warrants that the Software and Software Media are free from defects in materials and workmanship under normal use for a period of sixty (60) days from the date of purchase of this Book. If WPI receives notification within the warranty period of defects in materials or workmanship, WPI will replace the defective Software Media.

(b)   WPI AND THE AUTHOR(S) OF THE BOOK DISCLAIM ALL OTHER WARRANTIES, EXPRESS OR IMPLIED, INCLUDING WITHOUT LIMITATION IMPLIED WARRANTIES OF MERCHANTABILITY AND FITNESS FOR A PARTICULAR PURPOSE, WITH RESPECT TO THE SOFTWARE, THE PROGRAMS, THE SOURCE CODE CONTAINED THEREIN, AND/OR THE TECHNIQUES DESCRIBED IN THIS BOOK. WPI DOES NOT WARRANT THAT THE FUNCTIONS CONTAINED IN THE SOFTWARE WILL MEET YOUR REQUIREMENTS OR THAT THE OPERATION OF THE SOFTWARE WILL BE ERROR FREE.

(c)   This limited warranty gives you specific legal rights, and you may have other rights that vary from jurisdiction to jurisdiction.

6.   Remedies.

(a)   WPI's entire liability and your exclusive remedy for defects in materials and workmanship shall be limited to replacement of the Software Media, which may be returned to WPI with a copy of your receipt at the following address: Software Media Fulfillment Department, Attn.: *Microsoft Office Project 2007 For Dummies*, Wiley Publishing, Inc., 10475 Crosspoint Blvd., Indianapolis, IN 46256, or call 1-800-762-2974. Please allow four to six weeks for delivery. This Limited Warranty is void if failure of the Software Media has resulted from accident, abuse, or misapplication. Any replacement Software Media will be warranted for the remainder of the original warranty period or thirty (30) days, whichever is longer.

(b)   In no event shall WPI or the author be liable for any damages whatsoever (including without limitation damages for loss of business profits, business interruption, loss of business information, or any other pecuniary loss) arising from the use of or inability to use the Book or the Software, even if WPI has been advised of the possibility of such damages.

(c)   Because some jurisdictions do not allow the exclusion or limitation of liability for consequential or incidental damages, the above limitation or exclusion may not apply to you.

7.   U.S. Government Restricted Rights.
Use, duplication, or disclosure of the Software for or on behalf of the United States of America, its agencies and/or instrumentalities "U.S. Government" is subject to restrictions as stated in paragraph (c)(1)(ii) of the Rights in Technical Data and Computer Software clause of DFARS 252.227-7013, or subparagraphs (c) (1) and (2) of the Commercial Computer Software - Restricted Rights clause at FAR 52.227-19, and in similar clauses in the NASA FAR supplement, as applicable.

8.   General.
This Agreement constitutes the entire understanding of the parties and revokes and supersedes all prior agreements, oral or written, between them and may not be modified or amended except in a writing signed by both parties hereto that specifically refers to this Agreement. This Agreement shall take precedence over any other documents that may be in conflict herewith. If any one or more provisions contained in this Agreement are held by any court or tribunal to be invalid, illegal, or otherwise unenforceable, each and every other provision shall remain in full force and effect.